Steve Wilkens

SECOND EDITION

Beyond Bumper Sticker Ethics

An Introduction to Theories of Right and Wrong

IVP Academic

An imprint of InterVarsity Press
Downers Grove, Illinois

InterVarsity Press
P.O. Box 1400, Downers Grove, IL 60515-1426
ivpress.com
email@ivpress.com

InterVarsity Press® is the book-publishing division of InterVarsity Christian Fellowship/USA®, a movement of
students and faculty active on campus at hundreds of universities, colleges and schools of nursing in the United States
of America, and a member movement of the International Fellowship of Evangelical Students. For information
about local and regional activities, visit intervarsity.org.

While all stories in this book are true, some names and identifying information in this book have been changed to
protect the privacy of the individuals involved.

Design: Cindy Kiple

ISBN 978-0-8308-3936-0

Printed in the United States of America ∞

g green
press
INITIATIVE
As a member of the Green Press Initiative, InterVarsity Press is committed to protecting
the environment and to the responsible use of natural resources. To learn more, visit
greenpressinitiative.org.

Library of Congress Cataloging-in-Publication Data

Wilkens, Steve, 1955-
   Beyond bumper sticker ethics: an introduction to theories of right
and wrong /Steve Wilkens.—2nd ed.
      p. cm.
   Includes bibliographical references (p.   ).
   ISBN 978-0-8308-3936-0 (pbk.: alk. paper)
   1. Ethics. 2. Christian ethics.   I. Title.
   BJ1012.W515 2011
   171—dc22

                                                      2011013644

| P | 26 | 25 | 24 | 23 | 22 | 21 | 20 | 19 | 18 | 17 | 16 | 15 | 14 | 13 | 12 | 11 | 10 | 9 |
| Y | 39 | 38 | 37 | 36 | 35 | 34 | 33 | 32 | 31 | 30 | 29 | 28 | 27 | 26 | 25 | 24 | 23 | 22 |

*To my wife,
partner and friend,
Debra*

CONTENTS

PREFACE AND ACKNOWLEDGMENTS

THOSE OF US IN HIGHER EDUCATION who are committed to Christianity often hold on for dear life in a delicate balancing act called textbook selection. On the one hand, we want to avoid "ghettoization"—looking only at Christian ideas and critiquing them from a perspective that is familiar only to Christians. On the other hand, when issues beyond the specific confines of Christian thought are addressed, we would like the Christian tradition to get the recognition and attention we believe it deserves.

I have been surprised and dismayed at the number of otherwise fine texts in ethical theory that completely omit or severely restrict discussion of the religious dimension of ethics. This seems odd for at least two reasons. First, throughout the greater part of Western intellectual history it was assumed that ethics was closely integrated with religious considerations. Second, the vast majority of my compatriots will at least state that God has something to do with right and wrong. Thus to deprive people of the opportunity to explore ways the divine and the good may be related is to fail to address the questions being asked.

If you are looking for a Christian perspective on the usual range of ethical issues and topics, there are a number of very good texts to choose from. However, it seems that ethical theory has received somewhat limited attention. Often it is covered only briefly as an introduction to a consideration of specific topics; or when it is covered in depth, a significant academic background is assumed.

The thesis of this book is that ethical theory is an inescapable part of our world. We all think theoretically in this arena of life; we just do not always know that we do it. If this is true for Christians as well as non-

Christians, it is worthwhile to consider these ways of looking at the world. What distinguishes this text from most others available is that it assumes that certain fundamental features of a Christian worldview are valid tools to bring to the table in evaluating our moral bases. At the same time, it employs the usual means of critiquing ethical theory—logical consistency, possibility of universalization, consequences and the like.

Only one name goes on the cover of a book, but in reality there are many people who make it possible. Here are some whom I would like to thank for their contributions:

- My colleagues in the Haggard School of Theology, who have offered support and helpful suggestions—especially John Culp and Gayle Beebe, who read portions of the first edition.

- Azusa Pacific University, which offered institutional support in the form of writer's retreats, the Faith Integration Ethics Seminar, and the CREV summer seminar, in which portions of this book were written or revised.

- Tim Fenderson, who read the text and offered suggestions and encouragement.

- My students, who allow me to test ideas and constantly keep me aware of how much I have to learn.

- Flash and Zeke, for their careful supervision of the first edition from start to finish.

- Rodney Clapp, my editor for the original text, and Gary Deddo, who has shepherded this new edition through the revisions. The efforts of both editors and the rest of the terrific staff at IVP have made my twenty-year relationship with InterVarsity Press a real joy.

- Debra Wilkens, for supporting my teaching habit instead of insisting that I get a real job.

1

When in Rome,
do as the Romans do
ALL YOU NEED IS LOVE

MORAL
OF THE
STORY

BUMPER STICKERS
AND ETHICAL SYSTEMS

When in Rome, do as the Romans do.

Look out for Number One.

I couldn't help myself.

Survival of the ethical fittest.

The greatest good for the greatest number.

It's your duty.

Be good.

The moral of the story is . . .

All you need is love.

Do whatever comes naturally.

God said it, I believe it, that settles it.

FOR MOST OF US, life moves at a fast pace. Messages come at us from every direction and compete for our precious time. And if we have anything to say to the world, it had better fit into a "tweet," on a bumper sticker or in a five-second sound bite. Otherwise, our audience is gone. And it better have a "hook." If it isn't packaged in a way that sticks in our memory, competing messages will shove it aside. Companies pay big money to advertising agencies that are successful in imprinting the image of a product in the public mind. Candidates hire advisers to help them shape messages that will be heard and remembered. I recall hearing a radio interview that featured a man who makes a living by showing people how they can squeeze their philosophies of life onto seven-character personalized license plates. (It took him an hour to explain why this is important.) Whether you are a candidate vying for office, a reporter writing a story or a freeway philosopher tooling down the highway, you care about communicating succinctly and convincingly.

Ethical views are not exempt from this trend toward compacting our positions. When we ask for advice, overhear conversations at the next table or read the latest self-help book on getting our lives in order, the ideas often are communicated in a slogan format that can be delivered, received and digested quickly and easily. In other words, ethical counsel comes to us in quick statements, what I will call "bumper stickers" (for the sake of brevity, of course), like those at the beginning of this chapter.

Getting Beyond Bumper Sticker Ethics

It should not take too much reflection to conclude that we need to be careful about staking the important ethical decisions in our lives on bumper sticker catch phrases. The problem is not that any advice that can be delivered in a small amount of space is necessarily wrong. The problem is that the ideas expressed in these bite-sized pronouncements have broader implications.

Ideas are built on certain assumptions, and if the assumptions are untrue or only partly true, what we build upon them is shaky. More-over, the idea communicated in a bumper sticker is connected with other ideas. Thus, while the ethical aspect that is explicit in the bumper sticker may look good at first glance, other ideas that follow from it may not be so attractive. Most of us have heard or used the cliché "When in Rome, do as the Romans do," and it can sound like worthwhile advice. But what if the standard practices of the "Romans" stand in direct conflict with your moral or religious convictions? This is why we need to get behind the cliché itself. Such assumptions and connections are not made explicit in the shortened versions of ethical systems. Before we commit ourselves to any bumper sticker, we want to make certain that we can accept all that is implied in the slogan. In short, we have to get beyond "bumper sticker ethics" to see what else is in the package.

That is what this book is about. If you look at the bumper stickers at the beginning of this chapter, you may notice that they do not give specific solutions to specific problems (although in certain contexts an answer may be strongly suggested). Instead of direct answers, they provide the germ of a process for making decisions. For example, when we say "It's your duty," we imply that solving an ethical problem begins with recognizing our obligations to ourselves and other people, even when the results of following through on those obligations may not be attractive to us. Moreover, we can see quickly that this will involve a way of approaching moral decisions different from a bumper sticker like "Look out for Number One."

The process of how we work through moral issues is called an ethical system. My strategy in this book will be to use bumper stickers as a point of departure to explore ethical systems. This approach is possible because we can find a short, popular expression that captures the essence of just about every major ethical system. The difference between the bumper sticker and the system itself is not content; rather, the system makes explicit what is only implicit in the slogan. Instead of accepting bumper stickers at face value, the system fills in the blanks and provides arguments about why its views are better than other options. Only when we dig deeper into bumper-sticker-sized bits of moral directive can we know if an ethical perspective will bear the weight of a lifetime of moral decisions.

Ethical Options

Our world is a real marketplace of ideas. And whether the ideas we face are religious, political, economic or social, decisions about those ideas are unavoidable. We have to make choices. If we look at the list at the beginning of this chapter, we notice that some of the statements contradict each other. We cannot choose them all. It does not take a lot of thought to recognize that if we really mean it when we say, "I couldn't help myself," we have committed ourselves to a view that cannot coexist with the command to "be good." We can order people to be good as much as we want, but if they are not in control of their behavior, as the first assertion states, we will get nowhere.

Confronted with such a bewildering array of options, many people are tempted to retreat into skepticism. Given that there are so many choices, perhaps it is impossible to ever know the truth—or perhaps there is no truth to be known. Others retreat into subjectivism—they create their own truth, or at least think they do. But there are good reasons not to respond in these ways.

First, if you retreat first and ask questions later, you may not avail yourself of convincing arguments against skepticism or ethical subjectivism. In fact, you may never discover that such arguments exist. And being unaware of persuasive arguments against a position is no guarantee that no such arguments exist!

Second, many have retreated into subjectivism or skepticism because there is little moral consensus in society today. Practices once universally condemned as wrong—divorce, premarital sex, abortion—are now accepted by a sizable number of people. However, the question of what is right or wrong is different from the question of whether right and wrong exist. I suspect that many people who consider themselves skeptics or subjectivists do not really doubt that right and wrong exist. They just do not include as many things (or the same things) in the "wrong" category as others. Such people may not agree with more traditional beliefs about homosexuality or other areas of sexual ethics, but they would be morally offended if we said people should not be free to make decisions about their personal sexual activity. In this case, what we have is not a conclusion that there is no moral truth but rather a disagreement about what the truth is.

Finally, although many claim to be skeptics or subjectivists, it is difficult to be consistent with either claim in real life. If I stole a toaster oven from a guy who rejects the notion of absolute ethical truth, no one would be surprised at all if he argued that he had been wronged and gave reasons he expected rational people to agree with. In other words, he would appeal to some kind of truth.

The existence of conflicting views, then, does not necessarily mean that there is no ethical truth. But how do we explain why we end up with so many differing ethical perspectives? One possible explanation is that these differences arise for the same reason certain proverbs, clichés and slogans come into existence and become part of the popular currency. They contain a nugget of truth. They make sense of some aspect of our world and lead to positive outcomes in some situations. However, many of these bits of wisdom contradict each other. What is better, to "not put off until tomorrow what you can do today" or to "sleep on it"? Which is wiser: "A penny saved is a penny earned" or "You can't take it with you"? Each is good advice under certain circumstances, but we cannot simultaneously do all that these proverbs advise, because some of them are mutually exclusive.

When we look at the ethical realm, there are certain questions people naturally wonder about—or at least should wonder about. Why do we seem to find some basic areas of agreement in ethics? If ethical truth exists, why can't we fully agree on it? Are there rules that are valid for all people at all times? Are rules even a main component of a good ethical system? Each approach examined will answer some important questions well and will fit with certain ways of viewing the world. In short, the reason the ethical systems discussed in this book have staying power is that they contain at least some truth; this truth accounts for the appeal of each system.

But to say that truth is contained in a system is different from saying that the system is the best available. Unlike our proverbs about life, ethical systems are not meant to deal only with limited situations but are intended to be comprehensive. If too many gaps are present, the system falls apart.

So while it is important that we mine each system for whatever truth can be found in it, we also should examine them to see which one best provides the foundation for all moral decisions. It is probably unrealistic to think that any one approach is perfect, but some are better than others. Some may be acceptable with minor modifications. A few may be so flawed that they can be rejected outright. To borrow an analogy from Philip Devine, "All boats leak, but some boats leak more than others. And not all boats sink."[1]

Ethics as a Discipline

The idea that ethics is something to be studied can be confusing because making decisions about moral issues is something we do every day. When I entered my first ethics class, I wasn't sure what I was supposed to get out of it. In history, biology, physical education and speech I had a pretty good idea of what was coming. Some classes aim to give us information that moves us beyond our present knowledge; others help us develop a set of skills. But how does ethics fit in? Certainly we need information to make good decisions, but if information is all we need, we can get it elsewhere. I really did not want a class where someone told me all the "right" answers to ethical dilemmas. A skills class in which we would practice "being good" also did not fit my picture of what we should do. I concluded that since we already make ethical decisions, the discipline of ethics must be designed to help us do that better. How this was supposed to happen was still up in the air.

Confusion about ethics as a discipline is very understandable, because it is a unique area of study. Most disciplines deal with "is" questions. Who was Sigmund Freud? What is a dangling participle? How much does my car weigh? When are we going to get there? These questions involve a search for information. However, ethical questions belong to a different category. When we seek to untangle moral dilemmas we ask "ought" questions. Is maintaining the biological life of a person who is brain-dead the type of thing we ought to do? Should we participate in military operations?

In ethics, *right* means something different than *correct*. *Correct* is the label we attach to information that is factually true, while *right* is oriented to moral truth. Because the type of question is different, the means by which we look for and test answers in ethics will differ.

This does not mean that ethics is divorced from other areas of study. For example, it would be quite dangerous to come to conclusions about medical ethics without any information about the relevant medical facts. Nonetheless, the right ethical decision involves more than just correct information. It is how we move from information to ethical decision that is of concern in ethical systems.

As a discipline, ethics tackles two general kinds of tasks. The most obvious task is to examine ethical problems like euthanasia, abortion, capital punishment and homosexuality. This usually goes under the label of *applied ethics*. It is the "glamour" area of ethics, because there are clear points of contact with our lives. These are the hot-button issues we encounter daily. We discuss these issues with family and friends. Topics like these come up at the office during coffee breaks. Even when these matters are not a part of our lives in a direct way, they are part of our world, and decisions about them affect our lives.

A lot is at stake in these areas, whether we are personally struggling with questions about what is right and what is wrong, or whether our lives are affected by the ethical conclusions reached by those we live and work with. In any case, it is important to have confidence in the foundations these conclusions are based on. Ethical systems attempt to provide that foundation.

Examining ethical systems is the second general task that ethics tackles. This book takes up this task—examining and evaluating options in ethical theory. I hope to show how general ethical theory is useful (and inevitable) as we make important decisions about particular ethical problems.

Theory and Life

Most people don't get excited about studying theory. It's easy to assume that "theory has nothing to do with the real world." But I believe this perception is mistaken. Look again at the statement "theory has nothing to do with the real world." It is itself a theoretical statement about the way things work (or do not work), and if you truly believe it, it affects the way you live—your "real world." Even if you are unaware that such a statement provides a theoretical underpinning for your actions, it is there.

It works that way in ethics as well. Imagine that three people see a twenty-dollar bill on the front seat of an unlocked car. Each person walks past and leaves the cash there. Why? The first person wanted to take the money but passed up the opportunity for fear of punishment if caught in the act. The second rejected the temptation out of a conviction that God makes certain rules that people are to follow, and one of those rules is that we shouldn't take things that don't belong to us. The third refrained from taking the money because of empathy—awareness of how frustrated and angry she herself would be if some of her money were stolen.

The action is the same for each individual—no one took the money. But people do things for reasons, and the reasons behind the same action in the case above vary significantly. The bumper-sticker-sized version of the first person's ethics is "Whatever you do, don't get caught," while that of the second person is "Thou shalt not steal." The final person builds her morality around "Do unto others as you would have them do unto you." These different reasons grow out of differences in theories about what constitutes right behavior.

Though none of the three people may have been immediately conscious of these theories at work, the theories were there, and they guided each person's behavior. Each person's ethical theory did have something to do with life in the real world.

Furthermore, in ethical theory an action itself may not be the only factor in our assessment of that action. We also consider the motives or the reasons behind the action. Even though the three hypothetical individuals behaved the same way (leaving the money in the car), if we were able to know their reasons we might not judge all three to be equally ethical. Why they did what they did—the theoretical basis of their actions—is significant. Thus ethical theory is important not only to guide our own actions but also to evaluate the actions and theories of other people.

The reality is this: we cannot avoid either of the ethical tasks I have delineated. We must make decisions about the ethical issues confronting us, and we must have a theoretical foundation on which to build and evaluate these decisions. In other words, the issue is not whether we have a theory, but whether we are conscious of the theory we do have and believe it is the best available guide for our life. We do not choose to be ethicists; we cannot opt out of that. The real question is whether we are going to be *good* ethicists. If we want to make good ethical decisions, we need a solid ethical process.

Ethics and Worldviews

The only way we will know if we can invest our confidence in an ethical system is to test it. So how do we know what makes a theory a good one? This is not a simple matter, for not everyone agrees on the definition of "good ethical system." Usually the definition is part of the system itself. However, there is an external check that will help us evaluate the various approaches. Every ethical system is part of something bigger—something that can be called a worldview. Worldviews themselves can be complex, but the definition of *worldview* is fairly straightforward: a worldview consists of our beliefs and assumptions about how the world fits together. As is the case with ethical systems, everyone has one, whether it is acknowledged or not.

Since ethical beliefs and assumptions are part of our worldview, it is important to look at ethics in this context to make certain the pieces do in fact fit. For example, if we see the world as a giant machine in which everything (including us) functions strictly according to the rules of cause and effect, we may be inconsistent if we think of right and wrong in moral terms. After all, how can a machine be moral—or immoral, for that matter? Again, if you believe in a God who has a moral character and who is involved in the world, it is difficult to put this together with an ethical system that gives us carte blanche to act as we please. So when we look at ethics against the background of a comprehensive worldview, we can compare different worldviews and make certain that our view is internally consistent.

The broader context of a worldview also helps us ask all the relevant questions. If we get the right questions on the table, we won't leave out elements that are relevant. Since worldview questions come up in every ethical system, it is useful to be aware of them from the start. There are different ways to divide out the categories of a worldview, but for the sake of brevity let's look at them under two headings: ultimate reality and human nature.

Ultimate Reality

It is interesting that while we humans inhabit the same world, we have different models for understanding it. Is the universe an impersonal mass of energy functioning according to a set of unbending laws? An illusion? A collective tradition built on our relative perspective of the world? The random result of a primordial cosmic sneeze? The purposeful work of a master Designer? Or something else altogether? Not all of these options can be true, so we have to make choices. And these choices about the nature of the world outside ourselves will influence our ethical views.

You may well have a ready answer to the question of ultimate reality: God. If we start from this point, it is often assumed that the connection between God and ethics is obvious and there is little more to say. This is because our idea of God usually includes certain characteristics, such as moral goodness. It only seems natural that if God is a good God, he would expect us to abide by standards of right and wrong that are rooted in who he is. So if God is good and expects us to be good, that settles the problem of ethics, right? Not really. Even if we grant a Judeo-Christian understanding of God's moral nature, we should not suppose that all who subscribe to this perspective will adopt the same system. There are other significant questions, and most disagreements between Christians about ethical systems revolve around two of them.

First, how does God communicate his ethical desire? It is one thing to state that God wants us to be aware of his will for us; it is quite another to say how God gets the message to us. Are God's demands somehow imprinted in our minds at birth, so that knowledge of right and wrong is something like an intuition? Perhaps God's will comes to us through nature, and we pick it up through careful observation and processing of the world around us. Maybe God sends the message through Scripture or his church. Or perhaps the means by which God communicates his truth is more like a story that gives us a new identity. Ethical theory involves discussion of how we gain moral knowledge, and where we come out on this decision will determine the source we look to for authority.

A second concern takes us back to the issue of God's nature. To say that God is a moral being is not all we might say about God. We will need to answer questions about how God's goodness is related to other divine characteristics. What are the implications of saying that God is both good and reasonable, or that God is free from all restraints, or that he is a personal being who enters into a relationship with individuals? It may not be immediately clear how these questions matter, and they may seem a bit esoteric. But usually our picture of how God relates to us includes assumptions about these issues, whether we know it or not, and we will discover in later chapters that these assumptions can make a significant difference in how a system works out.

A number of ethical theories we will consider might be called "God-optional." They can accommodate belief in God, but they may be (and often are) outlined without any mention of God. Nothing in these theories requires that God be included, but he can be inserted without changing the essential nature of the approach. If you look for it, you will discover that this happens frequently on a popular level. Polls tell us that about 95 percent of all Americans believe in God. However, if we would ask a sample of these believing Americans how they make decisions about right and wrong, God would not be mentioned by many.

For example, a respondent to this question might tell us that morality consists in bringing about "the greatest good for the greatest number." Knowing that this individual believes in God, we might go on to ask whether God has anything to do with ethics. In response the person may revise the answer to say, "God arranges the world so that doing his will results in the greatest good for the greatest number."

This example brings us to a question that should be asked about such ethical theories—and often is not. Is ethics so closely tied in with God's nature that it will not hang together unless we integrate God with every aspect of the system? If God is the fundamental reality behind the universe, is it possible to correctly understand other aspects of this universe, such as ethics, without him?

If a person believes that God does not exist or that God's existence is irrelevant to ethics, this opens the issue of where right and wrong come from. It should be recognized that this is different from the question of where we learn about right and wrong. Here we are looking for the origin. If we reject God as the ultimate reality, we eliminate one possibility of explaining the origin of right and wrong, and will need to decide among the remaining options. Is human thought the most fundamental reality of the universe? If so, does something become right by our determining it to be right or by collective decision? Are the laws of nature the ultimate, with nothing or no one beyond or behind them? If so, then what we call right and wrong may be nothing more than sur-

vival strategies or social lubricants imposed on us by our genetic structure. Or we may conclude that traditional ways of thinking about ethics
are wrong-headed. Perhaps *right* and *wrong* are words we use to modify
the actions of people. Nothing is actually good or bad in a moral sense.
These are simply labels we attach to actions we want to encourage or
discourage.

In short, we need to recognize that in every ethical system there is a
connection between a concept of ultimate reality and the origin of right
and wrong.

Human Nature

Human beings have a lot in common with members of the animal
world. If we compare humans and higher primates physiologically, our
organs and theirs are similarly constructed and perform the same functions. We need the same kinds of food to stay alive. We breathe, drink,
excrete and reproduce along the same patterns. Some animal parts are
even interchangeable with human parts. Valves from pigs' hearts have
replaced defective valves in human beings, corneas from cows are used
for transplantation, and baboon hearts have replaced human hearts to
keep some people alive for a while.

For all these similarities, however, something about human beings
and human nature compels us to speak of ourselves differently from
how we speak of animals. This can be seen in ethics.

If my basset hound mustered enough initiative to rip the carpeting
from our living room, I would shout something like "Bad dog!" But
when I say "Bad dog!" I do not view my dog as morally responsible,
reprehensible and in grave danger of eternal punishment. It would seem
very odd to see any animal as a moral agent.

Now let's change the picture. If I discover an uninvited neighbor in
my living room removing our carpet, the words *bad neighbor* (though
I probably would not shout "Bad neighbor!") carry ethical connotations. Though we do not always agree on what constitutes moral
"badness," there is a universal tendency to describe human actions in
moral terms.

Most of us haven't thought much about why we find it natural to apply moral terms to human behavior but consider it strange to do the same with the actions of animals. This interesting difference may be ethically significant, however, because whatever differentiates humans from animals may be linked with the source of our moral consciousness.

What is different about human nature? Is it our freedom to make decisions? Our rationality? Spiritual sensitivity and awareness? Can it all be explained by a neurophysiology that is not qualitatively distinct from that of other animals, just quantitatively more complex?

In any case, ethics deals with human beings. Since we are talking about human ethics, any good ethical system must begin from a correct understanding of human nature. It will not work to say what it means to be a good person without assuming certain things about what a person is.

Besides considering what makes humans different from animals, we need to ask the question, Why do we do what we should not do? Ethicists disagree about almost everything, but they are unanimous on one thing: Humans have a problem. We are not where we ought to be in a moral sense. If we were doing everything right, there would be no need for ethics. But while ethicists agree that we have a problem, they disagree about what the problem is. The different definitions of the human problem are, to a considerable degree, what separates one ethical system from another.

Even if we have not explicitly thought about ethics from this perspective, the idea that something has gone wrong with us is implicit in our ethical answers. If you look carefully at the list at the beginning of this chapter, a pattern begins to emerge. These slogans are answers that assume a problem. Thus the problem is the flip side of the advice offered. If the answer is "God said it, I believe it, that settles it," the problem is that we are not listening and believing: faithlessness. If the advice is that we should "Look out for Number One," the problem is that we need to stop looking out for others.

As we look at the various ethical options, then, we will spend time examining whether they have the problem right. Getting the right answer depends on asking the right question.

A Word About Strategy

This book comes from a Christian publisher and is written by a Christian author who has in mind an audience that is composed primarily of Christian readers, but it is not limited to Christian ethics. The primary focus is to survey a broad cross section of ethical theory from a perspective that includes, but is not limited to, a Christian point of view. It is important that Christians have a broad understanding of ethics because we have a lot in common with those who are not Christians. First, there is commonality in ethical impulse; most people will acknowledge the importance of being good. Certainly there are few who pride themselves in being thought of as unethical (although the desire to be truly ethical is not always as strong as the desire to be thought of as ethical). We have a natural passion to know the right answers to ethical questions. Whether our way of viewing the world grows out of Christian conviction or some other approach, the belief that there is value in truth and goodness is mutual.

Second, there are numerous points of contact between Christians and others concerning ethical content. Knowledge of right and wrong is not proprietary information reserved exclusively for Christians. We see and live with non-Christians who embody moral principles that we agree with. We have no trouble finding non-Christians who encourage truthfulness, feel it is important to respect life and accept many values found in Christianity. The moral precepts of the Ten Commandments are not unique to Christian ethics.

Finally, Christians and non-Christians often use similar means in making and evaluating ethical decisions. While Christians know they don't usually get very far with a nonbeliever by prefacing an argument with "the Bible says," the discussion does not have to end there. Christians can advance their point of view by offering reasons that make sense to nonbelievers. We can empathize with non-Christians in matters of conscience, emotions, desires and goals. Christians, agnostics and atheists can all appeal to the authority of experience as a means of evaluation.

The points above have significant implications. First, they indicate that we can gain ethical insight from non-Christian sources. Too often ideas from outside the Christian world are rejected simply because of their origin. When we do this we risk missing the opportunity to discover valuable truth. Of course no idea should be accepted uncritically, even one that comes from Christians, but neither should we be hypercritical of non-Christian sources.

Second, our commonalities are significant for evangelism. Though this book is not about evangelism, effectiveness in sharing our faith requires that Christians know what people care about and that we have some common ground to work from. Because people do feel that there is value in being ethical, and because some ethical methods and content are shared, Christians have a foundation for moving particular discussions about ethics into broader discussions about Christianity. Believers could also be more effective in evangelism if they would think through and learn to express coherently why certain ethical approaches fall short of biblical standards.

So this book will survey various expressions of Christian ethics as well as moral theories that are not specifically Christian. Because it's impossible to consider every approach that is out there, I have selected eleven approaches that have significant followings today and that give us a broad cross section of ethical approaches. These have been grouped into three sections according to the role God plays in the systems.

The first section of the book looks at systems whose elements contradict basic aspects of a Christian worldview. Because these approaches are, as a whole, in fundamental tension with Christianity, they will be considered "dead on arrival" from a Christian point of view. However, even in such systems there may be something worthwhile that can be incorporated into our own ethical system. We often find valuable truths in unexpected places, so we will consider what is positive in these theories.

The middle part of the book considers ethical approaches that do not require a theistic starting point but that may be adaptable to Christian beliefs. The principle here is that it may well be possible to tap unknowingly into God's truth.

The final chapters give an overview of methods that consciously begin as attempts to express ethics from within the context of Christianity. As I mentioned earlier, beginning from the same set of basic beliefs does not guarantee complete agreement on all points. On the one hand, differences between these systems might correctly be classified as family squabbles. On the other hand, some of the squabbles involve important differences in how we understand God's work in our world.

In this survey of ethical systems I have tried to describe each theory as fairly as possible in a brief synopsis. Each view is then to be evaluated. I consider what truth may be contained in every theory I examine, with a view to understanding why people are attracted to it. Potential problem areas will also be studied. Valid questions can be addressed to every one of these systems. This questioning process does not automatically indicate that a system is hopelessly flawed, and the purpose is not to make us cynical about ever finding truth. Instead, my intent is to suggest where a theory may have to be defended and to highlight directions in which further discussion of the system must move.

The bumper stickers I use to introduce the ethical systems in each chapter are, to some degree, caricatures. They do not provide a complete and accurate statement of these approaches; in fact, they may distort or exclude important features. Despite this danger, starting with the slogans still has merit. Since these bumper stickers are abbreviated theoretical statements, they help us realize that we think in theoretical terms, often without being aware of it. They also help us recognize that the basic ethical ideas contained in these bumper stickers are what we find in the ethical systems. These same ideas can be set in the broader context of an ethical system, and in their respective systems the slogans can be presented in a more nuanced fashion. This may be comforting to those who suspect that what we find in textbooks and systems is far removed from "real life."

Learning about the ethical systems that are part of our world has value in itself. It helps us understand why people do what they do. But there is a second goal behind this book. These systems can be the crucible in which we test our own decision-making process. We should not uncritically adopt someone else's beliefs, but this does not mean that we cannot make use of the thoughts of others. There is no reason to reinvent the wheel. You may find a system that appears to give full expression to Christian ethics. If that happens, look carefully at what is involved in that system and do your best to answer the questions that others may raise. If you do not discover a system that successfully plugs all the gaps, you should at least find some starting points for constructing your own view. In any case, remember that this book is not intended to be the end of your exploration into Christian morality, but rather a beginning.

2

WHEN IN ROME, DO AS THE ROMANS DO

Cultural Relativism

THE WORLD IS BECOMING increasingly diverse culturally. More and more we come in contact with people who have different customs, religions and perspectives. Some of these cultural differences are ethically neutral. What people eat and wear, and how they celebrate their special occasions generally, though not always, stands outside the category of ethical evaluation. But this is not the case for all cultural practices. Often customs that are unquestioningly accepted in one part of the world are considered abhorrent in another. For example, female genital mutilation is practiced in numerous locations within Africa and Asia. Certain tribes in Papua New Guinea are widely believed to be cannibalistic. Both practices would not just be seen as different from what is acceptable in Western cultures; they would be considered highly unethical, even criminal.

Moreover, it is not just that behavioral standards vary from place to place; they also change over time within the same society. Restricting women to certain specific roles in the workplace was a given in years past, but reinstating those limitations would be seen as highly unethical by many today. Many of the ancient Greeks saw slavery as a natural part of life, but the vast majority of modern Greeks would consider it repugnant. While we could add to the list of examples in both categories, the primary observation is this: from one culture to another and from one time to another within the same culture, there is diversity in what is considered right and wrong.

Cultural Relativism

What are we to make of such diversity in ethical issues? Cultural relativism claims to have the answer to this. Diversity means that there are no absolute standards for moral judgment. Any standard for determining right and wrong is relative. Ethical relativism, the belief that there is no moral truth that applies to all people at all times,[1] has been around for a long time. The early Greek philosopher Protagoras opened his book *On Truth* with the words "Man is the measure of all things."[2] The specific version of relativism that we will consider, cultural relativism, is a more recent development. Cultural relativism says that it is not each person but each person's culture that is the standard by which actions are to be measured.

"When in Rome, do as the Romans do" provides a simplified statement of cultural relativism. In this bumper sticker, two beliefs of cultural relativism are close to the surface. First, the reason we should "do as the Romans do" when in Rome has nothing to do with the superiority of Roman ethics. No ethical system is better than any other. For us to be able to say that the ethics of the Romans is any better than that of Athens, or that the ethics of Islamic fundamentalism is any better than that of Confucianism requires a common standard outside of these cultures to which they can be compared. However, the existence of an absolute ethical measure is denied by cultural relativism. The only thing we can say about different practices is that they are different, not that they are better or worse. *Better* and *worse* are comparative terms that make sense only with a measure that is not tied to any culture.

So why should we do as the Romans do while in Rome if there is nothing about the Roman way of doing things that is superior to other ethical frameworks? This leads to the second point. Most people recognize that anarchy is destructive. Every society has to have some structure and order or it cannot survive. Included in this social structure are ethical standards. Although ethical standards differ from one place to the next, to preserve social order people are obligated to follow the norms of the culture they live in.

While we now have some of the basic tenets of cultural relativism in place, we need to break it down into its specifics, because as it stands it involves a leap of logic. The problem is this: just because cultures differ in what they consider right and wrong, can we conclude that one ethical answer is as good as another? Obviously not. When two answers conflict, we do not automatically assume that both are equally true. It is logically possible that one or both of them are wrong. For example, if two people came up with different sums to 2 + 2, we would not accept both answers as right. Why then should we view both cannibalism in one culture and criminalization of cannibalism in another as acceptable? We need something more than the fact that we disagree about beliefs to show that absolutism—the belief that an objective right and wrong exists which applies to all people at all times—is false.

Cognitive Relativism

Because the more nuanced statements of cultural relativism recognize that diversity in ethical practices does not require the conclusion that ethical truth is relative, the concept of *cognitive* (or conceptual) relativism is needed to bridge the gap.[3] Cognitive relativism extends relativity to any type of claim. It is not just ethical statements that are true only relative to culture. All "truths" are judged by cultural standards. Nothing, even the answer to 2 + 2, is simply true, at least as far as we can know. We have no neutral way of seeing the world, no Archimedean point from which to get an undistorted picture.[4] Truth is always perspectival; things are true only relative to something else, and that "something else," for cultural relativism, is one's culture.

What pulls cognitive relativism together with cultural relativism is the belief that culture is the filter through which we see and interpret the world, including its moral component. As Ruth Benedict puts it, "No man ever looks at the world with pristine eyes. He sees it edited by a definite set of customs and institutions and ways of thinking. Even in his philosophical probings he cannot go behind these stereotypes; his very concepts of the true and the false will still have reference to his particular traditional customs."[5] What this means is that our social background does not just influence how we see reality. It also creates the only reality we can know. We never see things "as they are." How we perceive what we perceive is determined by our perspective, which is culturally determined.

The idea that no single cognitive truth exists may sound very strange, but it is not difficult to see how one could draw this conclusion. If you have grown up in a Western culture, you probably believe that Western ways of seeing the world are correct. Therefore, when we try to predict future events, we rely on computer models, statistical studies, polling and appeals to laws of physics, motion or thermodynamics. However, individuals from other societies may stake their future on the exploration of chicken intestines by a shaman. It is important to realize that, as ridiculous as it seems to us that the inside of a chicken has any relevance for our major decisions, it seems just as strange in some cultures to rely on Western methods.

How do we know our ways are better? The consistent relativist would argue that there is no possibility of an unbiased point of view. The definition of *better* and the reasons that seem more reasonable to us grow out of our cultural conditioning. Therefore, relativism says that both the person who consults a physician and the one who goes to see the local shaman are equally right to conclude that their medical treatment is the best, provided their solution conforms to cultural customs.

If cognitive relativism is true, then cultural relativists feel that no outsider has a legitimate basis on which to criticize the customs and practices of another group. No absolute ethical judgment can be applied across cultural lines because there is no absolute knowledge about any aspect of the world. It is not just that we see only the world created by our cultural influences but that we also cannot evaluate other worldviews except by appeal to our own.

> Our own discussions of these matters of "taste" implicitly invoke the standards set by our paradigms and our way of going on from them, and here we can speak of right and wrong. But if we are talking of the views of another society we shall speak of what is true by their standards and by our standards, without the slightest thought that our standards are "correct."[6]

Moral Judgment

One question that is foundational to ethical theory is how we decide what is ethically correct. Most ethical systems look to an absolute yardstick, though they differ among themselves about what this standard is or how it is discovered. As we have seen, relativism rejects the existence of a universal and absolute standard. In one sense this simplifies the ethical task. We are not burdened with defending one set of guidelines over against competing claims. Nor do we have to justify how we get our ethical principles. Instead, we look at what is common practice within a particular society. What they do is what all in that society should do. Accepted practices constitute the moral obligations of that society. Since no culture has a corner on truth, this is a natural transition. The only standards we will ever have grow out of our social environment. Therefore, the means by which we measure the behavior of insiders is determined by what is considered acceptable by the group itself.

While right and wrong are not to be understood in an absolute sense, this does not mean that we should never make a moral judgment. There are extreme relativists who say that the same thing may be right for one person and at the same time wrong for someone else, but this is not the position of cultural relativism. Melville Herskovits argues that "*cultural relativism, in all cases, must be sharply distinguished from the concept of the relativity of individual behavior [extreme relativism], which would negate all social contracts over conduct. Conformity to the code of the group is a requirement for any regularity in life.*"[7] For stability and order in life, we need rules, but what we see as right and wrong is relative to a particular culture. Therefore, the cultural relativist is not involved in a contradiction if he says abortion is wrong in his culture but can be right in other cultures, as long as his society disapproves of abortion and the other cultures he refers to happen to approve abortion. Moral standards exist, but these standards are localized and vary from one society to the next and one time to the next.

While relativism does not entail the belief that we should refrain from all ethical judgment, it does say that we should not impose our standards on outsiders. This creates a very practical difficulty, however. What should be our attitude toward practices that other societies accept but which we believe to be not just wrong but horrific? For example, most of us would be revulsed by cannibalism or infanticide. The relativist argues that this negative reaction does not originate from knowledge of an absolute moral measure. Our feelings toward certain acts are simply a reflection of our culture. Because of this, we cannot see the same act in the same way that people from the other culture see it. But were we a part of a culture that practices infanticide, for example, our feelings toward infanticide would be very different. As D. Z. Phillips puts it,

> If I hear that one of my neighbours has killed another neighbour's child, given that he is sane, my condemnation is immediate. . . . But if I hear that some remote tribe practices child sacrifice, what then? I do not know what sacrifice means for the tribe in question. What would it mean to say I condemned it when the "it" refers to something I know nothing about? If I did condemn it, I would be condemning murder. But murder is not child sacrifice.[8]

Summary

The goal of cultural relativism is not merely to convince us to adopt a theoretical position. Instead, it sees its approach as a practical means of achieving a more peaceful and tolerant world. This seems to make a lot of sense since so much of the strife in this world has been caused by intolerance rooted in nationalism and ethnocentrism. Relativism argues that the first step toward eliminating intolerance is awareness of ethnocentricity. Ethnocentricity is unavoidable. This is the point of cognitive relativism; it is impossible for any individual to step outside the circle of cultural tradition and thought forms. As Herskovits puts it, as long as our ethnocentricity involves only "a gentle insistence on the good qualities of one's own group, without any drive to extend this attitude into the field of action,"[9] it is benign. It recognizes differences but does not judge them by some measure outside the culture in question.

However, ethnocentricity becomes arrogance when we make an evaluation of another culture's behavior from our own perspective and act on that evaluation. Using the previous example given by Phillips, it would be presumptuous for me to label the child sacrifices of another culture wrong and to argue that this practice be stopped. If I insist that child sacrifice is morally wrong, I assume that my ethical system is better than one which allows the sacrifices. However, cultural relativism rejects the idea that systems can be compared to each other in terms of better or worse. Unless I have an absolute standard by which all actions can be judged and to which all people are obligated, infant sacrifice is not worse, it is merely different.

Since relativism is convinced that no absolute truth about morality is available to us, it urges intercultural tolerance—a "live and let live" attitude. Our goal is not to convince others of the rightness of our views but to understand and be understood. Out of understanding and tolerance we find the hope of mutual respect between cultures.[10]

The Positive Side of Cultural Relativism

For its entire history as a nation, the United States has been a country mostly made up of people from somewhere else. While it used to be that the traditions and customs of immigrant groups blended together in the "melting pot" of America after a couple of generations, the more common metaphor today is that of the "salad bowl," where people maintain cultural identity, native languages and traditions. Cultural differences are increasingly viewed as positive because we can be enriched by different perspectives and benefit from the flavors, colors, moods and ideas of various groups.

In this way the insights of cultural relativism can be useful because they remind us that we should not simply assume that what is familiar is the right way or the only way. The cultural biases we all have often come to the surface when we are pushed to give a reason for a belief. Frequently, it comes down to "that's the way I was raised" or "that is what I was taught." The danger in this is easy to spot. Just because you were raised to believe something does not make that belief true (or false). Cultural relativism can open our eyes to this by questioning whether we accept a certain point of view simply because we are comfortable with it.

Cultural relativism also stands as a warning that we should not too quickly assume that technological advance is necessarily a sign of superiority in other areas. At one time or another, most of us have probably heard someone defend the superiority of Western structures, ideas and norms on the basis of scientific and technological progress. However, even in societies often seen as "primitive," observation tells us that there is social order and a means of governing. Marriages occur, children are born and raised, and people are fed, clothed and sheltered. The means by which different groups accomplish these common human tasks vary widely, but they work. These structures and institutions do not always function perfectly, but in view of the social, domestic and economic struggles in our culture, we might want to think twice before assuming that our way is superior to that of "primitive" people.

The relativist's recognition of the powerful influence exerted by culture is also instructive for the Christian. If Christianity is not intended to be limited to a particular culture, we must take care to distinguish between the gospel, that which is transcultural, and our particular expression of the gospel. The way we dress for worship, the style of music used and the architecture of church structures generally reflect our culture, but are not central to Christianity itself. This realization is increasingly being put into practice on the mission field. The Christian message can be integrated into another culture without changing many of the patterns of life that are comfortable and familiar. Therefore, on the one hand, we need to be careful not to load down Christianity with so much of our cultural baggage that someone from another culture is forced to accept our social values along with the gospel. On the other hand, it is important to remember that no matter how pervasive you believe Christian values are within your particular world, it is extremely dangerous to equate any culture with Christianity itself.

Potential Problems in Cultural Relativism

1. Who gets to be God? In chapter one I noted that all ethical systems are part of a more comprehensive worldview and that we should look for congruity between the two. It becomes apparent why this is important in evaluating cultural relativism. "When in Rome, do as the Romans do" involves certain assumptions about ultimate reality that are in direct conflict with a fundamental element of a Christian worldview.

Cultural relativism is built on the belief that there are no absolutes, at least none that we can know. This means that truth is always relative to a nonabsolute standard: one's own culture. Where does this leave God? In essence, relativism puts one's culture in the role of God. While God is the standard of right and wrong in a Christian worldview, this function is filled by culture in relativism. Not all cultural relativists deny the existence of God, but to stay consistent with their system, they must deny that we can know what God's moral will is for all people. This would be an absolute and universal standard. But such a view places God in the "so what" category. While God may exist, he is beyond our knowledge and thus is irrelevant.

However, this clearly contradicts what is assumed throughout Scripture. First, the Bible is clear that Christianity is not intended to be restricted to a particular cultural group or groups. Rather, the disciples are to go to "all nations" (Mt 28:19) and "to the ends of the earth" (Acts 1:8). Since ethics is an aspect of Christianity, it seems clear that moral truth is to be considered transcultural.

A second obvious shortcoming in relativism is that Scripture does not endorse the idea that what a culture does is right because it considers such a practice right. For example, Amos begins with a series of condemnations for the practices of nations that were neighbors of Judah and Israel (Amos 1:3–2:3).[11] Even though these cultural groups are outside the covenant, God holds them to standards that transcend their culturally accepted actions. This does not make any sense unless God's standards of right and wrong extend beyond the borders of his covenant people, so that Israel and Judah's neighbors are judged by those standards and not by just their own cultural perspective of right and wrong. In any event, the fact that cultural relativism involves an understanding of ultimate reality that leaves no place for God to have any ethical relevance disqualifies the system itself as an option for Christians. Most will agree that Christian thought allows for some diversity in the understanding of God, but the conclusion that God does not exist or is irrelevant to ethical evaluations about human actions goes beyond such allowances.

2. Do moral principles vary? Many critics of relativism go beyond the observation that some concepts are universal and argue that certain ethical principles are found in every culture as well. There seems to be good reason to do so. As noted earlier, the great diversity in ethical practices provides the crucial data for cultural relativism, which then goes on to explain these data as the reflections of different social truths. However, while one would have to live a very isolated life to doubt that there are differing moral *practices*, it is not as clear that societies disagree about moral *principles*. James Rachels provides the following illustration:

> Consider a culture in which people believe it is wrong to eat cows. This may even be a poor culture, in which there is not enough food; still, the cows are not to be touched. Such a society would *appear* to have values very different from our own. But does it? We have not yet asked why these people will not eat cows. Suppose it is because they believe that after death the souls of humans inhabit the bodies of animals, especially cows, so that a cow may be someone's grandmother. Now do we want to say that their values are different from ours? No; the difference lies elsewhere. The difference is in our belief systems, not in our values. We agree that we shouldn't eat Grandma; we simply disagree about whether the cow *is* (or could be) Grandma. It may be that there really is more commonality in ethical principles than would appear to be the case at first glance. It might even be possible to isolate a few core values that are truly universal, with the differences coming about because of differences in application because of differing circumstances.[12]

Rachels's point is that we should look beyond *what* cultures do to determine *why* they do it. The "why" question considers the principles behind the action. The "what" question is concerned with how the principle is applied. The application of these principles must be understood in the context of the unique social needs or different interpretation of facts within a culture. A certain tribe can believe the principle "You should not steal" is true and at the same time encourage stealing from neighboring tribes. This is possible because stealing from outsiders may be justified on the grounds that it is necessary for the tribe's own survival (social need) or on the grounds that members of neighboring tribes are perceived as less than human (different interpretation of facts).

When we get behind the observations of diversity, it can be quite credibly argued that all cultures embrace certain basic moral principles. It is important to remember that *universal* does not necessarily mean "true." Even if it was universally believed that the earth is flat, this does not mean that this view is true. However, the cornerstone of cultural relativism is that ethical norms differ from one culture to the next. As I have shown, there is good reason to doubt that there is cultural disagreement on ethical principles. If this is true, relativism's credibility is seriously undermined.

3. Is relativism self-contradictory? One of the most frequent charges against relativism is that it is self-contradictory or, at minimum, incoherent. This problem arises because of two foundation stones of cultural relativism: "There is no absolute truth" and "intolerance is wrong." When we try to put these principles into action, we end up with Orwellian-sounding concepts, such as "tolerant intolerance" and "absolute relativism."

To illustrate the situation, imagine a hypothetical absolutist society— that is, a society that believes its norms are true, and all norms that deviate from those norms are false. One of its rules is that all who refuse to fast on Tuesdays should be put to death. Not only does this group believe that this is absolute truth, but members act on this belief, putting to death at opportune times all who do not follow this rule.

What is the relativist's response to this absolutist view? On the one hand, our relativist cannot condemn this society because "there is no absolute truth" by which to judge these executions. On the other hand, this group has to be viewed as wrong by the relativist because, though it *claims* to possess absolute truth, in reality "there is no absolute truth." Similarly, relativism asserts that "we must be tolerant of the standards of all cultures," even of those cultures that have intolerant worldviews. At the same time, it states that "intolerance is wrong." In short, the relativist's position seems to be self-contradictory because it affirms two mutually exclusive things at the same time.

Relativists end up in this predicament because their two claims— "there is no absolute truth" and "intolerance is wrong"—are not viewed as true relative only to cultural norms. In fact, they contradict many cultural views. Instead, they are statements which relativists propose as absolutes and which must be absolutely true for cultural relativism to be true. As such, cultural relativists break their own rules against the existence of absolute truths. Because cultural relativism assumes some universal standard of truth, whether it admits it or not, it becomes self-contradictory. We cannot say "right and wrong is relative to social norms" unless we assume that a common basis exists upon which the hearer could assent to the reasoning behind it.

This same internal contradiction holds true for the whole of relativism. If all knowledge, moral and otherwise, is conditioned by environment, the absolutist society has just as much ground for claiming truth for an absolutist ethical system. To be consistent the relativist should say that relativism is true only for relativists. If there is no single "true for all," then the relativist's description of reality is not universally true. But this is not what relativism claims.

4. Is moral improvement possible? "Change is inevitable" is a statement we hear frequently, and much of ethics deals with how we should view new developments in the world. However, the concept of change presents serious problems for relativism. It is helpful to remind ourselves that the belief that truth and rightness are relative to culture is the heart of cultural relativism. What a culture accepts as ethical at a given time is what its members *ought* to do. This principle raises two issues: what is the motivation for ethical change, and how are we to evaluate change when it occurs?

Envision a culture in which slavery is practiced. A relativist cannot argue on moral grounds that this practice should be abolished. To do so would require an appeal to some standard other than the existing social mores, which allow slavery. Since customs are ethical truth for a society, slave-owning is a right for our hypothetical culture.

Some cultural relativists have argued that reasons for change can be offered but they cannot be *moral* reasons. But the use of nonmoral reasons also encounters difficulties. Argumentation, at least in its generally understood sense, implies giving reasons for a belief. Positions backed by the better reasons should win out. The sticking point is that *better* is a comparative term that presupposes a standard. Since the only standard the relativist accepts is what a society *believes at the time* is "better," these slave owners should not be persuaded to adopt a new position.

The result is that no possible reason could ever be offered for the rightness of changing slavery in this society, or of changing any practice in any society. Reasons from inside the culture will not work because what is currently accepted practice is the obligation of all within the culture: It is right for that group. There is no reason that can be given to change a practice that is right. Similarly, reasons from outside the culture are unacceptable bases for change because any attempt to judge from the outside is, in the relativist's view, arrogant. No one set of ethics is better than another. So why change the practice of slavery? Under cultural relativism, no good reason to do so can be given.

Even though no ethical reasons for why change *should* occur can be offered under relativism, ideas about what is right and wrong in fact *do* change within social groups. However, this creates a special challenge for cultural relativism because it cannot say the moral change is for the better. Let us say that a group of slaveholders decides to abolish slavery on January 1, 2016. What is considered ethical on December 31, 2015 (owning slaves), will be different from what is seen as good the very next day (not owning slaves). However, relativists cannot call the abolition moral progress, because from their viewpoint no single practice is superior to any other. This again raises the question of why ethical standards change within every culture. For if we do not believe we are making a change for the better, why change?

5. Is tolerance always good? A common argument for cultural relativism is that it promotes tolerance. The idea that we should always be tolerant of other cultures sounds great at first, but closer examination may cause us to question whether tolerance is an unqualified virtue. Under the definition of tolerance and respect that cultural relativism establishes, we have no basis to call on countries to stop the torture of political prisoners or end state-sanctioned racism. Such an appeal would be intolerant and arrogant since our truth is no more true than that of the truth in cultures we would criticize. To put it otherwise, we cannot appeal to the idea of human rights. No such concept is possible in cultural relativism because it assumes absolute standards. All human rights are granted by culture, so if a culture decides not to recognize certain rights, no other social grouping should attempt to impose their standards. That is intolerant.

This becomes even more difficult when we ask what to do when one culture must interact, voluntarily or otherwise, with another. Should we have been tolerant of Hitler's encroachment on neighboring nations and his extermination of millions of people in concentration camps? Some relativists would say that tolerance should not be unilateral.[13] However, a military response to the Nazis' claim to the rightness of their actions would require that we place a higher value on our "truth" than theirs, and this is inconsistent with relativism's central doctrine.

When we look at the implications of seeing truth as relative, what we see can be disconcerting. At the core of our discomfort is the relativist belief that whoever controls a culture is the final judge of truth. This can be frightening, even in a democratic society where rules are decided by majority, because most believe that it is possible for the majority to be wrong. However, tolerance is more difficult to accept when we recognize that not all cultural standards are established by a majority but are often controlled by a tyrannical minority.

Conclusion

Cultural relativism is an approach that we should consider carefully because it is just below the surface in many discussions of multiculturalism. We want to be careful not to overgeneralize, because multiculturalism can have different shades of meaning. Taken in its weaker sense, multiculturalism can be positive. It reminds us that no cultural group can claim final authority and that we have much to gain from learning about the customs and practices of other cultures. Many would agree that this is an idea that can be incorporated into a Christian worldview.

However, in its stronger sense multiculturalism picks up the idea behind "when in Rome, do as the Romans do" and takes on a very different meaning. It states that the beliefs of all cultures are equivalent. One view is as good as another. In other words, it is just cultural relativism with a new label. When defined in this way, multiculturalism is no longer compatible with Christianity but becomes instead a competing worldview. The basic incompatibility is that cultural relativism substitutes culture for God when defining the origin of right and wrong. Relativism does not launch a frontal assault on Christianity, but it undermines it nonetheless. As John W. Cooper puts it, "Instead of attacking, it trivializes. Instead of rejecting Christianity as false, it grants relative truth. The faith is true for Christians but not necessarily for anyone else."[14] In the end it must be recognized that relativism dramatically changes the usual definition of truth. When relativism calls something true, it does not bear the dictionary meaning of "conformable to fact or reality." Instead it means "what a given culture believes to be true."

Even apart from a Christian evaluation, cultural relativism has a number of flaws. Cultural relativism lacks internal consistency because it asserts that certain principles are absolute (for example, there is absolutely no absolute truth) even while it denies the existence of absolutes. Moreover, there is reason to believe that some cultures differ not so much in their foundational ethical principles as in how those principles are implemented. Finally, it seems counterintuitive to believe that no basis exists for judging certain practices better or worse than other practices and that people should tolerate any practice accepted in a given culture.

3

LOOK OUT FOR NUMBER ONE

Ethical Egoism

"**LOOK OUT FOR NUMBER ONE.**" The message of this ethical bumper sticker puts us in an awkward position. On the one hand, we have all given advice like this, even if we have not used these exact words. It is often a good recommendation for people not taking care of themselves or for people who are often taken advantage of by others. On the other hand, few will admit to holding this as a general ethical ideal. It is not hard to figure out why. As far back as most of us can remember, we have been told to be unselfish, to look out for someone other than ourselves. When we were children, we were encouraged (and ordered) to share our toys. As adults, unselfishness is still kept before us as a desirable virtue. Charities appeal to us to share with the less fortunate. Our government provides relief for those devastated by natural disaster within our borders and offers funds to assist in the economic development of other countries. Our heroes are those who give their time, money and lives for the sake of others. Sacrifice is valued over selfishness.

The principle behind this ideal is called "altruism." Altruism is the idea that we have obligations to other people and should act for the benefit of society. Because unselfishness is so highly praised, most of us would hesitate to say that "Look out for Number One" is the moral rudder that steers our life. The reason is that this bumper sticker promotes the opposite of altruism—selfishness. However, ethical egoism says we should not fear selfishness but rather embrace it as the highest principle of morality. Furthermore, egoists argue that altruism is not simply wrong in a theoretical sense; it is an ethical problem that damages people's lives.

Egoism can take several forms, but we will consider only a universalistic approach, which argues that each and every person should be self-ish. From this perspective the moral obligation of each individual is to perform only those acts that are advantageous to him- or herself. The primary advocate of this position is Ayn Rand, who at age twenty-one left communist Russia in the 1920s for the United States. In her career as a novelist, philosopher and social commentator, she advocated ego-ism as the virtue that made America great and railed against altruism, which she saw as the downfall of her native Russia.

In order to understand how selfishness is redeemed as a virtue in egoism, we need to define it correctly.[1] According to Rand we should adopt the simple dictionary definition: "concern with one's own inter-ests."[2] This distinguishes ethical egoism's concept of selfishness from two alternative meanings. First, this is not psychological egoism. The psychological egoist says that we cannot help but act from selfish mo-tives. Nothing we do has altruistic motives. Even if I sell my home to help victims of a natural disaster, the psychological egoist says that sup-posedly the reason I give the money away is that it makes me feel good or helps me avoid unpleasant feelings of guilt. This is a sign that I con-sider my psychological well-being more important than financial secu-rity. In other words, psychological egoism says it is impossible not to be selfish. Ethical egoism, on the contrary, says that it is possible to act altruistically. We can be unselfish, but we should not be.

Second, ethical egoism is different from what we might call egotism. Egotism says that we should do what is in our interest now. It is the pursuit of immediate desires and impulses. In contrast, Rand argues that satisfaction of personal goals is to be pursued rationally. We should take the long-term view and ask what is in our interest over a lifetime. Let us, therefore, enhance the dictionary definition given previously by distinguishing ethical egoism from both psychological egoism and ego-tism: We should choose to be concerned with our own broad-based and lifelong interests.

Ethics and Reason

Rand is fiercely opposed to altruism because she considers it irrational. The source of irrationality in altruistic ethics is what Rand calls "mysticism." Mysticism is the attempt to find warrant for ethics in appeals to faith, the authority of other people, God or social fashion. All of these are rejected outright as "whim" because, in Rand's view, they are all veiled ways of building ethics on our desires. We simply use structures such as authority, church, culture or government to justify our immediate wants. Under such ethical approaches, Rand says, "'society' may do anything it pleases, since 'the good' is whatever it chooses to do because it chooses to do it."[3]

By contrast, in rational (egoistic) ethics the moral distinction between good and bad is not something we decide on. The world is the way it is. It is objective, and what we want does not change it one way or the other. The laws governing aerodynamics are not affected by any desires we have for the design of our planes. If we do not want our aircraft to crash and burn, it is sensible to adjust our designs to these laws. Similarly, right and wrong is built into the structure of the world. Our task is to use our capacity for reason and observation to discover how the world works, and to live accordingly.[4] Instead of constructing ethical beliefs on subjective whim, we should build on that which is objective, observable and scientific.[5] When we do this, Rand is convinced that unselfishness is contrary to nature and thus unreasonable.

To begin our search for a rational ethics we must reexamine the question of human nature scientifically, starting with the observation of living entities. What do such entities strive for? Life—to remain living entities! Okra, pine trees and aardvarks do not do this consciously, but all living things, in the way they are put together, move toward this goal. Nature tells us this. Root systems drive deeper into the soil when water is scarce. The body turns inward to its own fat cells when the food supply dwindles. When the lion approaches, Bambi runs. Bambi does not know why he runs, but his instinct for self-preservation may save his life. Nature teaches us that life strives to preserve itself.

Since human beings are living entities, we share the same goal as plants and animals. The will to live is the origin of ethical value. "Metaphysically, life is the only phenomenon that is an end in itself. . . . To speak of 'value' as apart from 'life' is worse than a contradiction in terms. It is only the concept of 'life' that makes the concept of 'value' possible."[6] Rand is telling us that we need to put first things first. Life is the precondition of any act of valuation. We cannot assign value to anything if we are not alive, so our highest value should be our life.

Though we have the same goal as other living things, there is a difference in human survival. Lower forms of life get by on sensation and instinct. This will not do for us because our senses are not automatic guides to self-preservation, and humans have relatively few instincts when compared to animals. Instead, what is necessary for human survival is determined by human nature, which is characterized above all by rationality. "For man, the basic means of survival is reason."[7] We are not born with the knowledge that allows us to survive. Humans do not instinctively nest and hunt. We must learn (by using reason) to make the food, shelter and clothing we need to live. It is acquired knowledge.

When we have this knowledge, we must decide whether we will use it. Rationality is not automatic. We must choose to act rationally (that is, selfishly). We can also decide to function irrationally, but this has a cost. "Man is free to choose not to be conscious, but not free to escape the penalty of unconsciousness: destruction. Man is the only living species that has the power to act as his own destroyer—and that is the way he has acted through most of his history."[8] Every choice has its consequences, and these are not affected in any way by our hopes for a Disneyland ending. Nature acts in an ordered way. If we ignore the laws by which it operates, we do not break these laws but are broken by them.

This is what draws life, rationality and ethics together in Rand's philosophy. Life—our life—is of ultimate value to us, because we can make ethical decisions only when we have it. To act irrationally puts life at risk; rationality is the means by which we preserve our life. Since anything that threatens our life is evil, our life is the standard by which all decisions are to be evaluated.[9] Therefore ethics takes on an unusual urgency in Rand's thought. Ethics is not optional, something that can be switched on as an enhancement to life; it is necessary for survival.

This explains the intensity of Rand's attacks on altruism. With its focus on the needs of other people, unselfishness does nothing to enhance our capacity for survival. Instead it threatens our life by making others the beneficiaries of our actions. Its call to self-sacrifice, according to Rand, means that we have no value unless we act for the sake of others. Altruism, rather than making our life the standard of good, makes others the gauge of rightness and ourselves the measure of evil.[10] And since this, according to Rand's definition, is irrational, it is also unethical.

Egoism and Society

A frequent criticism of egoism is that it subverts attempts to live together. How can we get along if people everywhere look out for their concerns only? Doesn't this degenerate into anarchy? Egoists reject this criticism on the basis that it does not fully understand rational egoism. Their argument is this: if I pursue my long-term interests rationally, I will do nothing that damages my reputation, endangers my life or exposes me to punishment.[11] The interests of rationally selfish people do not conflict. Anarchy results only if we mistakenly interpret egoism to entail looting and thievery. The latter is not egoism but egotism, because it reduces us to our animal (irrational) nature. It cannot produce human happiness, because humans are rational.[12] Thus Rand says that it is possible for us to remain consistent with egoistic principles and still do what is beneficial to others. Of course, the benefits others receive from our actions cannot be our goal, but there is no reason they cannot be the result. In fact, egoists say that selfishness offers the best hope for the mutual enhancement of everyone's life.

Take an example from business. You have built a mousetrap factory for the selfish purpose of making money. As part of your strategy for success, you invest money from profits in research and development, looking for the proverbial "better mousetrap." In a sense you are making sacrifices: paying acceptable wages to a number of people, providing a safe and pleasant workplace, and doing all the other things necessary to motivate others to help you in your pursuit. However, these sacrifices have a selfish motive. You do them to make money.

Your efforts succeed; you discover a method for trapping mice that is better, faster, more efficient and cheaper. People buy more of your mousetraps, and as a result you become wealthy. Was anyone harmed by your selfishness? Not at all. Instead, everyone is allowed to achieve their selfish goals as a result of your self-interest: you are rich, your employees keep their jobs, and consumers get rid of mice. Everyone wins (except the mice).

Ethical egoism maintains that it will work this way across the board. If we allow individuals to do that which will get them to their goals, whether these goals are political, social or economic, society benefits from the resulting innovation and improvement.

Thus, for Rand, the virtue in selfishness is that it respects individuals and their choices. It allows them to define their interests and pursue them or, if they wish, evade them. But no one forces the choice on them. No one makes you go into the mousetrap business, forces employees to work for you or compels consumers to buy. These are decisions based on self-interest. The metaphor Rand prefers is that of the "trader." "A trader is a man who earns what he gets and does not give or take the undeserved. He does not treat men as masters or slaves, but as independent equals. He deals with men by means of a free, voluntary, unforced, uncoerced exchange—an exchange which benefits both parties by their own independent judgment."[13]

Rand argues that the model of the trader has social benefits. First, it establishes justice as a principle. People's rights are respected and protected. These rights are not imposed from the outside but grow out of individual self-interest. If you do not want to trade, you do not have to. Whether we are talking about our money, affections, time or vote, rational people trade only when they determine that the transaction will advance their personal interests. Therefore, freedom is enhanced. No one is forced to barter.

Second, egoism promotes self-esteem. What we get, we deserve. Our achievements are not the result of charity but of our efforts. Thus, we have pride in our accomplishments. This, in turn, allows us to honestly esteem others. It is one's view of oneself that determines one's view of human nature and one's way of relating to other human beings.

The respect and goodwill that persons of high self-esteem tend to feel toward other persons is profoundly egoistic; they feel, in effect: "Other people are of value because they are of the same species as myself." This is the psychological base of any emotion of sympathy and any feeling of species solidarity. But this causal relation cannot be reversed. A person must first value him- or herself—and only then can a person value others.[14]

We cannot divorce respect and love for others from self-respect and self-love. There is no "disinterested" love (as altruism advocates). The only way one is able to care about another is when a selfish interest exists. "If a man who is passionately in love with his wife spends a fortune to cure her of a dangerous illness, it would be absurd to claim that he does it as a 'sacrifice' for her sake, not his own, and that it makes no difference to him, personally and selfishly, whether she lives or dies."[15]

Summary

Rand credits altruism for recognizing the value of character traits such as justice, self-esteem and love for others. Where she faults altruism is in its failure to understand how we achieve these virtues. Its call to self-sacrifice makes these traits unattainable because we fail to love ourselves. Therefore, the best way to help others, according to egoism, is not to sacrifice oneself for others, but to act in such a way that others will be forced to help themselves. This allows them to gain self-respect.

The key concept behind egoism is our innate impulse toward life. We naturally strive to preserve it, and without it, nothing else matters. Therefore, we should use reason in ways that will protect and enhance life. This means that our foremost ethical obligation is to do that which is in our self-interest.

The Positive Side of Egoism

The initial response many have to the term *ethical egoism* is that it sounds like an oxymoron. How can one be both ethical and egoistic? Moreover, attacking altruism is kind of like attacking mom, apple pie and the flag. Who wants to advocate selfishness? However, if considered honestly, egoism has attractive elements. First, egoism forges a strong link between personal responsibility and self-esteem. Egoism stresses that individuals are responsible for what they do and should receive the benefits of their actions. Moral agency assumes that we accept responsibility for our own actions. If this is not the case, people will depend on others to solve their problems, and this soon becomes habit. Dependency, in turn, has negative consequences for those who are dependent because it is difficult to respect oneself when what is received is undeserved. It also has negative consequences for those who meet the needs of dependent people. Providers cannot focus their efforts on that which is most naturally their concern. Energy which could have been devoted to their interests and needs is now divided and diminished. We do not run as fast when we carry someone.

Second, after some reflection, most will likely agree that self-preservation and self-interest have a valid role in ethics. We can recognize the impulse toward self-preservation on both the biological and rational level. Our biological life is protected in numerous ways. We have built-in temperature, hunger and thirst controls to protect us. Each body comes with its own infection-fighting armies of cells as standard equipment. Adrenaline is pumped into our system in response to danger and gives us extra bursts of strength and speed. Nature tells us through our physical functions that life is important. Even where our natural defense systems are not sufficient protection, our mental processes work to keep us safe. Decisions are made daily that minimize potential dangers. We consider it rational to avoid certain areas of town, put on seat belts and watch our diets. In short, physically and mentally, we have a number of systems that protect our lives. Except in rare circumstances, we confirm these natural impulses in ethics by making preservation of our lives a moral duty.

Moreover, we can agree that the selfishness of others benefits us. As Nathaniel Branden states,

> [Do] we want our lover to caress us unselfishly, with no personal gratification in the doing, or do we want our lover to caress us because it is a joy and a pleasure for him or her to do so? And let us ask ourselves whether we want our partner to spend time with us, alone together, and to experience the doing as an act of self-sacrifice. Or do we want our partner to experience such time as glory?[16]

This makes the point that relationships require mutuality and would be unfulfilling if others received no benefit themselves, and this can be extended into other areas of life. People tend to do best at what they like. If they are free to follow their interests, we all share in the benefits of their productivity.

Finally, ethical egoism warns us that actions are not justified simply because they are unselfish. Altruism cannot be good solely because our actions are of no benefit to us. Otherwise Rand's diagnosis that the self becomes the standard of evil in altruism is correct. We have all seen situations in which a person's unselfishness was destructive for themselves or others. At times I have given money to people who said they needed to buy food, only to see them minutes later with liquor but no food. People have given so much time at church for good purposes that their own families have disintegrated for lack of attention. Thus, if altruism is going to work as an ethical perspective, something must be added to it that allows us to determine when an unselfish act is also a good act.

Potential Problems in Egoism

Ethical egoism has been in existence for a long time. As far back as the third century B.C., a philosopher named Epicurus advocated an egoistic ethics that resembles Rand's ideas in many ways.[17] It exists at present in those various versions of capitalism that stress the role of the self-interested individual.

Despite egoism's long history, not many people have embraced it, or at least they do not admit to it. But while egoism has always been somewhat on the fringe, lack of popularity does not necessarily make it wrong. Many have discovered that it is a difficult system to refute. However, there are several places where ethical egoism encounters criticism.

1. Does egoism properly understand ultimate reality? While cultural relativism sees one's culture as the final authority of truth, ethical egoism hinges on the belief that each individual's life is the ultimate source and measure of right and wrong. If this is not true, egoism collapses. From the beginning, then, this view encounters difficulty in relation to a Christian view of reality. Christianity does not deny the importance of the person and the significance of an individual's life. In fact, it stresses the value of each human being in the message of salvation. However, recognizing human value is different than making each person's existence the gauge of right and wrong, as ethical egoism does. It is also part of the Christian message that when left to our unchecked desires, all of us act in ways that are harmful to ourselves.

The most basic conflict between egoism and Christianity is a matter of worldviews. Egoism's worldview makes human nature the yardstick by which everything is measured. Our life becomes the ultimate reality, and when pursued rationally, our interests are infallible. In the Christian worldview, human nature is distorted. It is out of sync with the original intention of creation. If this is true, the best way to affirm our value is not by looking to ourselves as the source and standard of goodness but by seeking a standard of truth in something that has not been perverted. Rand's own atheism is significant in this matter, because when the individual is the final word, there is no room for God in the picture. Egoism may be the best of what is left if God is not the ultimate reality, but from the perspective of a Christian worldview this option is not open.

2. Is egoism overly optimistic about human nature? As noted earlier, Christians have a worldview conflict with putting human nature at the center of the universe. Closely related to this theological objection is the very practical question of whether, given egoism's optimistic view of human nature, such an approach is workable. Rand's thesis is that selfishness is not destructive for society but is constructive. Orderly cooperation and benevolent competition will prevail under egoism because reasonable people recognize that it is not in their self-interest to be punished if caught cheating, stealing or killing. But does social life actually work this way?

Suppose that you and a coworker are both up for a promotion and only one person can get the job. Reason tells you that four propositions are true:

1. Getting the promotion is in your long-term interest.

2. By most measures, your coworker has the slight edge for the promotion.

3. If your coworker's current project goes poorly, you get the promotion.

4. You can sabotage your coworker's current project with negligible risk of being caught.

What would you do? Under the tenets of egoism, sabotage of the coworker's project is not only desirable but required. You are morally obligated to act in your best interest, and this is advanced when you torpedo your coworker's project rather than just waiting to see what happens otherwise.

This presents a counterexample to the egoist's claim that rational selfishness leads to mutually positive results. Your interests are served by acting on proposition four; thus the action is right and rational by egoistic judgment. However, the coworker does not benefit but instead is harmed by something beyond her control.[18] The company is also harmed, because the project did not go as planned, and this in turn has negative results for society. Of course it is not beneficial to you if wrecking another employee's project does irreparable damage to the corporation that employs you. Therefore, contrary to the egoist's claim, the rational self-interest of one person may harm others.

3. Is egoism inconsistent and self-defeating? Most ethicists argue that any acceptable ethical theory must be universalizable. For egoism to be a valid ethical system, then, we must be able to say that everyone should be selfish. Does egoism pass this test? Rand certainly intends for us to understand it this way. However, it seems clear that attempts to universalize ethical egoism would run contrary to our self-interest. An old joke illustrates the difficulty. One year an organization decided to give a humility award. At the banquet they presented a medal honoring Mrs. Jones for her fine example of humbleness. But as soon as she pinned the medal on her blouse, the "humility committee" felt compelled to withdraw the award. The problem is that one cannot flaunt one's humility and still remain humble.

This is the situation for egoism. If I am truly selfish, it is not in my best interest to publicize it. It defeats my purposes to tell everyone else to be selfish as well. My needs will be better served if I am an egoist in a world chock-full of altruists. In such a world everyone (including myself) will look after my interests. If I convince others to adopt egoism, I am left alone to seek my own good while everyone else pursues his or her own interests, which does not benefit me.

This puts us in a contradictory position. On the one hand, my maxim is that "each person should do only that which is of benefit to him- or herself." On the other hand, it is not to my advantage if others adopt this maxim. I cannot universalize my rule without breaking it.[19] Similarly, it would appear counterproductive to reveal that I intend to act egoistically. If I believe that I should do only those things which are to my advantage, I can better gain the upper hand by appearing to be altruistic. If I can convince others that their well-being is my concern, even when it is not, there is a better chance of gaining their interest in my well-being.

The problem of universalizing egoism can be discovered if we return to an earlier illustration. In your plan to win a promotion over a coworker by sabotage, two things are required. First, the company must continue to operate. Otherwise you harm yourself. Second, you must inflict damage on the company (by sabotaging the coworker's project) in order to receive the promotion. What happens, though, if we universalize your course of action? Requiring that everyone act selfishly if it serves their self-interest will destroy the company, making it impossible for you and everyone else to achieve their goals. Thus, universalization of the egoist principle is self-defeating. Once again, your interests are best served if others act altruistically. This preserves the life of the company so you can benefit from its existence.

It will not help to agree with your fellow egoists that all must act fairly in order to preserve the company for the benefit of all. A true egoist may sign agreements and make promises, but he or she is morally bound to break them if doing so will be of greater personal benefit. The sole obligation of the egoist is to self. That which is good for all carries less moral weight than what is good for me. If we pass up an opportunity to act in our interest for the sake of others, we have become altruists.

4. Is justice possible in egoism? Some critics charge that egoism destroys our trust that all will receive just treatment. Since justice often involves third-party mediation, we will want to be certain that judges are impartial. At first glance this would not seem to be a problem, because egoism does not advocate giving preference to anyone on the basis of religion, gender, social status or any other factor. However, it does argue that we should give preference to ourselves, thus the fairness of a mediator may still be compromised by egoism.

For example, an egoistic judge has decided she wants to move up through the ranks. To accomplish the goal, she makes rulings with an eye to the political interests of those in a position to promote her. She stays within the limits of the law but uses whatever latitude available to play to a specific audience. As an egoist she makes decisions that do not depend on any principle of justice, concern for the well-being of society or desire to protect the rights of those accused or wronged (except as required by the law). The judge's guiding principle is self-interest, and she is ethically obligated to do whatever is necessary to achieve it, even if it violates principles of justice.

This concern is not limited only to courtroom justice. Professions such as medicine, psychology, social work, accountancy and the pastorate assume that the professional's power is not to be directed toward selfish ends. Instead societies sanction the practice of these professions for the good of society as a whole. The effectiveness of professionals depends on our faith that they are acting for the sake of the clients, not for themselves. The person who goes to the psychologist needs to have faith that everything said in counseling will be kept confidential, even when confidentiality is not in the interest of the psychologist. Thus rules governing the practice of psychology reject egoism when they require strict confidentiality of counselors (except when clients make explicit threats indicating danger to themselves or others). If egoism is adopted, the professional functions necessary to society are endangered. This again calls into question Rand's assertion that egoism is not destructive of society.

The background problem here could be in Rand's assumption that society is nothing more than a collection of individuals, all of whom are required by egoism to be dedicated to the pursuit of their own interests. In this model, society benefits from this pursuit only as a byproduct of egoistic successes. However, it may be that society should be viewed not as a collection of solitary individuals who happen to inhabit the same region but as an organic whole that can thrive only when individuals act for the good of the whole. This view, however, reverses Rand's program: the individual benefits as a byproduct of the good of society.

5. Does egoism misrepresent altruism? Rand, in defining altruism, states, "Altruism declares that any action taken for the benefit of others is good, and any action taken for one's own benefit is evil. Thus the beneficiary of an action is the only criterion of moral value—and so long as that beneficiary is anybody other than oneself, anything goes."[20] When we read such a definition of altruism, we get the impression that Rand is arguing against a view that no one holds. Just as Rand is careful to say that not all selfish urges are acceptable to egoism, no altruistic approach says that "anything goes" simply because an action grows out of unselfish motives. Altruism does not judge the goodness of actions by looking only at who benefits. It also considers whether we have achieved certain ends or honored commitments to defined moral standards.

Similarly, Rand caricatures altruism when she argues that it sets up the self as the standard of evil. No significant version of altruism proposes to do this. On the contrary, altruistic ethics generally bases our concern for others, at least in part, on the recognition that we are valuable. It is from our personal sense of worth that we are able to recognize the value of others and thus our obligation to them. While we really do not want to argue with Rand's view that self-love is necessary for us to love others, we can properly question her assertion that self-love is possible only in egoism.

It is possible that a third option exists between egoism and the kind of self-denial Rand describes. Perhaps self-interest and concern for others are two sides of the same coin. Maybe it is not possible to love another without self-love, just as it is impossible to love yourself without loving others. In other words, concern for others and self-interest may not be separable. This third option is generally what altruistic systems actually propose, not the self-hatred Rand puts forward as altruism. Altruism may emphasize our obligations to others more strongly than our obligations to ourselves, but that is usually done because we have little problem with wanting to pursue our own interests. It is the altruistic side of the equation that causes trouble for us.

6. What difference exists between us and them? Some differences between people do not warrant different treatment. For example, things like race, gender, ethnicity and educational level should not lead to denials of civil rights or due process. There are, however, times when certain differences do matter and justify choosing one person over another. We give those with higher GPAs and MCAT scores first shot at admission into medical schools. Superior work skills and years of experience are proper guides for who gets a job and who does not. Egoism says we should treat ourselves differently from how we treat others by giving priority to ourselves and our interests. Is there good reason for this? James Rachels argues, "We can justify treating people differently only if we can show that there is some factual difference between them that is relevant to justifying the difference in treatment. If we are to be the final word on right and wrong, we must find some rational guide for what sets our interests above those of others."[21]

Has Rand isolated any such factual difference between ourselves and others? She puts herself in a difficult position. On the one hand, she argues that respect for others is based on the fact that all have the same potentialities. At the same time she says that our interests have priority over the concerns of others. No rationale is given for this precedence except that our interests are ours. However, this difference has no relevance to the question of why another person should be treated differently than oneself. And if others' concerns and needs are similar to mine (which Rand admits), egoism is arbitrary in promoting selfishness. It simply chooses one set of interests over another.[22]

Conclusion

From a Christian point of view, egoism fails to provide a sufficient foundation for ethics on several fronts. First, it is a form of idolatry because it begins from the assumption that my life is of first and ultimate concern. This makes each individual his or her own god and leaves no place for God as our ultimate concern. Second, egoism fails to recognize the value of each person. When the sole standard of right and wrong is determined by self-interest, other people are seen as a means to achieve our interests. They are thus depersonalized. The result is that any possibility of functioning social systems and justice is undermined because both require that we recognize others as equally valuable. Finally, egoism fails as an ethical system because, if we attempt to universalize it, it becomes self-defeating.

Christianity and ethical egoism do have something in common: both believe that moral responsibility requires that we do what secures and enhances our lives. However, they disagree on how that is accomplished. Part of this tension arises from differing definitions of *life*. For Rand, life encompasses physical survival as well as social, economic and political interests. However, Christian ethics requires a broader definition of life, one that includes a spiritual dimension. Unless we incorporate the spiritual side of existence into our view of what it means to preserve and enhance life, we miss a very important dimension. Egoism, by restricting its view to the physical realm alone, does not address this side of human existence. And if we eliminate a central part of our lives from an ethical system, this does not appear to promote our interests.

4

I COULDN'T HELP MYSELF

Behaviorism

CONSIDER THE WAY WE EXPLAIN most things that happen. When we talk about objects—the growth of a spruce, the dent in the side of the car, rainfall patterns or the eruption of a volcano—we think in terms of cause and effect. These things do not simply happen out of a vacuum; they are caused. Something makes them happen. Moreover, these events do not involve a thought process on the part of the physical objects. Trees and fenders do not decide anything. They simply respond to the strongest cause. When we shift to explanations about human behavior, however, we use words like *decision, choose, will, deliberate, free* or the first word in this paragraph, *consider*. Our descriptions of the types of things humans do refer to or imply a mental process involving a choice between options. They also presuppose that people could select a course of action other than the one they have taken. In short, language about human action assumes that people are free in a way that spruces and fenders are not.

B. F. Skinner, a psychologist who taught at Harvard, understands human actions in a different way than what has been outlined here. He argues that the belief that human acts are free is mistaken. What we do is not the result of decisions we make. Instead, it is determined. Determinism is the belief that nothing happens either randomly or by choice. What we call choices are actually the result of some previous event: a cause. Actions that we think are the result of freely made decisions are only the effect of an unrecognized cause. In Skinner's view, we do not have thought processes in which we choose a course of action. "Acting" presupposes that we make decisions. Instead, our "actions" are really just predispositions to behave in certain ways as the result of physical causes. For this reason Skinner's approach is given the name "behaviorism."

If Skinner's behaviorism is correct, the freedom we feel is an illusion. We have no more freedom than trees, fenders or volcanoes. Therefore when someone says, "I couldn't help myself," she is more correct than she may want to be. Generally our "I can't help myself" statements are a way of talking about something that exerts strong influence on us. We don't mean to say that no other response was possible in the situation. However, Skinner says that this is precisely the case. Behavior is controlled by cause and effect, what behaviorists call stimulus and response. When a particular cause or set of causes (stimuli) are in place, a specific effect (response) must follow.

Freedom and Determinism

Traditionally, we have attributed human freedom to a soul or mind (as opposed to a brain, which is a physical organ). This is even reflected in the word we use to describe the study of our inner life—*psychology*, the study of the soul (psyche). This soul, or mind, is viewed as a nonphysical entity. It is a "something," but it is different from physical somethings in that it is immaterial and nonspatial. Because the soul is nonphysical, it is not subject to laws that govern physical objects. For example, God is a nonphysical being. Therefore it makes no sense to speak of trying to keep him out of a certain area by locking the door or building an air-proof container. God (a nonphysical being) cannot be stopped by a wall or Tupperware (physical things). Likewise, since the soul is viewed as an immaterial entity, it is free of physical causes. It is the soul's capacity for thought that makes freedom possible. Physical objects, on the other hand, do not have the capacity for thought and are therefore not free from the chain of causation.

Behaviorism rejects the idea of a mind or soul at the outset, because it seeks to adopt a strictly scientific approach to human existence. This approach considers only what we can confirm with our senses. Since we cannot see, touch or smell a nonphysical soul, nonphysical souls do not exist, and beliefs that include the concept of the soul must be understood in a new way. Skinner argues that if we reconsider evidence generally used to support belief in a soul, that evidence will be found wanting. Moreover, Skinner says, human behavior can be more accurately explained without it. For example, when we consider the way our bodies operate, we assume the same types of rules that govern other physical objects. I cannot reduce my size or lower my body temperature through mental activity. These changes are brought about by physical processes. This seems to be true of all bodily functions. They operate according to the laws that govern events in all other physical objects. If we recognize the physical causes occurring in our body and understand the laws behind them, we can anticipate the effects.

This ability to predict future events extends into our social behavior as well. Children raised in a culture that is primarily Buddhist are more likely to be Buddhists as adults. Those who spend a lot of time around hockey fanatics have a greater chance of developing an interest in the game. To a large extent, what happens to our bodies and what behaviors we will adopt is predictable. The ability to anticipate what individuals will do given certain circumstances leads behaviorism to conclude that we do not need the idea of a soul to explain what humans do.

Instead of talking about freedom of choice, Skinner proposes that we study human behavior the same way we study the external world: scientifically. Understanding human actions is a matter of discovering the unchanging laws that cause them. As Skinner states, "If we are to use the methods of science in the field of human affairs, we must assume that behavior is lawful and determined. We must expect to discover that what a man does is the result of specifiable conditions and that once these conditions have been discovered, we can anticipate and to some extent determine his actions."[1]

This is what leads Skinner to stress the importance of one's social environment. We cannot trace the firing of synapses in the brain to know which ones cause a particular behavior. However, there is an indirect way to understand why people do certain things, because the stimuli that move the brain to work in certain ways come from the external world. If we are careful observers, we can see the correlation between what people do and what is going on in their environment, and thus determine what it is in the environment that causes a particular behavior.

Skinner's views are not as strange as one might think. In fact, we use stimulus-response methods on a daily basis. For example, how do you change the behavior of a four-year-old who is throwing rocks at squirrels? Since throwing rocks at squirrels is a real temptation for the four-year-old, you will have to offer the child an attractive alternative behavior. The best option, according to Skinner, is to use a pleasurable experience to encourage the child to behave in a different way. You may smile at him when he begins to walk away from the squirrels. Or you might say, "If you drop the rock and come over here, I'll give you some ice cream." Skinner calls this positive reinforcement. Positive reinforcement occurs when we add something new to the social environment, such as a smile or an offer of ice cream, as a means of changing someone's behavior.

This stimulus-response means of influencing behavior affects everyone, not just four-year-olds. Stimuli that are effective with a four-year-old may not be effective for adults (although ice cream still works pretty well on most of us), but we are no more free of conditioning than a child is. When positive reinforcement is used in connection with a certain behavior, both adults and children are more likely to repeat the behavior in the future. The four-year-old does not decide to lay down the rock, the thief does not choose to steal, and we do not select whom we want to marry. These behaviors are caused by a social background that encourages such behavior by reinforcing it.

Behavioral Control

Many people are concerned about Skinner's belief that behavior is determined by the environment. But he goes even further and says that we should consciously mold behavior by manipulating our surroundings. To modify a quote from Marx, it is not enough to understand behavior, we should seek to change it. In fact, Skinner wrote a novel titled *Walden II*, in which he outlined his vision of a utopian community. In this community, behavior is modified by controlling the input to the inhabitants. Problems are corrected by changing elements in the social environment, which then leads to changes in behavior. As a result of behavioral manipulation, citizens of Walden II lead happy, creative and productive lives without personal and social conflicts. In Skinner's program, Walden II can be more than just a fictional place. Peaceful and fulfilling lives can be created by behavioral engineering.

If the idea of having your actions controlled by someone else makes you uncomfortable, Skinner wants you to consider two things. First, behavioral engineering is not some futuristic utopian ideal. We already do it (and have it done to us), although Skinner says its effectiveness is reduced because it is generally done unconsciously. Nonetheless, behavioral engineering happens through the educational system, the family structure, government policy, religious groups, peer pressure and all other institutions, formal or informal, we have contact with. Our failure to recognize this control does not mean we are free from its power. Behavior modification is inevitable; thus, Skinner states, "the problem is to free men, not from control, but from certain kinds of control."[2] This leads to his second point.

The belief that we are free is not just a mistaken notion; it threatens our survival. He illustrates this with a comparison of the physical sciences and the study of human behavior. The former has made great strides by applying scientific methods. Crop production is increased, diseases are cured, new forms of transportation and communication are invented, and space is explored. However, when it comes to human nature, we are still struggling with the same questions that perplexed the ancient Greek philosophers. Why do those who deal with the human world seem to be rehashing the same old issues? Skinner says it is because we will not let loose of the illusion that people are free. We are using a prescientific model of human nature. As long as we maintain this mistaken notion, we can make no more progress in repairing what is wrong with humanity than the person trying to increase crop yields by sacrificing small animals to fertility gods. On the other hand behaviorists argue that just as those who use scientific methods succeed in increasing food production, if we adopt a scientific model to shape human behavior, we will not just see progress, we will cause progress.

In Skinner's view the imbalance between the physical sciences and the understanding of human behavior cannot continue indefinitely. "It is understood that there is no point in furthering a science of nature unless it includes a sizable science of human nature, because only in that case will the results be wisely used."[3] The need to correctly understand how human behavior works can be summed up in one word: *survival.* If we cannot properly control our behavior, advances in our understanding of the external world will destroy us.

Behaviorism and Ethics

To this point our discussion has sounded more like Psych 101 than ethics. However, this background allows us to recognize important ethical implications in behaviorism. As a result of his understanding of human behavior, Skinner concludes that the traditional conception of ethics is headed in the wrong direction. Traditionally we have assumed that ethics deals with what people should do. However, if behaviorists are correct, the word makes no sense. We cannot choose, so what is the point of telling someone that they should tell the truth or respect life if they are not in control of what they say or do?

Where does this leave ethical statements? Behaviorism has a convenient way of incorporating them. Ethical claims are tools we use to modify people's behaviors. Skinner writes:

> "You should (you ought to) tell the truth" is a value judgment to the extent that it refers to reinforcing contingencies. We might translate it as follows: "If you are reinforced by the approval of your fellow men, you will be reinforced when you tell the truth." The value is to be found in the social contingencies maintained for purposes of control. It is an ethical or moral judgment in the sense that ethos and mores refer to the customary practices of a group.[4]

Ethical statements serve the same purpose as laws, religious doctrines and rules of etiquette. They tell us what society, or a portion of society, expects from us if we are to gain their approval. In other words, it is a way of shaping our behavior. However, we should be clear that ethical statements do not refer to choices we make. An imperative such as "Thou shalt not steal," Skinner tells us, "is no more normative than the assertion 'if coffee keeps you awake when you want to go to sleep, don't drink it.'"[5] The traditional idea that some things are wrong is lost when we forfeit the idea of freedom. What we are really doing in ethical statements, according to Skinner, is attempting to cause people to act in certain ways.

The behaviorist conception of ethics also has ramifications for moral responsibility. There is no reason to consider someone "responsible" for what they do if it is beyond their ability to do otherwise. Thus, Skinner argues that moral responsibility, as normally understood, is meaningless. Putting blame on someone who does what we consider wrong is cruel. How can we blame someone for what he or she did not choose to do? If this is the case, we must rethink the idea of punishment. Punishment only makes sense if people are free and could have taken a different path. If that is not true, punishing people for what they cannot change is ineffective and mean-spirited.

This does not mean that all behavior is acceptable. Some behaviors threaten the survival and well-being of ourselves and others and should be modified. Therefore, instead of punishing people for certain behaviors, we should see harmful behavior as problems to be solved and habits to be broken. In fact, Skinner makes almost no distinction between physical and behavioral problems. In setting a broken bone we change the position of the two ends so that the bone will grow back together properly. To put it differently, we reengineer the position of the bones by imposing causes on them that will lead to healing.

Likewise, when the murderer kills as a result of the environment's encouragement of that kind of behavior, it is necessary to reengineer that behavior by changing the social environment. If we are successful in the murderer's treatment, we will get a new set of behaviors from that person which will not threaten the lives of others. Both physical and behavioral problems are detrimental to the survival of an individual. Therefore we need to discover and then adjust the stimuli, either by removing those that cause unwanted behavior or by overriding them with different stimuli that will create positive responses.

Another point of ethical significance in behaviorism is the way human nature is viewed. Traditionally, we have set ourselves apart from the animal world by appealing to our freedom, moral responsibility and spiritual sensitivity. Since behaviorism denies that these qualities are real, it undercuts the idea that humans are essentially unique. If this is so, has behaviorism robbed humanity of dignity? Without freedom, are we reduced to the level of animals?

Skinner argues that if behaviorism makes us feel we have been stripped of our dignity, it is because we have become so familiar with the belief that we are free. Since we have always been taught that we are different from animals, of course we will react negatively to such a radical idea. However, Skinner is confident that this early negative reaction will change over time. At one point in history, people felt threatened by Copernicus's discovery that the earth was not the center of the universe. This too was seen as a challenge to human dignity. However, no one today worries much about the loss of geocentric cosmology. We do not feel that our place in the universe is sacrificed when we acknowledge that the planets and stars do not revolve around the earth. Similarly, Skinner is confident that as we become more familiar with the concept of psychological determinism, it will not be perceived as a threat.[6] Instead, it will open the door to a clearer understanding of our true place in the universe.

In Skinner's view there is a high cost in hanging on to the myth of "autonomous man" for the sake of human dignity. Warfare, poverty and struggle have been constants throughout human history. Where is the dignity in that? In Skinner's view we will be unsuccessful in solving the perennial problems of humanity as long as our understanding of human dignity is based on a romantic (and mistaken) idea of freedom. True dignity would result from solving these problems, and Skinner is confident that modifying behavior through scientific methods is the way to do it. Since human struggles are the results of causes, only a scientific approach will reveal the problem-causing elements and thus open the door for their elimination.

Finally, while human behavior is determined by outside forces, we are not left on the sidelines. "It is the autonomous inner man who is abolished, and that is a step forward. But does man not then become merely a victim or passive observer of what is happening to him? He is indeed controlled by his environment, but we must remember that it is an environment largely of his own making."[7] While we should not deny our control by external stimuli, that is not the whole story. We can create and change the stimuli, and thus we can create and change our world. We should not forget that we play twin roles as both manipulated and manipulator.

Summary

Skinner's concept of human nature has significant ramifications for ethics. Without human autonomy, ethics dissolves into the study of how society influences us. However, Skinner assures us that replacing freedom with determinism and viewing ethical statements as a form of behavioral control are not real losses. We are more than compensated by having an understanding of human behavior that is correct and which will increase our chances of survival. Behaviorists are convinced that our belief that we are free is based on ignorance. Freedom is a tool we use to explain what we did not understand. By replacing it with scientific methods, we will be in a position to understand human behavior. However, when we replace belief in freedom with behavioral engineering, we must also recognize that we have eliminated ethics in the traditional sense and replaced it with something very different.

The Positive Side of Behaviorism

Behaviorism is not the kind of ethical system many people want to accept. It makes us uncomfortable because we do not like to think that our actions are beyond our control. In addition, we get queasy when we consider the specter of others intentionally conditioning our behavior. Even if we could be convinced that it is "for our own good," the idea of being engineered to lead a happier life seems to reduce us to the level of lab rats running a maze in search of cheese. Regardless of whether we feel comfortable with behaviorism, there are some things to be gained from this perspective.

To best evaluate Skinner's position, it is helpful to divide his ideas into two categories: the methodological and the metaphysical. The methodological aspect of behaviorism deals with the means by which we understand and change human behavior. The metaphysical level, on the other hand, refers to an understanding of reality. These are not necessarily a package deal. We can agree with behaviorism's concept of the process by which environment influences behavior (methodology) without buying into his interpretation of the way the world is put together (metaphysics).

On the methodological level we observe the influence of positive reinforcement on human behavior. If someone consistently smiles at us as we pass, we are more likely to smile back at him or her than someone with a permanent frown. This person has modified our behavior. Similarly, we do not doubt that our most significant environments—home, school, church, work—exert a powerful pull on our actions. Behaviorism helps us recognize this influence and understand how it works. Without accounting for such factors, we will have a difficult time explaining why people do and believe certain things. Therefore, even if we disagree with behaviorism's claim that all our actions are the result of environmental stimuli, awareness that society does influence our lives can help us evaluate whether our views are the result of thoughtful decision or are simply borrowed from the world around us.

In addition, even though the words *manipulation* and *control* have negative connotations, we have to admit that we do attempt to change people's behavior through reinforcement. We teach children manners by rewarding certain actions and discouraging others. The coach's pregame pep talk is a means to get team members to feel certain ways and do certain things. We are exhorted to adopt certain beliefs in our churches and are rewarded when we do so. In short, we do use our institutions to influence behavior, even if we do not think of it in those terms.

If this influence is legitimate, we need to think carefully about how this influence is exercised so that we can be effective in using it. Such discussions occur daily. Management strategies, books on effective child rearing, and stop-smoking programs frequently involve forms of behavioral reinforcement. Many of the debates over public policy are actually debates about the best way to change behavior. For example, there is little disagreement that improving people's social environment reduces the likelihood that they will be involved in criminal activity. How we do this effectively is an important question, and behind it is the assumption that educational, religious, economic and media institutions are part of an environment that conditions behavior to some extent. Thus these influences should be studied to see which are the most effective. Since the institutions that influence us are social institutions, the social sciences can help us understand and enhance the effectiveness of their influence.

Freedom is something of a cultural icon for Americans, and to suggest that our decisions can and should be intentionally influenced meets immediate resistance from many people. However, Skinner is very effective in making two related points: We are not completely free of social influence (which is different from being free) in our decisions, and we cannot explain human behavior by referring only to a mind or soul. Our activities are swayed by the forces of our social world, and when we honestly acknowledge the way social structures work, society assumes that intentionally trying to influence behavior is acceptable. Therefore, Skinner makes some valid points when he speaks of the methodology by which behavior is shaped. This does not mean that his metaphysical assertions are correct, and this is where his views break down.

Potential Problems in Behaviorism

The means by which we evaluate behaviorism necessarily differ from critiques of other systems because it is, in a sense, an "antiethical" theory. It rejects the very premise of ethics: freedom and responsibility. Therefore we won't get anywhere by arguing that behaviorism calls us to decide ethical matters in the wrong way. From Skinner's point of view there are no ethical matters to be decided, because we are not free to decide anything. Because of this, critiques of behaviorism must begin with its understanding of the world. Skinner's conclusions about ethics assume certain truths about reality. If these metaphysical assumptions are incorrect, Skinner's statements about ethics are put in doubt.

1. Does God have a place in behaviorist metaphysics? Skinner's worldview has no place for God. Belief in the divine, like belief in human freedom, is considered an outmoded way of explaining things that we previously were not able to understand. Moreover, Skinner asserts that nothing is, in itself, right or wrong, and that ethical language is just another way to condition people's behavior. Ethical terms do not mean anything; they do things. Thus, Christian belief in a moral God who puts ethical demands on people is eclipsed.

Skinner's worldview understands the universe as a closed system. Everything that happens is explainable in terms of causes that occur within the system. No divine power intervenes in the process. The closest thing to God in such a view is the person who is able to comprehend the way the world works and manipulate it. Therefore, while to some degree the Christian may agree with Skinner concerning methods of influencing behavior, it is impossible to incorporate Skinner's understanding of ultimate reality into a Christian perspective.

2. Is everything the result of cause and effect? In the evaluation of the positive aspects of Skinner's view I stated that there is little doubt that our actions are influenced by our social environment. This is, however, much different from what Skinner says in arguing that our actions are determined by the environment. *Influence* refers to a power that exerts force on our actions, but can be resisted. Freedom and social influence can coexist. However, if something is determined, it cannot be other than what it is—it has to happen. Behavior is solely a response to the strongest stimuli. Freedom is compatible with influence, but it is not compatible with determinism.

What leads behaviorists to believe that we do not have freedom? To a large degree it is based on the predictability of human behavior. When we know a person well enough (which includes knowing something of his or her social history and background), we can rather successfully anticipate his or her actions. Thus one of Skinner's assumptions can be put in the form of a proposition:

(1) Determined behaviors are predictable.

We will accept this proposition as true. If an event is governed by laws of cause and effect, we can anticipate how it will turn out, provided we know all of the relevant data and the laws that relate to them. Therefore if we understand the governing laws and know the water temperature, the altitude and other relevant data, we also know how hot water must be to reach the boiling point.

However, what Skinner is trying to prove is something different from proposition 1. Instead he moves from the observation that human actions are predictable to the conclusion that they must therefore be caused. Therefore his view can be expressed as

(2) Predictable behaviors are determined.

One way to try to make the case for determinism is through a deductive argument, but this will not stand up. Proposition 2 does not necessarily follow from proposition 1 any more than "all birds are ducks" follows from "all ducks are birds." In other words, Skinner cannot prove deductively that human actions are determined.

The only way left open to Skinner to support his argument that humans are not free is to draw from observation evidence that indicates unambiguously that everything we do is caused by social forces. This does not seem possible either. First, the predictability of human behavior can be just as easily explained by social influence, which does not preclude freedom. For example, if you are an American driver, I can predict very accurately which side of a two-way road you will drive on. My correct prediction does not require us to believe that your behavior was determined. Your decision is very likely to be influenced by social pressures, but there seems to be no reason to believe you could not have decided to do otherwise.

Second, there is evidence that seems to indicate that we can act contrary to environmental influences. We can all think of people who should have turned out poorly in life because of their background. Instead, they beat the odds and became happy, well-adjusted and productive people. Of course, Skinner has a nice "out" when such counterexamples to his theory are pointed out. He can simply argue that causation is very complex and our inability to find a particular cause for unexpected behavior does not prove behaviorism false. We just do not know enough about the causal process to isolate all the relevant stimuli.

Here is where we are at this point: All sides agree that we can often foresee what actions people will take. Skinner interprets this to mean that everything we do is predetermined by our social environment.

However, this conclusion encounters three rather difficult problems. First, it cannot explain (at this point) why people sometimes seem to act differently from what we would expect. Second, predictable behaviors can be explained just as easily by social influence. Thus, even if environmental influence is so powerful that it overrides a person's potential for choice, this does not mean we are determined. It does not damage the nondeterminist's argument to say that we do not, or even cannot, exercise freedom at certain points. Finally, Skinner's position runs into the difficulty of explaining why virtually all people have the impression that they can and do make choices when, if Skinner is correct, this feeling is false. We will consider this issue next.

3. Why do we ask why? For Skinner's argument against freedom to be accepted as true, he has to convince us that things work in the human world the same way they work in the nonhuman world. In other words, we must be convinced that there is nothing different about human behavior and animal behavior except the complexity of the influences on human actions. However, the difficulty with this position is that human behavior does not seem to be simply "bigger and better" than animal behavior. Human behavior and animal behavior are qualitatively different. We seek understanding. We want to know what is right and wrong (and why we talk about right and wrong), why we consider Yosemite Valley more valuable for its beauty than for its potential as a large landfill, why there is a universe instead of nothingness, why the universe manifests consistency rather than chaos, and why we believe we are free when we may simply be drones manipulated by the world around us.

Humans do not just do a better job of asking questions; we are the only species to try to understand ourselves and our universe. We should not be so blind as to ignore the uniqueness of the actions we engage in daily. Whether we reflect upon what God is like, critique the latest Steven Spielberg movie, tell someone we love them or deliberate on where we will attend college, humans perform tasks that are not replicated outside the species. While it may not be apparent at first glance, all of these unique actions assume freedom. Our lives are not consumed by the events that surround us. We are able to step outside the flow and reflect on them. We can detach ourselves from the immediate situation and ask what it all means.

How all of these uniquely human actions occur is a mystery. As previously noted, uniquely human actions traditionally have been attributed to a nonphysical soul. There is no physical process we can point to that explains what causes these types of behaviors. However, using the concept of the soul to explain human behavior does not sit well with the scientific method, which cannot account for nonphysical causes. So Skinner rejects the existence of a soul. However, in trying to unravel the mystery of human actions by reducing them to mechanical stimulus-response behaviors, Skinner leaves us with an even greater mystery. Even when language about the soul, freedom or God is eliminated, we still have to answer the question of why we are aware of what we do, why we ask why and where moral or spiritual sensitivity comes from. If Skinner is correct that "man is a machine in the sense that he is a complex system behaving in lawful ways,"[8] why are human actions not simply more complex than the actions of beast or machine but rather are of a completely different category from these? We may not be able to provide a full explanation about how we are able to act freely. However, human freedom does seem to give us a better explanation of the empirical evidence than determinism.

Everyday experience tells us that human beings are an exceptional part of creation in that we do things that no nonhuman species does. These are not just different things that humans do but are activities that presuppose freedom and responsibility. In *Beyond Freedom and Dignity* Skinner states that "man is much more than a dog, but like a dog he is within range of a scientific analysis."[9] This is not much comfort to his critics, however, because we are "more than a dog" only in terms of the complexity of our biological functions and the sophistication of the environment that controls us. And this does not seem, to many, to be a sufficient foundation for understanding human dignity.

4. Is Skinner consistent? The central doctrine of behaviorism is that we have no ability to make choices. However, opponents frequently argue that behaviorism is inconsistent at this point because no behaviorist can really speak or act as if the theory is true. It is amazing when you stop to consider how many of the words in our vocabulary assume or imply that we are free to make choices.[10] As Skinner himself notes, without freedom we cannot have attitudes or pride. We cannot think, plan, intend, will or take initiative. Faith and frustration are also impossible. All such actions assume processes in which we weigh alternatives and make decisions. Generally, Skinner is careful to filter out words that presuppose mental activity (as opposed to brain activity). At times, he puts such terms in quotes, indicating his belief that we could express the same thought in terms that conform to behavioristic theory if needed.

While it may be possible to rid our vocabulary of words that presume human freedom, it is not as clear that we can purge the idea of freedom from our speech. For example, Skinner argues that since behavioral manipulation is a fact, we ought to understand how it works and use it to engineer a better world. This becomes problematic if we stop to think about what is involved in the phrase *ought to*. *Ought* assumes that we can decide to use behavioral engineering or reject it, so what sense does it make to tell people they ought to do something? If, as Skinner argues, those who read his words are determined by their environment, it is impossible to choose a behavioristic method, or any other method for that matter.

The problem for any approach that wants to remain purely scientific is how to find a way to move from statements that are factual to statements that are obligatory. It is clear that Skinner holds (although behaviorism cannot allow for beliefs) that his position is factually correct. However, it is hard to deny that he also asserts that we have an obligation to adopt any view that is factually correct. But once again, to say that we should act on the basis of factually correct statements presupposes capacity for choice. Remember, *should* requires the assumption that we can do otherwise. Skinner can say that acting according to a correct understanding of reality is necessary for our survival as a species. But he cannot tell us why it is right to be concerned about survival without invoking a moral principle (which is not allowed in behaviorism). A similar problem occurs when Skinner says that we should reject the idea of punishment. He can be consistent if he means that punishment is an inefficient means of modifying people's behavior. However, his theory does not allow him to extend the argument to maintain that we should not punish people. This implies that there is an obligation to be efficient.

The charge of inconsistency is not just a logical puzzle one uses to trip up people. It involves the very practical matter of whether Skinner's views can be put into practice. Take his view that scientific method is a prerequisite for our survival and should have a role in directing life in the future. Skinner acknowledges that "it would be quite inconsistent if we were to exempt the scientist from the account which science gives of human behavior in general."[11] This means that the theories of scientists such as Skinner cannot be different from what they are. Skinner did not choose to be a determinist. And if the task of science is to engineer behavior, it must be acknowledged that this understanding of science's task was not chosen by scientists or by nonscientists submitting to the control of scientists. For in behaviorism there is no freedom. Therefore, Skinner cannot state or imply that behavioral engineering is what we should do in the future (*do* implies intention, which assumes freedom). If he is correct, the most he can claim is that behavioral engineering is the correct prediction of what will happen in the future as a result of observation of people acting according to unbreakable rules of behavior. However, his conclusions are not presented as the findings of social science based on research but as an agenda (a word that, once again, assumes intention).

Conclusion

My hunch is that this chapter is one of the most challenging to understand in this book. The nature of the system makes it this way, because behaviorism's ethical views depend on a particular understanding of reality. In order to get to its conclusions about ethics, you have to understand and evaluate its metaphysical views. Behaviorist ethics provides a good illustration of how important worldviews are to our conclusions about morality. Skinner's understanding of reality presupposes that nothing exists that cannot be discovered through the scientific method. This rules out God from the start because God is not the type of reality that can be touched, tasted or seen. Moreover, Skinner's view of reality vetoes the possibility that there is something within human beings not detectable by the senses, but something nevertheless that allows us to act freely.

Since his assumptions about what is real lead to the conclusion that human beings are not free, Skinner promotes a radically different interpretation of ethics. Without freedom, moral statements have no ethical meaning. Ethics is reduced to a behavioral strategy in which people are trained to behave in certain ways. We lose much more than just ethics, however. Behaviorism's understanding of "I can't help myself" applies to all aspects of human life. Thought, belief, love, responsibility, sin and reward all cease to exist in the traditional sense. With this reduction of ethics and human existence, the premise of Scripture that we are a special part of creation that is responsible before God is lost.

5

SURVIVAL OF THE (ETHICAL) FITTEST

Evolutionary Ethics

AS MENTIONED IN THE introductory chapter, bumper stickers generally don't venture beyond the delivery of a simple, compact message. Occasionally, they respond to other bumper stickers, such as those announcing, "My kid beat up your honor student" or "My border collie is smarter than your honor student" as replies to the omnipresent "My kid is an honor student at Bart Simpson Elementary School." In rare instances, however, bumper stickers engage in something that approximates debate. This is the case when the "ichthus" Christian fish bumper sticker draws fire from the Darwin footed-fish bumper sticker, which is counterattacked by the rotund "truth fish" swallowing the mutant Darwin fish.

This back-and-forth bumper-stickering offers limited insight into Christianity and evolution, but tells us a lot about the owners of these bumper stickers. First, it is obvious that some folks have strong opinions about Christianity and evolution. Second, both sides of the debate imply that their bumper symbol represents an overarching worldview— a benchmark idea that answers life's biggest questions. One task in this chapter is to ask whether evolution offers an explanation for everything, including ethics, or if its scope is more limited. Finally, this bumper sticker debate implies that Christianity and evolution are either-or choices. If you are a Christian, you must reject evolution, and vice versa. One fish swallows the other. We will challenge this assumption by asking whether Christianity and evolution are indeed an either-or matter or if they are potentially compatible.

The Roots of Evolutionary Ethics

The Christianity-evolution debate has been around since publication of Darwin's *On the Origin of Species* in 1859. However, *Origin of Species* is not the origin of biological evolution; the concept had been around for decades. Darwin's contribution, a decisive one, was his theory of natural selection, which seeks to explain the mechanism by which evolution functions. Therefore, before turning to recent versions of the controversy, we will take a quick glance at natural selection to see what ethical implications Darwin and a contemporary, Herbert Spencer, drew from this theory.

Natural selection begins with the observation that in any species the offspring may vary from the parents. Some of these variations are beneficial to the offspring; many are harmful. In domestic husbandry, we weed out harmful attributes so they will not be passed on, and select advantageous variations. For example, we might choose larger bulls for breeding because larger size is hereditary and thus will be transmitted to the offspring. Smaller bulls are weeded out by being transformed into steers. Outside the "planned parenthood" of domestic breeding, Darwin says, nature itself "selects" which variations pass on to future generations, although he emphasizes that nature's selection process is not intentional. In natural settings, then, if a particular shift in insect coloration makes it less likely that predators will find and eat it, the bug possessing this characteristic is more likely to survive, reproduce and impart this trait to its offspring.

The example above also illustrates the critical role environment plays in natural selection. With the exception of intelligence, no particular trait is universally advantageous for survival. Advantage always depends on the environment. Certain insect colorations provide great camouflage in a deep green jungle, but offer a lousy disguise against desert sands. Thus, the evolutionary motto "survival of the fittest" assumes that "fitness" always refers to the surrounding environment. Environments, however, are never static. Climate changes, shifting migration patterns, introduction of a fungus and a myriad of other factors alter an environment, and this process is ongoing. Thus, a species once well adapted may become less fit over time. If a variation appears that makes its possessor a better fit for new environmental circumstances, this variation may become so pronounced over many generations that a new species emerges from an earlier one. In some cases the original species without the survival-enhancing variation becomes extinct; in other cases it continues to exist alongside the new species or in a more hospitable environment.

Darwin's *Origin of Species* says remarkably little about natural selection's implications for humans. However, his later book *The Descent of Man* (1871) spells these out in detail. One aspect that was implicit in *Origin* now becomes explicit: Because human beings evolve from non-human species, we are not qualitatively different. Not even rationality distinguishes us in any categorical way. Darwin says, "The difference in mind between man and the higher animals, great as it is, is certainly one of degree and not of kind."[1] Based on this, he concludes that moral attributes, which are built on intelligence, are present also in the animal world, although in lesser complexity. Thus Darwin says, "Every one has seen how jealous a dog is of his master's affection if lavished on any other creature; and I have observed the same fact with monkeys. This shows that animals not only love, but have a desire to be loved."[2] Antecedents for human moral qualities such as love, honesty, cooperation and faithfulness to kin are all found in the social behaviors of the animal world.

At first glance moral attributes that encourage unselfishness seem contrary to evolution's push for individual survival. However, Darwin says that social qualities that enhance the survival potential for one's group also increase the survival potential of individuals within the group. Group survival is not then contradictory to individual survival. Thus Darwin argues that nature "selects" unselfish moral predispositions and passes them on to future generations of human beings as well. This prosocial evolutionary tendency gives rise to optimism. "Looking to future generations, there is no cause to fear that the social instincts will grow weaker, and we may expect that virtuous habits will grow stronger, becoming perhaps fixed by inheritance. In this case the struggle between our higher and lower impulses will be less severe, and virtue will be triumphant."[3]

While Darwin only reluctantly took evolution beyond biological boundaries, Herbert Spencer, a contemporary of Darwin, had no such qualms. He viewed evolution as a single, all-encompassing process that explains every facet of our world, and he dove headlong into its implications for social life by formulating what is often referred to as "social Darwinism." One implication of social Darwinism is that human nature cannot be conceived in static terms. As he put it, "Between the naked houseless savage, and the Shakespeares and Newtons of a civilized state, lie unnumbered degrees of difference."[4] This reveals a strong progressive element in Spencer's thought. Evolution is an upward, purifying movement that improves the human species.

Spencer admits that evolutionary processes required the eventual extinction of less evolved "naked houseless savage" societies by the more advanced "Shakespeares," primarily by means of warfare. However, he was confident that social progress had made warfare unnecessary. For future evolutionary improvements, "what remains to be done, calls for no other agency than the quiet pressure of a spreading industrial civilization on a barbarism which slowly dwindles."[5] Spencer's view of evolution sounds pretty heartless toward less advanced cultures. However, he reminds us that he didn't make the rules. Nature's evolutionary laws punish the ignorant with suffering and death. On the brighter side, evolution's laws also provide the means to correct these miserable conditions. The truth available from a scientific understanding of evolution's rules will set us free.

Social Darwinism was very popular in the late nineteenth and early twentieth centuries, but thereafter quickly fell out of favor. The horrors of World War I revealed that barbarianism did not dwindle in highly evolved industrial civilizations. In fact, the more "advanced" cultures proved extremely adept at barbarianism. World War II also pointed out that the eugenic aspects of social Darwinism could be directed in very ugly directions. If nature extinguishes barbarians, why not nudge nature along by exterminating those who are a drag on the human race? As a result the assumption that evolution brought about irreversible progress in human goodness was shattered.

A second problem for social Darwinism was more philosophical; it appears to commit the so-called naturalistic fallacy. Briefly stated, the naturalistic fallacy says that we cannot jump from *is* to *ought*. Thus, the evolutionary process of nature may reveal certain facts about human nature ("is" claims), but these are very different from statements about how we *ought* to act. For example, even if it *is* a fact that natural selection eliminates "the naked houseless savage," it is quite a different thing to say that we *ought* to eradicate them. As a result of these problems, evolutionary ethics lay dormant for several decades until its recent revival.

Sociobiology—A New Start for Evolutionary Ethics

A new phase in evolutionary ethics began in 1948 when sociologists and biologists set out to integrate the two fields and sociobiology was born. However, sociobiology gained little traction until the appearance of E. O. Wilson's book *Consilience: The Unity of Knowledge*. The main title acknowledges a gap between the empirical sciences such as biology, genetics and physics and transcendentalist approaches to knowledge. *Transcendentalism* refers to the methods and assumptions of the humanities, social sciences, philosophy and theology because they generally assume that answers for life's biggest questions transcend natural entities or causes. Wilson hopes to bring consilience, or reconciliation, between empiricism and transcendentalism in order to give unity to our knowledge, as Wilson's subtitle indicates.

The terms of this reconciliation should be noted, however. As Wilson puts it, "The choice between transcendentalism and empiricism will be the coming century's version of the struggle for men's souls. Moral reasoning will either remain centered in idioms of theology and philosophy, where it is now, or it will shift toward science-based material analysis."[6] He clearly chooses the latter because he believes that only empirical science explains causation.

To transcendentalists, then, this looks more like a hostile takeover than a reconciliation. At the same time, Wilson says that the natural sciences must give up something as well. Empiricism must surrender the assumptions (1) that scientists should focus exclusively on their particular field, and (2) that they should be content with describing *how* things happen. Instead, Wilson argues scientists should move into the transcendentalists' domain and address questions of meaning, ethics and purpose. The majority of scientists, however, believe that science is ill-suited for addressing these issues.

The Core Beliefs of Evolutionary Ethics

As an indication of evolution's pivotal role in evolutionary ethics, Richard Dawkins says, "If superior creatures from space ever visit earth, the first question they will ask, in order to assess the level of our civilization, is: 'Have they discovered evolution yet?'"[7] In addition to the framework provided by natural selection, evolutionary ethics retains three key ideas from Darwin and Spencer—human beings are not qualitatively unique, evolution's processes are oriented toward survival and reproduction, and moral characteristics are beneficial for survival. The new factor in the discussion is provided by genetics. Darwin knew that traits were passed from parents to offspring, but didn't know *how* this happened. Genetics provides a means for contemporary advocates to explain how traits of all kinds are transmitted to offspring. Our task is to see how evolutionary ethics traces our evolutionary path from simple genes to the emergence of ethical traits, and what that tells us about our path forward.

In the Beginning: Matter, Genes and Survival Machines

"In the beginning was simplicity," Dawkins tells us.[8] *Simplicity* refers to a relatively static universe filled with raw, fundamental elements. As natural forces acted on these materials, the first simple molecules formed, and eventually a new kind of molecule evolved—a replicator. Replicators could reach into the primordial soup around them, draw out materials similar to their own and reproduce themselves. Because the environment had a finite capacity to support life, natural selection dictated that "the replicators that survived were the ones that built *survival machines* for themselves to live in." While early "survival machines" were protective coatings, the more complex forms were plant, animal and, eventually, human bodies. Thus after billions of years of evolution, these replicators "created us, body and mind; and their preservation is the ultimate rationale for our existence. They have come a long way, those replicators. Now they go by the name of genes, and we are their survival machines."[9]

With this brief description of evolution from molecule to human being, we can see how genetics has shifted the discussion. In Darwin's day "survival of the fittest" described organisms struggling to survive in a competitive environment. However, evolutionary ethics argues that individual organisms, human beings included, are simply vehicles—survival machines—that serve purposes dictated by their genes. The real battle for survival occurs on the genetic level.

The predominant quality that allows DNA to make the evolutionary cut is, as Dawkins puts it, "ruthless selfishness," an attribute that "will usually give rise to selfishness in individual behaviour."[10] The second shift in the discussion grows from the claim that our genes create us "body and mind." Dandelions, manatees and human beings are products of genetic strands whose genealogies stretch back over eons. Our shape, size, intellect and moral capacities are ultimately reducible to our genotype. Thus no accounting of human morality can be given until we know how genes turned us into moral creatures.

How Genes Became Moral

Nothing thus far appears to offer a promising beginning point for ethics. Indeed, Wilson says that genes themselves "feel nothing, care for nothing, intend nothing."[11] How then do unfeeling, uncaring, purposeless, selfish genes generate beings capable of moral qualities such as feeling, caring, intention and selflessness? Evolutionary ethics reminds us that these genes did not survive for millions of years without some pretty slick tricks up their metaphorical sleeves. These tricks are referred to collectively as "epigenesis," which paves the road from prosocial behaviors to unconscious altruistic behaviors, resulting ultimately in moral behavior.

Epigenesis refers to regularities within an organism's internal processes that allow for its life-enhancing characteristics. For example, a prairie dog (which, for the uninitiated, is a rodent, not a canine) will yip to warn others to dive into their holes if it senses a coyote nearby. This is a regular behavior that employs the prairie dog's internal processes, its brain and sense of smell, which has obvious benefits for survival. Evolutionary ethics argues that such prairie dog behaviors arise because its genes "desire" to live and reproduce. To increase this possibility, genes encode safety strategies into this critter's sensory and brain functions. Moreover, this behavior has a social benefit; it increases the survival potential for other prairie dogs in the kin group. In this case the benefit comes with little risk to the one who helps the group. The next link in the chain toward morality, then, requires prosocial activities involving individual risk.

The movie *March of the Penguins* documents the arduous trek emperor penguins endure every year to propagate. Without stopping, these animals walk over barren tundra for days to reach their breeding area. After pairing up, the female lays a single egg and, following weeks without food, takes the long hike back to water to find nourishment. In her absence the male keeps the egg warm between his feet in horrific subzero weather. The chick is already born when mom returns two months later. Dad, starving and weak, waddles several days back to get renourished himself while the female assumes parental duties. Predators, hundreds of miles of waddling and the worst weather imaginable make the breeding ritual extremely perilous for the penguins, and many do not survive.

Evolutionary ethics sees this self-endangering behavior as an important link in the evolutionary chain toward morality. The penguins' epigenetic rules compel behaviors that parallel the social character of moral action. Penguin parents work together to achieve a goal, lavish great love on their offspring and are highly loyal to each other (at least during that particular breeding season) and to their chick—all social behaviors. In addition, these social behaviors involve significant deprivation and sacrifice, even to the point of death. In short, the epigenetic rules governing penguin reproduction result in *altruistic* behavior, behaviors that put individual interests and life at risk for others.

Behind penguin altruism are selfish genes seeking to replicate. They accomplish this by prescribing epigenetic rules governing the reproduction of new "survival machines" for themselves (i.e., baby penguins). Penguins whose genes do not compel such altruistic behaviors don't reproduce; altruistic penguins do. Thus, as Wilson puts it, "If the reduction of survival and reproduction of individuals due to genes for altruism is more than offset by the increased probability of survival of the group due to the altruism, the altruism genes will rise in frequency throughout the entire population of competing groups. . . . The individual pays, his genes and tribe gain, altruism spreads."[12]

This attempt to demonstrate how epigenesis explains altruism still has two difficult hurdles to cross. First, no one pretends that an emperor penguin's unselfish behaviors are moral actions. They are genetically programmed, not free, choices. The question, then, is how genetically determined behavior can be transformed into consciously chosen action. The second issue is that the same epigenetic rules that lead nonhumans to sacrificial actions on behalf of a kin group also prescribe aggression against outsiders, who are competitors for necessary resources. Animal altruism thus appears to have strict limits. Evolutionary ethics must therefore explain how the same genetic legacy that (1) determines animal behavior and (2) leads to hostility toward outsiders can also account for (3) freely chosen actions and (4) altruistic impulses toward complete strangers or even enemies. The answer, it claims, is found in our genome's creation of mind and culture.

Minds, Culture and Religion

Wilson asserts that at a certain level of complexity and integration between the senses and the brain, mental activity appears "as an emergent process."[13] Mental activity, or mind, differs from brain activity because it has capacities like volition (choice), rationality and intention. Thus, while brain-equipped penguins unconsciously behave unselfishly, mind-equipped human beings make choices about their actions, consider alternatives for action within a broader framework of ideas about the world, and attribute motives to what they do. In addition, the mind's capacity for forming ideas allows for the emergence of culture, which Wilson defines as "the total way of life of a discrete society—its religion, myths, art, technology, sports, and all the other systematic knowledge transmitted across generations."[14] Culture, then, formulates ideas about the world, turns them into doctrines, laws, rules and etiquette, and passes on these ideas through social structures such as religion and political systems.

While culture may seem far removed from genetics, Wilson argues that cultural ideas are reducible to genetic impulses. Consider, for example, cultural taboos against incest. On the one hand, given our strong genetic predisposition to propagate, one might suspect that we would look first toward kin. On the other hand, contemplation of sexual activity with one's closest relatives elicits a definite "yuck reflex" in us, and this "yuck reflex" is expressed in virtually every culture through laws, religious sanctions and social isolation.

While incest taboos are generally communicated through cultural structures, Wilson says that ethical precepts "are very unlikely to be ethereal messages outside humanity awaiting revelation, or independent truths vibrating in a nonmaterial dimension of the mind."[15] Instead, he locates morality's origin in biology. As evidence, he points out that incest avoidance is not just a human phenomenon but one commonly found in mammals with no cognitive awareness that incest results in fewer live births and a higher incidence of defects. Moreover, human societies had incest taboos well before they understood the biological ramifications.

The question, then, is how unknowing mammals and humans "know" that incest puts a species at a disadvantage in the survival sweepstakes. The answer evolutionary ethics gives is that our genes guide us to cultural restrictions before we humans even suspect what they are up to. Thus social taboos that cite the divine will or strictly moral reasons for prohibiting incest do all the right genetic things but are based on illusion.

The implication of this is that our DNA is responsible for foisting the illusion of transcendent powers and divine realities on us. How does this happen? Some evolutionary ethicists have suggested that consciousness came at a cost: Human beings driven by a will to live were now also conscious of their mortality. This awareness led to despair, which presented a danger to our survival-oriented genome. Epigenetic rules created religion as a response to this threat. Since religion gives purpose to life by conferring meaning on our existence, it has survival value. Moreover, it benefits society by offering reasons to live that transcend individual existence. Sacrificial acts can now be justified by appealing to the divine will. Individuals resistant to group norms and ideas can be brought into conformity with threats of divine punishment, and the tribe benefits. This illusion had such powerful life-preserving tools that the genetic code transmitting it quickly spread throughout the whole species.

This presents a quandary for those who want to replace religion with a scientific worldview. As Wilson puts it, "The essence of humanity's spiritual dilemma is that we evolved genetically to accept one truth [religion] and discovered another [empirical science]."[16] He believes that we can live without God, but people still need a "sacred narrative" that provides a sense of purpose and unity. If empirical science robs us of that, we are left impoverished. Thus, while we need to abandon the old religious worldviews, Wilson believes that

> the true evolutionary narrative, retold as poetry, is as intrinsically ennobling as any religious epic. Material reality discovered by science already possesses more content and grandeur than all religious cosmologies combined. The continuity of the human line has been traced through a period of deep history a thousand times older than that conceived by the Western religions. Its study has brought new revelations of great moral importance. It has made us realize that *Homo sapiens* is far more than a congeries of tribes and races. We are a single gene pool from which individuals are drawn in each generation and into which they are dissolved the next generation, forever united as a species by heritage and a common future. Such are the conceptions, based on fact, from which new intimations of immortality can be drawn and a new mythos evolved.[17]

Summary

Wilson says that empirical science indicates that all living things arise from "a single gene pool," evolving over billions of years. The gene pool has flowered into an astounding diversity of forms united by a common impulse for longevity and reproduction. This idea, derived from scientific investigation, must be couched in a narrative that uses religious-type language (what Wilson calls "mythos"). The mythos then can inspire a universal concern for all life, regardless of race or tribe. While the language may be poetic, the content is grounded in empirically based rules consistent with our genetic mandate to succeed as a species while also nurturing all other forms of life. Thus, the final chapter of *Consilience* is a call to environmental responsibility so that we can achieve and maintain the broadest possible range of biodiversity.

Positive Elements in Evolutionary Ethics

Wilson's desire to ground ethics in empirical science allows evolutionary ethics to contribute to a description of what we might call our ethical infrastructure. *Infrastructure* refers to a framework within which things happen. For example, a transportation infrastructure includes things like road and rail systems, fueling facilities, airports and various vehicles used to provide transportation. In a similar way, evolutionary ethics focuses on the physiological components of our ethical infrastructure.

In our moral decisions we depend on our senses to gather data, our nervous system to communicate this data to our brains, and our brains to process the data. While the infrastructure does not constitute ethics itself, our ethical processes cannot work outside this infrastructure. And if glitches arise in the infrastructure, ethical deliberation will be hindered in some way. Thus, if an individual's brain becomes debilitated by a serious cranial injury, a tumor or a significant chemical imbalance, individuals may act in ways they themselves would consider highly immoral apart from the impairment. In short, evolutionary ethics reminds us that our moral life relies on a physiological infrastructure, and the capacities and incapacities of that infrastructure have a strong bearing on how we process moral data and assign responsibility.

An additional aspect of infrastructure arises because of the issues generated by circumstances. Population densities, geography and costs are all factors in our design and use of a transportation infrastructure, and the interests represented in each of these factors must be considered against the others. In a similar way, evolutionary ethics examines the genetic factors that determine how our moral infrastructure is used. It makes a plausible case that many of our strongest impulses—group loyalty, aggression toward outsiders, individual survival instincts, selfishness, parental protectiveness and reproductive drives—are universal because they are genetically based. Moreover, these impulses create the circumstances that require moral decision because they often conflict. Thus, we must choose between drives such as national allegiances and family duties to determine, for example, when to send a child to war or ship him or her to a neutral country to avoid war.

Our discussion of ethical infrastructure refers to an aspect of ethics known as "descriptive ethics." Descriptive ethics is concerned with factual matters such as why people are inclined to act in certain ways or embrace a particular set of moral values. Evolutionary ethics, with its reliance on empirical methods such as observation, testing and quantification, is well-suited for this task, and we can benefit by taking its findings into consideration. However, descriptive ethics supports a second aspect of the discipline—"normative ethics." Normative ethics is usually what people have in mind when they hear the word *ethics*. It considers how we should live and what type of people we ought to be. In short, it goes beyond description and prescribes what people *ought* to do. As we will see, evolutionary ethics faces severe limitations in this normative function.

Potential Problems with Evolutionary Ethics

1. Evolutionary ethics can't tell us how to get from **is** *to* **ought**. While evolutionary ethics is very interested in descriptive ethics, it isn't content to stop there. Thus Wilson's determination that we *are* genetically predisposed toward survival and reproduction leads to a normative conclusion: we *should* act in ways that promote survival and species continuation. To this end, then, he asserts that we should be environmentally responsible in order to nurture and protect the broadest possible range of biodiversity.

Wilson's normative statements clearly indicate that he cares a lot about preserving life of all kinds. What we don't find, however, is any explanation about *why* he, or anyone else, *should* care. We might conclude that our genetic construction causes us to care about our life and that biodiversity extends our longevity and ensures the future of our species. Even if these are factually true claims, he doesn't explain how they justify a very different claim such as "our survival is ethically good." To say that something *is* differs significantly from saying that something is *good*. This presents a particularly sticky problem for evolutionary ethics because it says that we must choose between a variety of clashing genetic predispositions. In other words, our conflicting drives present the problems ethics has to solve. If evolutionary ethics is to resolve the conflicting "is's" presented by our genetic nature, it must go beyond them to find our moral "oughts." This, however, requires dependence on the very transcendent ideas that evolutionary ethics rejects.

2. Evolutionary ethics cannot explain or justify altruism. Nothing in the list of human drives that might be plausibly explained by genetics—reproduction, individual survival, group loyalty, parental protectiveness and so on—appears to be compatible with a robust type of altruism. At best, evolutionary processes might explain why I would act sacrificially in order to gain something valuable in return. However, evolutionary ethics wants to go beyond this *quid pro quo* altruism and prescribe an ethics that takes us beyond family, kin or tribal loyalties to a universal benevolence toward all people.

Natural selection creates difficulties for this endeavor, however. Why, for example, would I donate money to help earthquake victims a continent away? These victims cannot reciprocate and will never even know the source of their assistance. So how can my genes generate the idea that I have a moral obligation to help them? After all, such acts run contrary to natural selection; they reduce the resources available to my kin group and thus decrease our reproductive prospects.

The problem becomes even more difficult if I know that some of the earthquake victims I feel compelled to help would exterminate me if they had the means or opportunity. Every genetic impulse points away from acting altruistically toward those who hate me. In short, we can't make sense of universal altruism in a system built on natural selection, which views outsiders as competitors in the contest for limited resources. Why would my genes endanger their own survival by prescribing altruistic attitudes toward hostile competitors outside my immediate gene pool?

3. The reduction of humans to genetics is problematic. Skinner's behaviorism and evolutionary ethics both believe that human nature can be fully explained by reductionism, or reducing human functions to more basic physical functions. Skinner's reductionism, as we have seen, requires abandonment of traditional ideas about ethics because we cannot squeeze freedom out of material components operating according to the deterministic laws of physics (see chapter four). Wilson, on the other hand, wants it both ways. He believes that humans are reducible to physical realities, genes, *and* that we possess the capacity for free choice that makes ethical responsibility possible. He asserts that this is possible because minds, which evolve from brains that achieve a certain degree of complexity, transcend the mechanistic limits of brains. Wilson, however, is vague about how this quantum jump occurs and offers only a promise that science will eventually explain it.

Maintaining that determined matter can become free and moral creatures is only one way that Wilson tries to have it both ways. Because he is committed to genetic reductionism, he argues that humans differ from nonhumans only in terms of complexity or quantity. At the same time, he cannot accurately describe what human beings actually do without recognizing that many of our activities are qualitatively unique. Thus Wilson says that while all creatures inhabit an environment, only human environments are shaped by ideas, laws, constitutions, traditions and religious doctrines. In other words, humans create culture, pigs don't. He argues that all living creatures are products of their genome. At the same time, ethics is a one-way street in which genetically created human beings have ethical obligations to nonhumans such as camels, but genetically created camels cannot be held morally responsible for their treatment of humans. A male praying mantis is genetically compelled toward a mating process that propagates the species while often leading to his own death, but only human beings *choose* to mate and to sacrifice life for some greater good.

Evolutionary ethics is not the first worldview to entertain the hypothesis that these and other uniquely human endeavors are merely the products of a larger and more complex brain. Great thinkers have considered this option for thousands of years, because, on the surface, our connection to the nonhuman world is striking. After all, we bear many physiological and behavioral similarities to nonhumans, especially primates. We have the same organs in the same places that perform the same functions, die from many of the same causes (although the orangutan death rate from traffic accidents is pretty low) and eat many of the same foods. Humans and nonhumans alike have territorial tendencies, family loyalties and selfish inclinations. We even share a very significant genetic connection.

Despite all this, the vast majority of history's greatest minds have concluded that human beings cannot be fully explained by genes or any other material function. The reason is that we have to account for the human capacities that allow us to analyze poetry, speak of wisdom, choose between survival and martyrdom, debate the meaning of penguin altruism, care about biodiversity, or feel a moral tug to love both our family and our enemies.

Wilson acknowledges the gravity of these unique human activities, which is why he feels compelled to attribute minds to human beings. The difference is that he believes that minds can be reduced to physical stuff, while most of history's best thinkers have argued that minds (which they usually use as a synonym for soul) are realities whose capacities transcend explanation by genes, which, as Wilson puts it, "care for nothing, intend nothing." The irony, then, is that the very transcendentalism that Wilson portrays as irrational came into existence because history's best minds concluded that physical reductionism is itself irrational. The exceptional capacities of the human species put far too much strain on the explanatory powers of material causes.

4. Evolutionary ethics cannot explain our purpose. Wilson's claim that human beings are reducible to our genes creates a difficult tension with his belief that evolutionary ethics offers an "ennobling" narrative that gives meaning and direction to human existence. From evolution's narrative, he claims, we discover "new intimations of immortality" that offer purpose to human life. This purpose arises from the fact that "We are a single gene pool from which individuals are drawn in each generation and into which they are dissolved the next generation, forever united as a species by heritage and a common future."[18]

The implication of Wilson's genetic reductionism, however, is that this "ennobling narrative" is not really a story about human beings at all. It is a narrative about our genes. Individuals are created by these genes and then "dissolved" into the next generation. The essential link to the future is not provided by us. We are only vehicles for our genes. In fact, the "single gene pool" of which Wilson speaks is not limited to the *human* genome. All life—algae, mosquitoes, sparrows, human beings—has the same "heritage and a common future."

The bottom line on Wilson's "ennobling narrative" is that my individual existence only serves the purpose of handing off a genetic code to the next generation. Even the limited role the human species plays in genetic transmission is merely a matter of chance. Dawkins, in the concluding statement of *The Selfish Gene*, reminds us that, according to his theory, "the individual [human] body, so familiar to us on our planet, did not have to exist. The only kind of entity that has to exist in order for life to arise, anywhere in the universe, is the immortal replicators."[19] Even though our genes use human organisms as vehicles for transmission, billions of other possible organisms could do the job just as well.

In the end, if Wilson's narrative implies that moral ideas like goodness, justice or respect for a diversity of life forms point toward a purpose for individual human beings, he promotes the very type of illusion he claims to find objectionable. The real narrative is about our genes; they are the beneficiaries of our moral activity. This may be a narrative, but it seems highly misleading to claim that it ennobles us or provides any purpose for our existence.

5. Evolutionary ethics assumes that science will purify human nature. When evolutionary ethics assigns blame for the ethical shortcomings of the past, it sees ignorance as the culprit. This explains its emphasis on laying a rational, factual foundation for ethics. The assumption then is that an ethics constructed on empirically grounded facts will succeed where transcendentalism has failed.

In addition to my objection to Wilson's caricature of transcendental-ism as blind faith, my problem with this premise is twofold. First one must ignore much of our recent history to believe that empirical science can scrub us clean of our moral failings. In the past century those socie-ties that envisioned a world purified by scientific method were also re-sponsible for two world wars that killed more people than all other wars in recorded history combined. In fact, it seems a bit odd that the eco-logical degradation Wilson is so concerned about has accelerated along with our scientific expertise. I could multiply examples, but the point is clear. Advanced scientific knowledge does not seem to yield morally advanced people.

The reason scientific breakthroughs do not seem to be correlated with ethical progress brings us to the second problem: Normative ethics seems to transcend the scope of science's expertise. Wilson portrays rejection of evolutionary ethics as a rejection of science, but this seems far too simplistic. I don't doubt science's expertise in dis-covering facts about observable and quantifiable entities and using these facts to devise amazing and useful technologies. In fact, my family history of Alzheimer's disease and cancer has me cheering sci-ence on to even greater discoveries. Science has a good track record of telling us what we *can* do. I am less certain, however, that its expertise extends to an ability to illuminate what we *should* do with all these discoveries. Most scientists, by the way, agree with these limits on science. For example, Stephen Jay Gould, a prominent scientist who has no qualms about evolution, says, "scientists cannot claim higher insight into moral truth from any superior knowledge of the world's empirical constitution."[20]

In the end, these two problems bring us full circle to the birth of evolutionary ethics. Social Darwinism died in the early twentieth cen-tury because it could not show us how to get from *is* to *ought* and be-cause the events of that period demonstrated that scientifically ad-vanced people were not necessarily good people. Unless social Darwinism's successor, evolutionary ethics, can prove that future scien-tific advances will purify our moral nature, the belief that empirically based ethics generates benevolent people rings hollow.

Conclusion

At the beginning of this chapter I questioned whether the "great bumper sticker war" had misled us into believing that we had to choose between science/evolution and God/transcendence. Evolutionary ethics, it is clear, believes that this is an either-or choice, and it comes down squarely on the science/evolution side. Others, especially theists, embrace God and transcendence, and reject the other side of the equation. I think both sides are wrong.

Wilson is critical of transcendentalist ethical approaches that move directly to normative claims before having the facts that descriptive ethics can provide. To him, this looks like we have built our ethical theories in midair. His desire, then, is to lay a factual foundation under our ethics. To the extent that he sticks to the factual matters of what I have called our "ethical infrastructure," he offers a useful contribution. Wilson reminds us that we cannot ignore the numerous intersections between human and nonhuman physiology and behavior, and that we should not shove questions about how humans have come to assume our current physiological structure or behaviors under the rug.

Moreover, while I believe that purely naturalistic models of evolution are problematic, I see no reason why his explanations about how evolutionary forces have shaped our moral infrastructure should be dismissed out of hand. I also think it unwise to completely ignore the role our physiological elements play in this ethical infrastructure. Even if our mental, cultural or ethical actions cannot be reduced to purely physical causes and interactions, they don't occur apart from them either. To put it in more philosophical language, our physiology/genes provide the *necessary conditions* for ethics. Our physiological infrastructure is necessary because we couldn't do what human beings do if it didn't exist. Where I part ways with evolutionary ethics, however, is that I think it is highly improbable that the evolution of genetic materials provides the *sufficient conditions* for ethics.

A "sufficient condition" refers to an explanation that has sufficient power to explicate all the data that needs to be explained, and this is where evolutionary ethics fails. Combining an evolutionary process with an animal's physical components may sufficiently explain what nonhumans do because their behaviors remain within the limits of matter functioning according to laws of cause and effect. However, these factors are insufficient to explain human abilities to exercise freedom, establish and reflect on motives, compose national constitutions and sonatas, think about and worship God, or create ideologies built around evolution. Only transcendent realities provide the sufficient conditions for such uniquely human pursuits.

Wilson makes big claims for empiricism's potential as an explanation for everything. For example, he says that, "The natural sciences have constructed a webwork of causal explanation that runs all the way from quantum physics to the brain sciences and evolutionary biology." Immediately after this, however, he admits, "There are gaps in this fabric of unknown breadth, and many of the strands composing it are as delicate as spider's silk."[21] He is confident that the natural sciences will bridge these gaps and reinforce the delicate explanatory strands. However, these "gaps in the fabric" are quite considerable. Scientific answers are still pending for basic questions such as how we get from is to ought, explain altruism or our purpose in life, vindicate our moral capacities, and explicate why scientifically bright people are not always morally good people. Ironically, then, evolutionary ethics, which portrays itself as the rational alternative to faith, turns out also to be a faith system. And all these intellectual IOUs demand significant quantities of faith. Too much faith, in fact.

These first four ethical systems have all tended to turn traditional concepts of morality upside down. In each, we have noted specific points worth considering, but as complete systems they are of little help to Christians. They are particularly problematic in that they leave little or no room for a moral God, or any God at all. The next four systems more easily accommodate belief in God, but hang together as moral theories without such a belief.

6

THE GREATEST HAPPINESS

Utilitarianism

MANY PEOPLE ARE UNCOMFORTABLE with ethical egoism because it advocates the selfish pursuit of happiness. The factor that disturbs people about egoism is not the emphasis on happiness but the emphasis on selfishness. What would happen if we kept the pursuit of happiness, eliminated selfishness and devised a more socially inclusive system? Can we create an acceptable ethical theory around a bumper sticker that advocates "the greatest happiness for the greatest number"?

"The greatest happiness for the greatest number" is not a new slogan. This phrase was coined more than a century ago to express the essential idea of an ethical system called utilitarianism. This theory, which has its roots in the movement toward democracy in the eighteenth and nineteenth centuries, is a form of hedonist ethics. Hedonism is the view that the good that people should seek is happiness or pleasure (the terms are used as synonyms in this chapter). There is often a negative response to the term *hedonism* because it is associated in popular use with immediate physical or hormonal pleasure. However, hedonistic ethics usually refers to happiness or pleasure in a broader sense. It refers not to an emotion or immediate feeling, but to a state of overall well-being that includes, and usually emphasizes, the intellectual, spiritual and social aspects of happiness.

Although Aristotle cannot be classified as a utilitarian, the argument for happiness as the guide to determining the good goes back to him. His ethics begins with a simple question: What do our actions tell us about what we want? When we go on vacation, advance our education or invest in the stock market, what are we really after? You may believe these questions have three different answers, but Aristotle says that ultimately the answer to all these questions is the same. We do want to relax, learn more and make money, but these are not ends in themselves. We can still ask why we pursue relaxation, education and money. Aristotle's answer is that we believe (though not always correctly) that such things are means to happiness.

If we try to push this further and ask people why they want to be happy, we get puzzled looks. The answer generally sounds something like "I want to be happy because it makes me happy." We end up with circular explanations because it is difficult to get behind happiness to a more ultimate goal. That is because, says Aristotle, "everything that we choose we choose for the sake of something else—except happiness, which is an end."[1] Or, to use different terminology, happiness is the only thing that has intrinsic value. It is good in itself, not just a way to get to something else. If pleasure is the only thing that is intrinsically good, then pain (including physical, intellectual, spiritual or social pain), its opposite, is the only thing that is intrinsically bad.

The name *utilitarianism* comes from the idea of utility, or usefulness. Utilitarianism says that acts are morally right when they succeed in (or are useful for) bringing about a desired result. The result that should be desired is happiness, because it alone is intrinsically good. This is incorporated into the basic statement of utilitarian ethics, the "principle of utility." As Jeremy Bentham defines it, "By the principle of utility is meant that principle which approves or disapproves of every action whatsoever, according to the tendency which it appears to have to augment or diminish the happiness of the party whose interest is in question."[2] Acts are good when the result is happiness, evil when the result is unhappiness. We can seek after other virtues, such as kindness, justice or fairness. But these are good only when they lead to happiness. They are a means to an end. Only happiness is an end in itself, therefore it is the only true standard of goodness.

For the Greatest Number

While the "greatest happiness" principle is central to utilitarianism, the other part of the equation, "for the greatest number," is also significant. In his definition of the principle of utility, Bentham speaks of "the party whose interest is in question." This "party" refers not only to one-self but also to everyone affected by a decision. Our decisions involve other people, so asking only about the good that will result for us is inadequate. We are obliged to consider the well-being of all who are touched by our decisions.

Two things are involved in requiring happiness "for the greatest number." First, this principle includes what egoism leaves out. Each person is valuable, therefore, one person's happiness is as important as another's. Equal regard for the interests of all is the basis of democracy. Thus utilitarianism is an altruistic approach to the extent that whenever the majority will receive greater happiness, you have an obligation to honor its decisions even if it is not to your advantage.

This leads to the second observation. Utilitarianism acknowledges that happiness "for all" cannot be achieved in every situation. People's interests conflict, and some people will have to concede their interests for the sake of "the greatest number." If a vote does not go your way, the will of the majority should be accepted. This requires a bit of sacrifice from everyone. However, the sacrifice is not good in itself. As John Stuart Mill puts it, "The only self-renunciation which [utilitarianism] applauds is devotion to happiness, or to some of the means of happiness, of others."[3] Therefore, sacrificing our desires to the will of the majority is good because respecting its opinion will result in the greatest happiness for the most people. Everyone wins in the long run.

Utilitarianism as Consequentialism

Utilitarianism began as one aspect of a broad-based revolution. I have already mentioned its association with the democratic trends of the last 250 years. Both utilitarianism and democracy are part of a more comprehensive rebellion against authoritarian structures in which power and law came from the top down. In such structures, ethics was generally based on rules, and those who followed the right rules from the right sources were considered good.

Utilitarianism's response to authoritarianism is twofold. First, it builds on the assumption that truth comes to us through our senses. We do not need to rely on a source that must be accepted by faith or under coercion. Truth is discovered through observation and can be verified by the senses. We know when we are happy because our senses tell us. Thus, our senses provide the empirical evidence that accompanies good actions. Second, utilitarianism does not judge actions by their conformity to rules like "do not murder" or "do not commit adultery." Instead, if we want to know if something is right or wrong, we look at the results. We ask how a potential course of action will turn out. This is what is called a consequentialist system. Ethical truth is found in the consequences of our actions; it is subject to testing. For utilitarians the right ethical question is whether an action will have the result of creating the greatest happiness for the greatest number. Since the consequence we seek is happiness, right and wrong is determined by whether this is the result we get.

Although utilitarianism rejects faith as a sufficient basis for ethics, it does not necessarily leave God out of the picture (but some utilitarians do). Theistic utilitarianism simply argues that we need to understand how God communicates his will to us—that is, that God teaches us through our senses. Christian utilitarianism says that proper observation of the world should tell us what God expects from us, since the universe is God's creation. We are created to be happy, and the result of doing what God intends is happiness. In fact, Mill argues, utilitarian ethics is the system that best fits a religious view of the world. "If it be a true belief that God desires, above all things, the happiness of his creatures, and that this was his purpose in their creation, utility is not only not a godless doctrine, but more profoundly religious than any other."[4]

Quantitative Utilitarianism

The first major advocate of utilitarianism was Jeremy Bentham (1748-1832). Bentham's goal was to make ethics quantifiable; if indeed goodness results from happiness, then we need a way to determine which choices lead to the greatest amount of happiness. Bentham suggested that there is an objective way to quantify right and wrong (which fits well with utilitarianism's stress on observation and testing). In fact, the concepts of measurement and objectivity are reflected in the name of his method: hedonistic calculus (or calculus of felicity). He divides happiness into seven categories: intensity (how intense is the happiness?), duration (how long will it last?), certainty (what is the probability of obtaining desired results?), propinquity (how soon?), fecundity (will it lead to similar pleasures?), purity (how much pain comes with it?) and extent (how many are affected?).[5]

Once these categories are in place, making ethical decisions by means of Bentham's hedonistic calculus is a two-step process. First we quantify how much pleasure we expect to gain in each of the seven categories. Then we compare the totals to see which of the options available scores highest. The option that provides the greatest quantity of happiness is the ethical choice. It's a bit like doing ethics by spreadsheet

Bentham did not think there was anything novel about his method. In fact, he believed that most people use a similar process without realizing it. For example, if you have ever made a major decision by listing positives and negatives on opposite sides of a sheet of paper, you have engaged in a process similar to Bentham's hedonistic calculus. Should I change jobs now or stick with my present one? What is included on one side or the other of your sheet probably reflects several of Bentham's categories. One option may offer more satisfaction in the long run (duration), lead to advancements down the line (fecundity) and have a positive impact on the greatest number of people affected (extent). The other choice may have greater immediate benefits (propinquity), be more secure (certainty) and have less aggravation attached to it (purity). In other words, Bentham's hedonistic calculus has a natural feel to it. His concern is to provide a way of measuring happiness and, by breaking it down into the seven categories, to ensure that we consider all the important aspects of happiness.

Bentham's utilitarianism takes a purely quantitative approach to right and wrong. The only question that matters is how much pleasure will we receive. Do we lose something, though, if we do not also ask how good the pleasure is? In other words, if we do not consider the quality of happiness, have we forgotten something important? For example, what would happen if government reviewed its allocation of funds for cultural education? It has been determined (hypothetically) that the cost of education in the arts, classics and philosophy is two hundred dollars per year for each household. Someone suggests an alternative: Why not give voters a choice? In the next election we should let the people decide whether continued funding for cultural education or a two-hundred-dollar voucher for video equipment for each household brings about the greatest good for the greatest number. Which would win?

Qualitative Utilitarianism

One person who feared that culture did not stand a chance against things like video gadgets was John Stuart Mill (1806-1873). While he believed Bentham's fundamental idea was sound, he modified utilitarianism to emphasize the qualitative aspects of pleasure. Mill argues that quantitative utilitarianism is incomplete because it does not recognize that humans have both "higher" and "lower" desires. The higher desires are those of reason and intellect (like cultural education). The lower desires are based on our immediate and biological needs and wants (like video players). One problem with Bentham's "hedonistic calculus," as Mill saw it, is that the lower desires are quantifiable (although many question whether this is true for categories other than extent and perhaps propinquity) but the higher desires are qualitative. How do we calculate quality? Mill argued that we cannot, and thus that a hedonistic calculus leaves out qualitative considerations.

A second problem with a quantitative approach is that not everyone has experienced the higher pleasures. Thus, in a choice between two pleasures—one which appeals to the higher desires, the other to the lower—Mill would expect video to win out over cultural education because the majority of people have not experienced the higher pleasures. As Mill puts it, the "capacity for the nobler feeling is in most natures a very tender plant, easily killed." Thus, Bentham's quantitative utilitarianism needs to be supplemented with a consideration of qualitative elements if we are to avoid becoming barbarians with highly sophisticated video equipment after a few generations.

How do we know which pleasures are higher? Mill's solution is relatively straightforward. If a person has experienced two pleasures and is under no pressure to choose one over the other, the pleasure he or she freely chooses is the higher. Once again, we test claims via experience. Of course, Mill was certain that the pleasure selected would be that which employed the higher faculties. Therefore, while those who have not tasted the higher will choose the lower, individuals acquainted with pleasures of the intellect will not revert to a lower level of life. As Mill put it in his famous statement, "It is better to be a human being dissatisfied than a pig satisfied; better to be Socrates dissatisfied than a fool satisfied. And if the fool, or the pig, are of a different opinion, it is because they only know their own side of the question. The other party to the comparison knows both sides."[6]

The fool does not have a clue about the pleasures of wisdom, but Socrates understands the lower pleasures that appeal to the fool. Thus, Socrates is in a better position to make qualitative judgments about ethical options. This reveals an element of elitism in Mill's brand of utilitarianism. Not everyone has sufficient experience with happiness of the higher quality to be counted on to function according to the "higher desires." This does not mean that the value of anyone's happiness can be disregarded in our decisions, but it does mean that not every person is in a position to be a competent judge of moral matters.

Positive Aspects of Utilitarian Ethics

The essentials of utilitarian ethics can be summarized in three main points:

1. Happiness is the only thing that is intrinsically good. Only pain (or unhappiness) is evil in itself.

2. No individual's happiness (including one's own) is more valuable than that of any other. Therefore, we should seek the pleasure of the greatest number.

3. The only thing that is ethically significant in judging an action is the result. Since happiness is the only intrinsic good, it is the result to be pursued.

To many, these three essentials seem to contain a lot of common sense, and this has made utilitarianism an extremely popular ethical system from the time of Bentham and Mill to the present. This was, of course, part of their argument. Why should ethics run counter to human intuitions? It makes sense that a good ethical system would have a high degree of natural plausibility.

One reason utilitarianism looks so plausible is that it links doing good and happiness. That we do naturally seek happiness is hard to deny. If we want something without trying to want it, this seems to be a powerful indicator that there must be something good about it. And if we look at it from the other direction, what kind of world would it be if goodness made people miserable? In utilitarian ethics, opposing that which causes pain is an obligation. If we think of pain in utilitarian terms, as a disruption of a person's overall well-being, it is difficult to envision a system which does not seek to eliminate pain as ethical. Thus, connecting happiness with good and unhappiness with evil rings true.

Another attractive feature for many is that utilitarianism is oriented to results. Because it requires that beliefs be empirically verifiable, it gives people a way to keep subjective elements from creeping into their ethical decisions. Utilitarian ethics does not rely on any person's or group's claims to revelation, intuitions, feelings, authority or other bases that may be in reality nothing more than opinion. Instead, it looks for concrete results that are observable by everyone. Since many people have more confidence in that which can be measured, tested and tracked, the bottom-line orientation of utilitarianism has great appeal.

A third positive point is the versatility of this approach. The principle of utility can be applied to both individual and public decisions. When we make social policy decisions on such diverse issues as taxation, education or criminal law, it is difficult to think of a better approach than respect for the greatest happiness for the majority. It seems just as natural to apply this principle to decisions of personal morality. While fewer people are affected by our personal decisions, we still consider those individuals and their happiness important. Thus, utilitarianism helps us avoid an ethical schizophrenia that requires one approach for personal ethics and a different ethical system for social concerns.

Finally, utilitarianism offers a means of balancing individual freedoms with social obligations. On the one side it allows for equality: The happiness of each person is of equal importance. Individual interests receive consideration alongside the desires of all others. On the other side it recognizes that society cannot survive without concessions by individual members. Thus, with the "one person, one vote" concept implicit in utilitarianism, each person is free to say what will bring him happiness, but ultimately each person has to accept the decision of the majority.

Even though utilitarianism does not presuppose a Christian worldview, all four of these features can be incorporated into Christian ideals. First, it would be hard to conceive of a loving God who wants his creatures to be miserable. In spite of what some—both Christian and non-Christian—have believed, Christianity has nothing against happiness. In fact, the word that introduces each of the Beatitudes, *makarios,* can credibly be translated as "happy." The term is usually translated as "blessed" because it points us away from the idea of short-term emotional feelings and toward the idea of general well-being, but the latter is what the utilitarians have in mind when they speak of happiness. Thus, Christian utilitarians can argue that when Jesus says "blessed" (or happy) are the poor in spirit, those who mourn and so on (Mt 5:3-11), he is advocating the same concept as we find in utilitarian ethics. If we believe that our desire for happiness is God-given, there is good reason to believe that happiness is related to goodness.

Second, utilitarianism also fits well with the belief of most theists that when we do things the way God wants them done, the results ultimately will be good. In other words, if we assume that God built some kind of logic into his universe, we would anticipate that the observable results of human actions could be indicators of whether a behavior was right or wrong.

Third, Scripture speaks of ethics in both individual and corporate terms. Since right and wrong have their source in one God, we would expect to find one method of ethical decision making and one set of standards that applies to both private and public decisions.

Finally, while God does choose specific individuals for special tasks, the fact that all are judged according to one standard and loved equally by God matches well with utilitarianism's stress on the equal importance of each person.

Potential Problems of Utilitarianism

Utilitarianism makes a good first impression, and part of the reason for this is its emphasis on results. However, building an ethical system on consequences creates certain problems that we might not have noticed at first.

1. Can we know the results? One common difficulty of consequentialist approaches is found in their orientation to the future. If actions are judged by their consequences, then decisions about the goodness of our actions are dependent on knowing something that is still future (the result). And because the future is, by definition, unknowable, we are left in a kind of ethical limbo until we know whether the results we anticipate come to pass. But if good is determined by future happiness, how can we know whether a decision is good or bad until we know the results?

The following hypothetical case illustrates the problem. Faced with a lack of energy-generating capacity, your region of the country had to determine the best solution to a problem. This problem was not just political, because it involved questions of taxation (appropriating the private property of people), possible relocation of people from homes or jobs, subjecting those nearby to potential health hazards, and other ethical concerns. According to utilitarianism, the moral solution would be the one that involved the least amount of pain and maximized happiness. Every form of power facility considered (hydroelectric, nuclear, coal-burning, solar, wind-generated) had its good and bad points. While nuclear power did very well in several categories, it was passed over because of risk in the event of malfunction or damage to the plant, and because of nuclear waste disposal problems. However, one year after an alternative plant was constructed at a much higher cost (that is, greater unhappiness) than a nuclear plant, breakthroughs in technology solved the problems associated with nuclear power generation.

Usually we would say that no wrong was done, because there was no way to know when or whether such problems would be successfully resolved. But that is just the point. Utilitarianism cannot escape responsibility for present decisions on the basis that we cannot know how things will turn out in the future. There is no standard of judgment other than consequences, and every consequence occurs after the decision. Thus, because our choice did not result in "the greatest good for the greatest number," don't we have to say that our decision not to build the nuclear generating plant was morally inferior?

This case points out the very practical difficulty of basing decisions on future events. It also illustrates that utilitarianism cannot tell us at what time in the future we can judge whether a decision was a good one. What if we had built the nuclear power plant but had not found a way to neutralize nuclear waste? When do we know if happiness was maximized? The next year? Ten years? One thousand years? Nuclear fuel remains potentially dangerous for thousands of years. Would we have to wait until the risk disappeared before we could evaluate our action?

2. How do we compare results? When we make a decision, one path is chosen and others are not. We do not know with certainty how things would have turned out had we made a different choice. This is important to remember, because *greatest* (as in "greatest good") is a comparative term. When we make a decision, we compare the anticipated results available in two or more options. But how can we evaluate our decision when we actualize only one option? To put it otherwise, can we know with certainty whether we have chosen the greatest good when it is impossible to know whether alternatives we did not choose would have, in fact, brought about less good?

To illustrate this problem, consider the following question: Can we say that the events of September 11, 2001, were evil? It is conceivable, for example, that one of the planes that was flown into the Twin Towers held a terrorist, unknown to the terrorists who hijacked the plane, who had the intention, know-how and materials to construct and explode a nuclear device in New York City. Had he been successful, the death toll would have been several hundred thousand rather than several thousand. And the result would certainly have been a great deal of unhappiness for a tremendous number of people. Thus, the actual events of that tragic day might have been a far superior moral outcome to what would have occurred if the planes had reached their scheduled destinations and our undiscovered terrorist had detonated his nuclear device. But we can never be certain, because there is no way of knowing the intentions and capabilities of the passengers on the planes that were intentionally crashed. Without doubt, the death and destruction of 9/11 caused great unhappiness to many people, but it would have been minimal compared to the nuclear nightmare that might have occurred otherwise. Remember, only the results count, and the greater happiness or least amount of pain determines the winner. So how can we know that the actions of the 9/11 terrorists were evil unless we know what to compare it to?

The point is this: while most of us consider results important, it is questionable whether only the outcome carries moral significance. Regardless of what might have happened as a result of the unknown terrorist's future plans, most people would still consider the work of the actual 9/11 terrorists evil. If we view these events as wrong regardless of what might have happened otherwise, we are not adhering to a pure form of consequentialism. Somewhere along the line, other standards have been used beyond those offered by utilitarianism.

3. Can we know the extent of consequences? While the first criticism dealt with consequences themselves ("greatest happiness"), we also can find problems concerning the extent ("greatest number") of actions. If goodness requires the happiness of "the greatest number," we must consider the effect of our actions on those who are touched by our decisions. This means that we must know two things.

First, who will be affected? The difficulty here is that we do not usually know this beforehand. Decisions have a tendency to move in directions we cannot anticipate. If an individual decides to have an abortion, can she be certain that she is able to determine how many and who will fall within the sphere of her decision? If we contemplate moving to another state, will we know whose lives will be affected? If we do not know the extent (number affected) of our actions, how is it possible to know, as required by utilitarianism, whether the majority will benefit from our decision?

Second, even if we are certain about who is included in the sphere of our decisions, we still have a "greatest happiness" problem. We have to know what constitutes happiness for those our decisions affect. If morality consists in producing the "greatest happiness," we must know whether our actions will result in happiness for them. Since happiness is defined differently from one person to the next, it is doubtful that we can be sure which decision will deliver the greatest happiness.

4. What happens to justice and other ethical virtues? For utilitarianism, rules are unimportant for deciding whether we are acting rightly. In a utilitarian worldview, traditional ethical precepts such as fairness, honesty, respect for life and justice are not standards of good and evil. They are ethically significant only when they contribute to the happiness of the greatest number. However, many critics of utilitarianism argue that we cannot safeguard the rights of people without rules and virtues.

Imagine that a town has experienced a rise in the incidence of jaywalking and a corresponding increase in pedestrian injuries and deaths. To end this suffering the town council decides to make jaywalking a capital crime: anyone caught will be executed by hanging. Can this law be justified under utilitarianism? To determine this we need to ask how much pleasure or pain will result, and for whom. Probably no one would risk a hanging just to avoid walking to the corner to cross a street. Thus not much unhappiness will result from the law. At most, you probably have to hang only one person to completely eliminate the jaywalking problem. A jaywalker execution would clearly bring about unhappiness for some people. But would this unhappiness outweigh the happiness resulting from preventing the injuries and deaths that would have occurred without the law?

In real life, no one is going to propose the hanging of jaywalkers, and if we ask why, the answer reveals a problem in utilitarianism. Most will say that jaywalking is a minor infraction that does not deserve execution—the punishment does not fit the seriousness of the crime. In other words, the sentence violates a sense of justice. However, what is to keep us from exemplary punishment (hanging jaywalkers) under a utilitarian approach if justice is not an intrinsic value? It is true that most utilitarians will argue that happiness, if properly defined, would not allow execution of jaywalkers. This can be debated. What is clear is that utilitarians cannot appeal to a rule of justice as an argument against hanging jaywalkers. So if we can make a case that the principle of utility is best satisfied by exemplary punishment, then utilitarians would say this is what we should do.

To this point we have considered justice from the perspective of punishment. However, we encounter similar problems with utilitarianism on the positive side of justice. Under utilitarianism we cannot contend that people deserve to get their wages simply because they have earned them. If the greatest number will benefit from confiscation of wages rightly earned, then confiscation can be considered right by utilitarian standards. Utilitarians may argue that the best results are obtained when people get what they earn, but that it is just that we get what we deserve is secondary. The only ethical standard is happiness.

5. Does motive count? Under utilitarian standards the motive behind an act is ethically unimportant. Only results count. Thus if two individuals provide one million dollars each to fight hunger, and the money provides a great service to those in need, it is assumed that the actions of each donor are equally good as long as the happiness that results from each donation is equal. But does this seem right if we know that one person gave out of great conviction for the work of the charity, while the other did it only for the tax write-off or public recognition?

Utilitarianism, in most versions, looks only at the objective results. Therefore, *why* people do what they do has no significance for our evaluation. However, to call each act equally good when the motivations are so different runs counter to our ethical intuitions.

6. Is morality dependent on the success of an action? Let's change the previous example a bit. Once again, we have two one-million-dollar donors. This time each gives with the same motive. However, while the money of donor A is put to great use, the contribution of donor B ends up in the pockets of an unscrupulous treasurer who is now enjoying the lifestyle of the rich and dishonest somewhere in Brazil. If we consider consequences only, do we say that donor A's action is morally superior since her gift was successful in bringing about great happiness? Even though the actions and the motives are equal, it appears that if results are our guide, unsuccessful attempts at doing good have no moral value.

7. Who is ethically responsible? Our final criticism concerns the means by which we determine responsibility for actions. When we assign guilt or praise for an act, it seems natural that responsibility is attributed to the one who acts or responds. However, it is not clear that this is true for utilitarianism.

If a family with twelve children moved into a small community, that family would make an impact. But imagine that such a family moves into a small town where a great majority of the citizens believe that zero population growth is a moral imperative for everyone. The citizens are fanatical about their belief and are not at all happy with the presence of this family. They have been very proud that their community is a model of population-control ideas, and the new family undermines their message. The new family is also unhappy. Because family members are unrepentant about the size of their family, they are shunned in town, they have no friends at school, and they receive nasty calls at home.

Few people would say that having twelve children is morally wrong. Crazy perhaps, but not wrong. However, in this case, we have unhappiness, which, by utilitarian standards, means there is a moral problem somewhere. Who then is responsible for the unhappiness (evil)? If having a large family is not considered evil, that leaves only the townspeople as the cause of unhappiness. However, under utilitarianism, the factor that creates the unfavorable consequences must be seen as wrong, because the outcome would have been different without that factor. Therefore it seems that the couple who decided to have a large family is guilty of doing wrong.

Conclusion

Because it is a tricky business to say which ethical rules or virtues are valid and why, many find utilitarianism attractive. It allows us to bypass the entire question of rules and concentrate on results instead. However, it is common to hear people who claim to be consequentialists say things like "That just isn't fair!" Why, when faced with instances outlined here, do people tend to default to the rules?

One reason is that rules protect people's rights. We have rules against stealing because people have a right to property. There are rules against excessive punishment because there is a right to fair treatment. These rights assume that people have value. This helps us understand the opposition to utilitarianism. The charge is that while utilitarianism emphasizes the value of each individual's happiness, it does not recognize value in people. Happiness is what has intrinsic value, not people. People are only coincidentally significant as the "owners" of happiness. Unless people are viewed as intrinsically valuable, the possibility exists that people can be used as a means to an end.

A final distinction that might be noted in transition from utilitarianism to our next ethical perspective is that goals are different from results. Life may work in such a way that when happiness is the standard we use to test decisions, happiness itself becomes unattainable. It may be that happiness is the result of desiring something else.

If we return to the Beatitudes, Jesus never says, "Happy are those who seek happiness." Instead, the happiness that Jesus promises to his followers may be the byproduct of fulfilling certain duties. These concepts—duty, inherent human value, rights—are central to the ethics of Immanuel Kant, who faulted utilitarianism for making results the measure of right and wrong.

7

IT'S YOUR DUTY

Kantian Ethics

AT THE COMMAND OF HIS CAPTAIN, a young soldier attacks an enemy gun position at the top of the hill. He is part of the first wave and faces withering gunfire. There are no illusions; he knows that he stands a good chance of becoming a casualty.

A woman sits in a jury room. The defendant has a long criminal record. All her instincts tell her that the man is guilty and would continue to terrorize innocent people if he was released. However, the judge's instructions stated that cases are to be decided on the basis of evidence, not intuition or past record, and the evidence presented in the trial was just not strong enough for conviction. To the dismay of the other jurors, she votes again for acquittal.

Neither person is doing what they want to do. The soldier would like nothing more than to cut and run. With a guilty vote the woman could escape the displeasure of fellow jurors and leave the courthouse reasonably certain that the defendant got what he deserved. However, both believe strongly that what they want is irrelevant. They have a duty, and regardless of the consequences it is important to fulfill their responsibility.

The bumper sticker "It's your duty" seems appropriate as a guide in these situations. For most of us *duty* is not an attractive word. It certainly isn't a word we associate with fun. As soon as someone begins to talk about our duty, we can be sure that we will have to sacrifice, make commitments and fight strong impulses to do something else. However, we should also realize that *duty* is a word that comes up in the most important things we do. We have duties to our country, our family and our job. These are too significant to leave open to whim and inconsistency. Some things need to be done because they are right, not because we want to do them. The question we may want to ask, then, is this: If "It's your duty" is a good guide in the most central aspects of our lives, why not use it as a guide for all the ethical decisions of our lives?

Duty is the centerpiece of Immanuel Kant's moral philosophy. Being good is a matter of reverence for duty. Kant's emphasis on obligation is very different from utilitarianism's emphasis on happiness. People who follow Kant care about rules and motives, while utilitarians want to know about results. At the root of the disagreement between the two systems is the question of authority. What determines what is right and what is wrong?

Unlike the previous scenarios, Kant's concept of ethical obligation is not founded on criminal or military law. These systems of law do not apply to everyone in every circumstance, but Kant argues that ethical duties are the same for all. He also asserts that ethical duty should not be based on the opinions of any individual, group, tradition, faith, cultural norm or even God's will. These all require that we first believe some nonethical truth in order to embrace the ethical system built on it. For example, if Confucianism is not true, we have no reason to believe that Confucian ethics are true. Kant argues that moral truth stands by itself; it is autonomous and self-contained. We do not go outside the realm of ethics to find a justification for ethics.

This also tells us why Kant would reject utilitarianism (as well as all other forms of consequentialism). Consequences only tell us what is. The way to test the truthfulness of a claim about physical objects includes many things that have nothing to do with right and wrong. The weight, sound, smell or color of an object is ethically irrelevant. Ethics, on the other hand, is about what should be. Since consequentialism relies on results (*is*), it can never get us to ethics (*ought*). Thus Kant argues that we need to begin from some foundation other than consequences.

The previous paragraphs eliminate the foundation for just about every ethical system available, whether it is self-interest, religious tradition, survival, culture, collective decision, God or results. So what is our authority for ethics? For Kant, reason alone is the foundation. The only ethical rules that should be adopted are those that show themselves to be logically consistent and which do not result in self-contradiction. Kant says moral principles that meet the demands of reason are always valid for everyone. He even goes so far as to state that each individual, acting rationally, creates universal moral truth. Reason is not just the judge, but also the source of right and wrong.

Kant grants reason such a high status because rationality is what allows humans to be moral beings. Our actions are not the result of instincts embedded in our genetic structure or reactions to the world around us. Instead, reason gives us freedom to deliberate between options and make a decision. And freedom gives us something that animals do not have: moral responsibility to duty. Since we choose what we do, unlike animals, we must answer for our choices. While we do not speak of penguins or whales as morally good or evil, reason requires that we hold people responsible for freely made decisions. Thus rationality is the source of human freedom, value and duty. The positive side of our heightened responsibility is the elevation of human worth. It is reason that gives humanity value.

The role of reason is to direct the will, the instrument of freedom. Will in itself is neither good nor evil. The real issue is what we do with it. When properly used (rationally guided), will is good. In fact, Kant begins the first chapter of his *Groundwork of the Metaphysics of Morals* by stating, "It is impossible to conceive anything at all in the world, or even out of it, which can be taken as good without qualification, except a good will."[1]

This brings us to the role of motive. Kant moves ethical evaluation to the beginning of the process instead of putting it at the end, as utilitarianism does. Rather than relying on results to tell us whether we have done the right thing, we look at the motive. Even if we do not reach our goals because of unforeseen twists in events, if we act out of an intention to fulfill our duties (or goodwill), we have met our ethical obligation. Thus if the soldier at the beginning of this chapter gets no farther than the edge of his bunker before breaking his leg, he has still done what is morally required. It is not success that counts; it is his motivation to do his duty. Nothing is good except reverence for duty. It is duty for duty's sake.

The Categorical Imperative

The question, then, is how to discover which duties we are obligated to fulfill. First, we should recognize that duties imply rights. Kant tells us, "A duty is what in one being corresponds to the rights of another. Where there are no rights there are no duties."[2] A defendant at the beginning of the trial has a right to be tried on the facts of the case. Therefore, the juror has an obligation to reach a decision on the basis of evidence. Her duties are outlined by rules. To assure that the defendant's rights are honored, our juror is obligated to rules that prohibit discussion of the case with nonjurors, outside contact with the defendant and other acts that might influence her judgment. If we are going to respect people's rights, says Kant, we need the right rules.

Rules tell us what we ought to do. However, Kant recognizes that the word *ought* can be used in two different ways. Consider the following statement: "If you want to get from New York City to London in less than a day, you should take a plane." The word *should* is contained in this claim and identifies it as a rule of some type, but it is not an ethical rule. It is instead what Kant calls a hypothetical imperative. "Hypothetical imperatives declare a possible action to be practically necessary as a means to the attainment of something else that one wills (or that one may will)."[3] Such imperatives are conditional ("if you want to") because they are based on a person's wishes and goals. If we want to get from New York to London in less than a day, the *ought* or *should* introduces the proper strategy for fulfilling this desire. Given Kant's argument that personal desires have nothing to do with ethics, there is no moral obligation to travel from New York to London in less than a day. This particular strategy is not morally binding on us if we change our goals and decide that we would be satisfied with a more leisurely trip.

There is, however, a second type of "ought" statement, which is intended as a moral command. An example might be "We should make promises we cannot keep." Kant says that moral rules are to be tested by reason. We do not yet know whether "We should make promises we cannot keep" qualifies as a rational ethical statement (we will test it a little later), but we do know that it is a rule that has an ethical meaning.

"Ought" statements with ethical meanings, when they satisfy the test of reason, are what Kant calls categorical imperatives. "A categorical imperative would be one which represented an action as objectively necessary in itself apart from its relation to a further end."[4] *Categorical* refers to that which is absolute. A categorical imperative, then, is a command or law that allows for no exceptions. There is no room for the "if you want" of the hypothetical imperatives. Regardless of your desires or goals, your "further ends," moral duties are "objectively necessary."

How do we arrive at these universal rules of conduct? Kant says that individual imperatives grow out of a principle he calls "the Categorical Imperative" (which will be designated by capitals to distinguish it from individual categorical imperatives). The Categorical Imperative is a general axiom that is not itself a moral rule but a means of arriving at specific moral rules that apply to everyone (categorical imperatives). It tells us how to know which ethical rules should be acted on. The Categorical Imperative states that we should do the following: "Act only on that maxim through which you can at the same time will that it should become a universal law."[5]

Two important elements are discovered when we break the Categorical Imperative into parts. First, "act only on that maxim" contains the idea that human deeds involve decisions about rules. Whenever we humans act, we do so on the basis of some maxim, a proposed rule of action.[6] Kant provides an example of a man who borrows money, promising to pay it back at a certain time even though he knows this is not possible. The maxim, or proposed rule of action, behind this potential act is "Whenever I believe myself short of money, I will borrow money and promise to pay it back, though I know that this will never be done."[7] We must then choose whether we will act on this maxim or reject it. The same is true of any moral decision. Maxims stand behind all of our choices, even when we are not aware of them. Thus a first step in applying the Categorical Imperative is to uncover the rule that will govern what we do.

The second half of the Categorical Imperative tells us how we determine whether a maxim should be put into action. We ask whether we want everyone to act on this rule. Should it be elevated to the position of universal imperative? Any moral rule should be absolute (categorical). So if we would not have our maxim "become a universal law," we should not act on it ourselves. Thus, to determine whether it is morally acceptable to make an unfulfillable promise to repay a person by the agreed time, the first step is to locate the underlying maxim (which we will abbreviate to "We should make promises we cannot keep") and, second, to see if we are willing to universalize it. In other words, do we want everyone to abide by the rule "We should make promises we cannot keep"?

Kant says the answer to this question is no. Universalizing a maxim like "We should make promises we cannot keep" is ultimately self-defeating and irrational. When we make a promise to repay a debt when we know it will not be possible, we deceive someone. But deceit is parasitic; it cannot exist without trust. People can only be deceived when they trust us. If all people always lied, there would be no truth left to deceive someone about. Therefore, universalizing the maxim "We should make promises we cannot keep" would defeat the very purpose of using deceit because no one would believe any promise.

Since universalization of a principle that says we promise to do what we cannot do makes it impossible to deceive someone, it is self-contradictory. Thus it violates what Kant considers to be the ultimate and sole ethical authority: reason. The same process is used to test any other maxim that is a candidate as a categorical imperative. We should not act on any maxim we would not want to be universalized. Stated positively, if we would want everyone to act on a maxim under consideration, it is our moral obligation to do it ourselves. It is not simply permissible to do it. It is our duty.

The Categorical Imperative: Version Two

Kant also provides a second version of the Categorical Imperative. While we will see later how the two versions are related, there is a difference in emphasis in this form of the Categorical Imperative: "Act in such a way that you always treat humanity, whether in your own person or in the person of any other, never simply as a means, but always at the same time as an end."[8]

This gives us Kant's second test for ethical principles: Do our actions "treat humanity . . . as an end," or do they use people "as a means"? This restatement of the Categorical Imperative reveals Kant's view that people are inherently valuable. If people are intrinsically valuable, they should not be manipulated to achieve a goal.

It may have occurred to you that "We should treat people as ends, and not as means" sounds a lot like the golden rule ("Do unto others as you would have them do unto you"). There is a strong similarity, but two notable differences exist. First, in the golden rule what we do is determined by what we want others to do to us. If we would prefer that others not lie to us, we should not lie to them. However, Kant wants to eliminate our desires, which are often irrational, from ethical consideration and focus instead on our duties, which are, by his definition, always rational. What is right is different from what we want, and it is not always the case that we desire that people do right by us. A masochist may want others to inflict physical pain on him, but that does not mean that it is right for a masochist to inflict pain on others.

A second difference is that the golden rule does not cover acts involving only ourselves. For example, it does not address the ethics of suicide, for suicide does not directly involve "doing unto others." However, suicide is addressed by the Categorical Imperative, because it specifies that we should not treat ourselves as a means ("whether in your own person or in the person of any other"). One would contemplate suicide only if he thought some benefit could be achieved by it, such as relief from great anxiety. However, Kant sees this as morally wrong because, in killing ourselves, we use a person (ourselves) as a means to an end (freedom from pain).[9]

Kant justifies this version of the Categorical Imperative in two ways. First, people are to be treated as ends because when they are used as a means to an end, they do not have full freedom to make decisions. For example, if I am lying when I compliment your appearance because I want you to like me, you are being treated as a tool and not as a person with inherent value. Why is this? Your freedom of response depends on your ability to trust what I say, and insincere compliments that manipulate your behavior limit your choice of responses. You are not able to freely respond to what I really think. I have used you as a means to get something I want.

Second, people have inherent value because they are valuers. No matter how sincere people are when they say, "We should not judge," judging is impossible to avoid. ("We should not judge" is itself a moral judgment against those who make moral judgments.) It is part of our makeup to evaluate moral decisions. Because Kant goes so far as to state that the reason of each person is potent enough to create moral law for everyone, the individual must be seen as inherently valuable. This idea links the two versions of his Categorical Imperative. Kant says, "Every rational being, as an end in himself, must be able to regard himself as also the maker of universal law in respect of any law whatever to which he may be subjected; for it is precisely the fitness of his maxims to make universal law that marks him out as an end in himself."[10] Our capacity for moral judgment requires that we be treated morally.

Kant argues that treating people as inherently valuable corrects a problem in consequentialist systems. Consequentialism views the happiness of the majority or some other end as inherently valuable. However, this opens the door for exploiting people in order to gain these ends. It is often noted that slavery could be justified under utilitarianism. If the majority of people derive the greatest happiness from enslaving a segment of the population (for instance, all green-eyed people), what is to stop the majority from enslaving a minority? Against this position, Kantian ethics says that humans have inherent value, thus they can never be used as means. Since enslaving green-eyed people constitutes the use of these individuals for the happiness of the majority, slavery cannot be tolerated.

Summary

Kant says that there are two ways of knowing because there are two general categories of things to be known. One category involves physical objects that are accessible to the senses. This category includes things about which we make "is" statements. An iron bar has a particular weight, shape and color, and we discover these characteristics by our senses. However, there is another side of reality that the senses cannot get to. This includes subjects like God, freedom and ethics. The senses can tell me that an iron bar has smashed the windows in a number of cars in a parking lot, but they can never tell me whether such an act is right or wrong. Right and wrong cannot be tested by hearing, sight, taste, touch or smell. Even so, Kant asserts that we can still make truthful statements about morality. Instead of checking ethical claims by sense data, we test by internal consistency between the ideas. This is what the Categorical Imperative is all about. Does a maxim pass the test of logical consistency, or is it self-contradictory?

The abstract nature of Kant's ethical system is one of the reasons his ideas are somewhat difficult to grasp. But even though people often have little confidence in abstract arguments because they want something that is tangible, Kant's point here is worth considering. Right and wrong are not the kinds of things that can be seen or touched, so if we insist on using our senses to make ethical decisions, we can never even get to the most basic ethical question, What should we do? Abstract arguments may not be easy to comprehend, but this does not make them wrong or less certain. And if we look carefully at the components of Kant's ethics, it is obvious that the ideas are closely interwoven. Beginning from his concept of reason, logical connections can be made between a number of concepts central to ethics, such as human freedom, universal obligation, rules, the will and duty.

Positive Aspects of Kantian Ethics

While some see the abstract nature of Kant's ethics as a negative, others are hesitant about his theory for a different reason. The heavy emphasis on words like *duty* and *rules* gives his system a dry and dreary feel. However, these very terms are what attract others to Kant's system, and for good reason. *Duty* takes us back to the intuition that some things are right no matter what. It helps anchor morality so that we are not swayed by changing moods and emotions, or sidetracked by unpredictable consequences. We court danger when the basis of our choices is arbitrary and changeable. Relying on the concept of duty seems like a good way to avoid that danger.

Rules can be aggravating because they illuminate our shortcomings.

Because a law like "do not steal" has an objective status that separates it from our emotions and wants, it does not care how we feel about stealing. This detachment can be of great benefit if we are interested in knowing what is true. We often fight a battle between what we would like to be true and what is actually true. We do not always want "do not steal" to be true. Thus, as Kant points out, our desires may blind us to what is right. His system tries to take us beyond the nonethical question, What do I want? to the ethical issue, What is right? and this seems to move us in the right direction.

Furthermore, if ethical truth is truth in the normal sense of the word, we have to acknowledge that ethical beliefs are either right or wrong. Mathematicians and scientists do not see truths in their fields as something that can be compromised. They might change their beliefs about what is true when it is reasonable to do so, but the universe itself does not change. All that has changed is their view of it. Kant says the same thing is true about ethics. Ethical laws are not open to negotiation. It is possible to hold unreasonable beliefs about ethics, but this is a problem with our understanding of right and wrong, not a problem with right and wrong itself. This is why Kant's ethics has so much appeal to people who are not simply looking for a way to justify what they want to believe, but who really want to know what is right.

Another positive point follows from this. Irrationality can be frightening when it comes to ethics, so there is merit in stating that ethics should be rational. Most people are willing to accept the authority of reason, at least in theory. We may disagree about what is reasonable, but people generally seem to agree that of two conclusions, the one with better reasons to support it is the better conclusion. Therefore, it is difficult to disagree with Kant's assertion that an ethical conclusion that can be rationally supported is preferable to one that is not rationally supported.

Moreover, Kant connects rationality with the universalization of categorical imperatives in a way that coincides with the moral intuitions of many people. Kant says we should put ourselves in other people's shoes. If we would be unwilling to have other people adopt the maxim we are considering, we should not act on it ourselves. If what we propose to do uses someone as a means to an end, we should not do it. This may not make us want to do what we should. However, most will agree that it provides a good way to check whether our wants are ethical.

Although Kant affirms the existence of God, God has no place in Kantian ethics. Kant wants reason alone to be the foundation of moral truth. Despite the absence of God from Kant's ethical system, many have found much in it that is compatible with Christianity. For example, the idea that ethics is objective—that things are right and wrong regardless of what anyone thinks about them—matches well with the ideas of most Christians. Moreover, many of the ethical rules Kant comes up with through the Categorical Imperative parallel what we find in the Ten Commandments. Finally, Scripture's assumption that its basic ethical directives are intended for everyone fits well with Kant's demand that rules be universalized. For these reasons many have argued that, with some modifications, his approach is an option for Christians.

Potential Problems for Kantian Ethics

1. What happens when there is a conflict of duties? If a murderer came through the door seeking to kill an innocent person, would you lie when the killer asks where the intended victim is? There is a good chance you will say yes to this question. There is also a good chance that you believe the lie is justifiable because it causes less harm than aiding in the murder of an innocent person. In other words, you would look at the results. However, we should recall Kant's position that results have no bearing on whether something is right or wrong. It is rationality, not consequences, that judges the rightness of human actions.

The example of whether we should lie to a murderer comes from Kant himself, and he concludes that we should not lie, even if it leads to murder.[11] His rationale is that, were we to allow lying to murderers, our behavior would be guided by a maxim like this:

It is right to lie. (Let's call this maxim 1.)

But this is not a maxim we would want to universalize. As we have already seen, lying requires the existence of truth. It is useless to tell a lie if the lie will not be believed. When maxim 1 is universalized so that everyone is morally obligated to lie, truth would no longer exist, and lying ends up in absurdity because we would not believe anything we were told. Lying is thus self-contradictory, so we should allow our decision to be guided by another rule:

We should not lie. (Maxim 2)

Kant says that this is a rule we would want everyone to adopt and therefore it is a duty—a categorical imperative. We should never lie, even when confronted by a murderer seeking a victim.[12]

What Kant does not appear to recognize is that it is possible to universalize more than one rule in this case. Our decision about whether to reveal the whereabouts of an intended victim also turns on whether we will decide to adopt a maxim like the following:

You should help those who seek to murder innocent people. (Maxim 3)

Using Kant's Categorical Imperative, it would seem irrational to universalize this law as well. Therefore we should not act on it. However, we would be able to universalize its opposite:

You should not help those who seek to murder innocent people. (Maxim 4)

Here is the problem. We have two maxims (2 and 4) that we would be willing to elevate to categorical imperatives. However, they conflict in this case. If we adopt maxim 2, as Kant says we should, we cannot adopt maxim 4. On the other hand, the only way we can put maxim 4 into action is by lying, thus violating maxim 2. This presents real problems for Kant's ethics, because he relies on the premise that it is never ethical to violate a categorical imperative. It does not look like we have a choice here. Sometimes choosing between two rules that can be universalized is unavoidable, and Kant does not have any way to resolve this problem.

2. Does Kant avoid circumstances completely? Kant says consequences are irrelevant to the question of whether an act is right or wrong. Instead, we know what is right by embracing laws that can be willed for all people. When that requires us to help a person who intends to murder someone, we might question the wisdom of completely ignoring consequences in making ethical decisions, as Kant argues we should. Moreover, it is also questionable whether Kant himself successfully eliminates a consideration of results from his system.

Suppose we do not have enough money to buy a car. Is it right to steal it? Kant's answer is no, and his reason would be something like this: Stealing assumes that people have a right to their property. If everyone stole, the concept of property would be undermined. We would have only temporary possession of things, not ownership of property. However, you cannot steal something that no one owns. Therefore, the rule "You should steal" is irrational.

Did you spot the inconsistency? It may be more apparent if I rephrase this slightly: Stealing assumes that people have a right to their property. If everyone stole, the result would be that the concept of property would be undermined. We would have only temporary possession of things, not ownership of property. However, you cannot steal something that no one owns. Therefore the rule "You should steal" is irrational.

How do we know that a pro-stealing ethic is self-defeating? Because the result or consequence of such an ethic is irrational. This reveals an inconsistency in Kant's position. On the one hand, he says consequences tell us nothing about ethics. On the other hand, consequences are consulted in determining whether a proposed rule is rational.

3. Is every rule we would universalize a moral duty? Kant argues that we can know which rules are morally obligatory by determining whether we would will that everyone act upon the maxims under consideration. However, consider the two maxims below:

People should smile at strangers.

People should keep their shrubbery properly trimmed.

It is not unreasonable to believe that people should will that everyone smile at strangers and keep the shrubs neat and trim. Thus these maxims pass Kant's Categorical Imperative. However, it is difficult to see smiling at strangers and trimming bushes as moral obligations.

This is a problem in Kant's ethics, because willingness to universalize a maxim is how we discover our moral duties, but this method does not work in these two rules. While this may seem picky, it raises an important question. We universalized a law about hedge trimming in the same way that Kant universalizes a maxim about telling the truth. If we can conceive of laws derived from the Categorical Imperative which do not have moral significance, how can we be certain whether laws about honesty are any more ethically significant than laws about gardening?

4. Is reason sufficient? Putdowns of human reason are common among some Christians because reason is sometimes seen as the opposite of faith. This position is unwarranted, since God is the Creator of our minds, and reason is part of the creation that God declares "very good" (Gen 1:31).

However, Kant's position that reason is the absolute and autonomous moral authority could be too much of a good thing. From the Christian point of view, a certain amount of restraint in our confidence in rationality is warranted. While Scripture does not promote irrationality as a virtue, neither does it view reason as an autonomous judge and source of right and wrong.

First, like all created things, human reason is finite. To make our limited reason the sole standard of right and wrong leaves any ethical system open to error. Moreover, as we will see in chapter nine, some question whether Kant's confidence in attaining an unbiased rational perspective is misplaced. And this creates a greater problem for Kant's ethics than for other systems because Kant maintains that categorical imperatives are universal and absolute. Building absolute laws on the finite powers of human thought throws the whole system into question. Kant's claim that reason should function autonomously leaves us with less than the certainty he wants for ethical conclusions.

Second, since reason is part of human life, it is not immune from the effects of sin. This makes us liable to the type of error that goes beyond the natural limits on human reason. Sinfulness means that even the best motivations are not fully pure. Even the good will, which Kant sees as the only thing that is inherently good, never by itself measures up to God's standard. Nowhere in Kant's ethics is there any mention of our need for God's help. It is a do-it-yourself plan of ethics (and salvation) that assumes that the ability to overcome our moral shortcomings is within our power. It is not clear how fulfillment of our moral duties is possible given the absolute demands of moral law in Kant's system. What is clear, however, is that Christian thought denies that it is possible to live up to the demands of morality without grace.

5. *What happens to love?* Within a Christian worldview, discovering what is right is linked with the question of what God is like. Christian tradition is nearly unanimous in describing God as a rational being, so making a place for reason in ethics is not controversial for most Christians. However, rationality is not the only divine attribute that is relevant for ethics. If ethics is based on reason alone, as Kant suggests, it reflects less than the full nature of God. God's mercy, forgiveness and love are left out. The Christian can appreciate and agree with Kant's emphasis on justice and duty, but in Kant's ethics we can fulfill our duty to treat people justly without loving them. This is not possible in Christianity.

By excluding love, either love for God or love for other persons, Kant's system becomes cold legalism. There is no sense of fulfilling the demands of ethics because of our love of God and our fellow human beings. Instead, it is duty for duty's sake. Jacques Maritain summarizes the results well:

> One might say that [Kant's] ethics of Pure Reason is a Christian ethics whose theological root has been severed, leaving only the stiffened moral branches. Thence what could be called the Kantian hypermoralism. There is no longer any order of grace, and consequently no order of charity, of infused virtues and gifts. . . . There remains only the order of the Law.[13]

Conclusion

Kant includes many of the elements many people expect to see in an adequate ethical theory. Duty, moral law, reason, justice and the dignity of all people play central roles. There are, however, two significant gaps often cited in Kant's approach. First, for all his talk of human value, this system still seems to lack humanity and concern for persons. Reason certainly has a place in ethical systems, but when reason allows someone to be murdered in order to avoid lying to a murderer, something is wrong. Maybe we need some standard to provide a balance to reason. This does not require that our ethics be irrational. It may be that human reason alone cannot build an ethical system adequate to the demand of life.

Second, though it happens infrequently, there are times when moral rules do conflict with each other. Kant gives us no help in determining what to do when this occurs. The next system we will consider attempts to keep much that is good about Kant's system and at the same time escapes the sterility of Kant's logic-chopping approach and his inability to resolve conflicts between rules.

8

BE GOOD

Virtue Ethics

"BE GOOD." My guess is that you would be wealthy if you had a nickel for every time these words were said to you while growing up. Although the intent was probably to put a stop to some immediate behavior, "be good" can have a deeper significance. There is a difference between doing good and being good. The first refers to a single action at a given moment, while the second focuses on who someone is. "Doing" is fixed on activity, but "being" draws our attention to character.

An evil person can do good things occasionally, but that does not make such an individual a good person. Generally, when we refer to someone as good, we are talking about more than sporadic acts. Instead, it is a matter of character. The idea that ethics demands more than just occasional good deeds is at the heart of virtue (or character) ethics. Virtue is the predisposition to do good things, an internal motivation that not only does the right but also loves what is right.

Virtue ethics had its heyday in the classical Greek period, and the primary representatives of this theory will be drawn from that age. However, while it has been out of favor for some time, it is making a strong comeback today. Until recently, modern advocates of virtue ethics have largely stated their case in books written for the academic community. Today, virtue has burst into the headlines. Many schools now emphasize the development of character, with character awards given to students who exemplify various virtues. In response to headline-making corporate abuses, business schools have incorporated ethics classes as standard fare for MBA programs, most of which offer a healthy dose of virtue ethics. We hear a lot of debate today in newspapers, talk radio and periodicals about "the character issue." Indeed, ethics has become a hot topic, and virtue and character are frequently offered as the antidote for society's ills.

While the idea of virtue is often left vague in many of the debates today, it is worth examining whether this theory can provide the answers for contemporary questions. Is virtue the answer to street crime and poverty? Is it the catalyst that will restore respect for teachers and help right a struggling educational system? How important is the connection between someone's private and public life? Should a person's past moral lapses disqualify him or her from certain jobs or offices? Should we care what people do after hours if they get the job done between nine and five? Perhaps some two-thousand-year-old ideas about virtue hold the answers to these questions, and those who argue that ethics is about being good are onto something.

What Is Virtue?

Before we get too far, we need a definition of *virtue*. First, while *character* is often taken today to mean one's personality type, the classical meaning refers to an internal predisposition to act in certain ways in certain situations. Although personality type is primarily a matter of genetics, virtue is learned. Moreover, while personality types vary from person to person, the virtues can be the same for all. For instance, one person may have an intense personality and another may be easygoing. However, virtue ethics says that both can and should have character qualities such as courage, self-discipline and benevolence. How we manifest these attributes will differ according to our circumstances, but a newspaper editor, a student, a full-time parent or a police officer all need them.

Second, virtues are not just any internal dispositions that lead to action. They are good character traits that result in good acts. Thus, virtue ethics involves a belief in ethical truth. It sees a real difference between good and evil, and between good people and evil people. These terms do not simply refer to our preferences or tastes; they point to some kind of objective truth about the way we ought to be.

Third, character ethicists are more concerned with virtue than with virtues. The Greek term *areté*, usually translated as "virtue," means something like "excellence." While we may be able to isolate particular areas of intellectual and moral excellence in a person, the ideal is that they reside in individuals as a package. It is not enough that an individual be only courageous, fair or self-disciplined. Virtue is not a multiple-choice affair in which people pick and choose the virtues they like. The goal is to be a good person. This involves possession of all these moral excellences and others as well.

Recognizing the Virtues

But how do we know when a particular character trait can be called good? Let us consider tests from two classical advocates of virtue ethics. The first is Plato, who teaches that each person functions on three different levels, each of which correspond to different activities of the soul. Our lowest function is what he calls appetite. Appetite refers to our urges to satisfy physical needs such as hunger, thirst or sex. This function is one humans share with animals. The second level Plato calls spirit. This involves human drives like anger or ambition. These higher desires are different from the appetites, as shown by the fact that spirit and appetite are frequently in conflict with each other. For example, a runner's ambition to win a race (spirit) may cause her to press on even when the pain (appetite) is great. The third and highest human function is reason, which should channel appetite and spirit into their proper uses.[1]

Each human function has its own virtue, or as stated earlier, its most excellent expression. When appetite is kept under control, the virtue is *temperance*. Thus, an appetite that is tempered or moderated represents the ideal use of our physical desires and allows us to concentrate our attention on the higher activities. Spirit, when functioning correctly, manifests the trait of *courage* and puts reason's commands into action, even in the face of resistance. *Wisdom* is the virtue of our reason, and since reason is the highest of our functions, it should control appetite and spirit. Finally, Plato adds the virtue of *justice*, a harmonizing trait that applies to all three facets of life. Justice gives each part of our life its proper due. Thus, it balances our life to assure that the needs of appetite and spirit are kept under the control of reason. Proper balance results in a life that is healthy, one that functions properly. In other words, a balanced soul is virtuous because it is used in the best way possible.[2]

For Plato nothing in the physical world is perfect, whether we are talking about physical objects, the attributes of things or human actions. These are only wavering, temporary and imperfect copies of a deeper reality. Instead, perfection exists only in a nonphysical realm that Plato calls the world of forms. Forms are nonphysical realities known by reason, not by any physical organ or capacity. (This explains why Plato sees reason as our highest faculty.) These forms are ideals, the perfection of the virtues we see only imperfectly enacted in this world. For example, no human act of courage is perfect. Some acts can be called courageous, though, because they reflect, only dimly, the perfect form of courage. Thus, the forms of temperance, courage, wisdom and justice are ideals toward which the ethical person strives.

Aristotle, like Plato, views ethics primarily in terms of character. However, there are two notable differences. First, Plato's understanding of the virtues is based on a world of forms beyond our senses, whereas Aristotle built his ethics closer to earth. For Aristotle the virtues are known through observing and comparing actual events. The second difference is that Plato argues that acts are virtuous to the extent that they emulate an ideal, such as the form of courage. If a deed fails to participate in the form of courage, it is cowardly. Thus, Plato pairs virtues and vices. Acts of virtue resemble ideals while acts of vice do not.

Contrasting a virtue with an opposing vice seems very rational, but there are gaps in this approach, and these gaps led Aristotle to define virtue differently. The deficiency can be illustrated in a situation that occurred several years ago and raised a considerable amount of controversy. A man plunged into an icy lake in an attempt to save a drowning puppy. Not only was the rescue attempt unsuccessful, but the man also drowned in the process. The debate that followed focused on how to evaluate the man's rescue attempt: Was it courageous?

If we decide the issue by choosing between courage and cowardice, we would have to pick the former, because it is clear that the person did not exhibit a cowardly character by jumping in after the drowning puppy. Aristotle, however, tells us there may be another way to evaluate this case. Instead of seeing virtues and vices as paired opposites, Aristotle sees virtue as "a mean between two vices, that which depends on excess and that which depends on defect."[3] In this approach, courage is still distinguished from cowardice, which is a lack (or defect) of courage. But it is also set apart from a vice on the opposite end of the spectrum, a foolhardiness that throws caution to the wind and takes excessive risks. In order to know whether the man's attempt to save the puppy was courageous, we must ask if the act exhibited such excess. Thus, while not presuming to know how Aristotle might evaluate the attempted rescue, whether courageous or foolhardy, his definition of virtue does give us a tool that can bring greater focus to the debate.

Aristotle says all virtues can be understood in the same manner. Remorse is the midpoint between indifference, which is a deficiency of repentance, and chronic guilt, which takes sorrow for wrongdoing to excess. Liberality (generosity) is the mean between prodigality (wasteful use of resources) and stinginess. Proper pride is the mean between empty vanity and undue humility, while righteous indignation is the midpoint between envy and spite. Aristotle's method has often been described as the search for the "golden mean" (although he does not use this phrase). Every virtue can be distinguished from the "not enough" and "too much" at the extremes.

Aiming at the Ideal

It is clear that Plato's understanding of ethics directs us toward an ideal, a perfection. However, even though Aristotle differs in the means by which we discern a virtue, his own approach also involves a sort of idealism. Virtues are not a matter of personal preference or taste. We can miss our ethical target by a great deal or only slightly, but there is an objective right to aim for. Thus, for both Plato and Aristotle, that which is virtuous is not decided by us; we discover it and accommodate our character to its ideal.

Virtuous persons, then, are superior to evil persons because, as measured by the objective standards, they have become more excellent persons. We are not all of the same moral status. There are more virtuous and less virtuous people. As Bernard Mayo points out, "There certainly are degrees by which we approach or recede from the attainment of a certain quality or virtue; if there were not, the word 'ideal' would have no meaning."[4] This superiority is achieved only through a process of character education. Thus Plato and Aristotle agree that the ethical life is never a "done deal" but rather a process of growth toward a perfect standard.

Proponents of character ethics see a significant advantage in incorporating ideals with moral theory. As Mayo puts it, the concept of an ideal fits more closely with our experience and intuitions about right and wrong than does a rule-oriented ethics. Rules are "black and white"; you either keep them or you don't. But choices, and our judgments about choices, do not come only in black or white. We recognize shades of goodness and badness.[5] Our evaluative vocabulary reflects these degrees. An action we label "tolerable" is not the best possible, but is better than a hateful deed. Certain choices are morally necessary, but others go beyond this to qualify as sacrificial.

For example, if the story of the good Samaritan ended after he had stopped to bandage the wounds of the man waylaid by bandits, the narrative perhaps would be known as "the pretty good Samaritan." This Samaritan did indeed meet the minimal expectations of moral responsibility. However, he went beyond "pretty good" when he loaded the injured man on his donkey, took him to the inn and paid his room and board. This is more than simply following a rule or fulfilling a duty; it is moral excellence. Virtue ethics, with its focus on ideals, helps us express what we already recognize: that there is more to ethics than a bare good or bad. While rule-based ethics reduces our evaluations to right and wrong, character ethics can speak easily of acts as good or better (or bad and worse) insofar as they exemplify an ideal to a greater or lesser degree.

Character

As advocates of this approach point out, character ethics does not start from the question, What should I do? Instead, the primary issue is, Who should I be? This does not ignore what we do, but encompasses behavior under the broader category of character. Virtue makes us good and causes our actions to be good. While virtue is not primarily about what someone does, we cannot be virtuous without doing good.

In Aristotle's approach, good character should manifest itself in behavior, and three conditions must be present before a certain behavior can be called a good act. First, we must understand what we are doing and why it is good. Second, what we do must be freely chosen. Finally, the "action must proceed from a firm and unchangeable character."[6] The last condition means that telling the truth does not itself make someone honest. An honest act is virtuous only if one does it because one is honest. Thus, while doing good deeds is a part of character ethics, we must be careful not to confuse inner dispositions with a habit of following rules.

To separate character from mere habitual rule following, Aristotle distinguishes between temperance and continence. Temperance means that a person moderates or abstains from certain activities because he or she wants to. In contrast, the continent person abstains, but not willingly. For example, Aristotle says that a coward may stand his ground against something that is terrible, but really wants to bail out. The fact that the coward does not run means that he is continent, but not yet good. He becomes virtuous only when he wants to take a stand because it is right. This positive attitude toward virtuous action requires that our sense of pleasure and pain be educated so that we take pleasure in doing what is virtuous, even if it comes at great cost.[7]

The distinction between character and merely adhering to rules adds a dimension missing from many forms of duty or utilitarian ethics. One can fulfill a duty without any personal desire to do so. For example, you may visit your grandmother in a convalescent home only because it is a duty. Similarly, utilitarianism gives little weight to inner motivation. If the desired results are achieved, then the visit was good. However, both of these options seem ethically inferior to going to visit out of a caring disposition with a genuine desire to see Grandma. The inner qualities that lead to the behavior are, for virtue ethics, the most important moral issue.

Virtue and Reason

Aristotle's distinction between virtue and mere continence also helps us see how wisdom fits with the virtues. The moral value of temperance, courage and justice is obvious, but how does wisdom fit in? The latter seems to be more an intellectual value than an ethical matter. One of Aristotle's three conditions of a virtuous act, as we saw earlier, is that acts must be done with knowledge. Wisdom reminds us that living well involves more than just habitually following a group of rules. We also need to understand why virtuous traits and the actions that follow from them are good.

For example, someone may train a horse to thump its hoof twice anytime it hears the word *nine*. If you would then "ask" the horse the total of "11 minus 9" or the sum of "2 times 4 plus 3 minus 9," you would get an appropriate response. What you do not get, however, is a horse that understands math. Similarly, we may consistently act in the way a virtuous person acts, but we are not actually virtuous until we know why virtues are good or why they make people good. Wisdom, then, while not specifically ethical in itself, is the necessary foundation for morality. If reason is to direct our lower impulses, as Plato tells us, it must understand why it is best to direct them in a particular way.

This points to the important place reserved for character education in virtue theory. Many skills in life are not automatic, and natural aptitude only takes us so far. If a person wants to become a master musician or a maker of fine furniture, he or she will need both good teachers and much practice. Mastering any skill or trade requires the repetition of certain actions and patterns until they become habitual. In the same way, character is not something people are born with; it is shaped. Like musicianship, virtue is born from the repetition of certain types of actions. If we consistently behave in a self-indulgent manner, we become self-indulgent people. If we consistently exercise self-discipline, we become self-disciplined people. As Aristotle puts it,

> States of character arise out of like activities. This is why the activities we exhibit must be of a certain kind; it is because the states of character correspond to the differences between these. It makes no small difference,

then, whether we form habits of one kind or of another from our very youth; it makes a very great difference, or rather *all* the difference.[8]

We can be said to be virtuous only when these actions become so internalized that they are part of who we are.

This is why reliance on example is more prominent in virtue ethics than in other theories. To progress toward ethical ideals, we need models to point the way to show how it is done. As Mayo states it,

> Heroes and saints are not merely people who did things. They are people whom we are expected, and expect ourselves, to imitate. And imitating them means not merely doing what they did; it means being like them. Their status is not in the least like that of legislators whose laws we admire; for the character of a legislator is irrelevant to our judgment about his legislation. The heroes and saints did not merely give us principles to live by (though some of them did that as well): they gave us examples to follow.[9]

In virtue ethics, then, the concept of the hero is different from most current views. Heroes of virtue gain their status not because of fame, wealth, athletic ability or musical skill. Their heroism is not based on the ability to perform a task but on living well.

Why Be Virtuous?

We are frequently encouraged to be good, but why being good is important is seldom explained. However, every ethical system must ultimately address the question, Why be good? For virtue ethics the answer is that goodness is necessary for a good life. The good life is not one of fame or wealth, but one lived in accordance with reason: a balanced life. Virtue means that everything is functioning as it should. Thus, Plato and Aristotle both reject the belief that we can separate ethics from the other things we do. Anything worth having is connected with character: Ethics is an integral part of a worthwhile life. And, as we have seen, character should be guided by reason.

For Aristotle the result of living virtuously is *eudemonia*. This term is generally translated as "happiness," but that can be misleading because we usually think of happiness as an emotion. Aristotle has a much broader definition. Happiness "does not consist in amusement" but is a state of well-being. It refers to a life so arranged that it allows an individual to achieve the highest levels possible for a human being. This does not happen in a moment or even a few years. Aristotle states it in the following way:

> Human good turns out to be the activity of the soul in accordance with virtue, and if there are more than one virtue, in accordance with the best and most complete.
>
> But we must add "in a complete life." For one swallow does not make a summer, nor does one day; and so too one day, or a short time, does not make a man blessed and happy.[10]

Since happiness is not a feeling but a state of balance and well-being over a lifetime, people are not happy just because they believe themselves to be. As with ethical ideals, happiness is conformity to an objective measure. Thus, not everyone who believes him- or herself happy is actually happy. We are not the final judge on that matter. Instead, the standard of happiness is not simply personal opinion but how one measures up to virtue.

Christianity and Virtue

It should not be surprising that a number of Christian ethicists have adopted virtue theory, and it does not take much ingenuity to see how this approach can be "Christianized." Instead of viewing Plato's moral forms and Aristotle's golden mean as impersonal ideals, they can be understood as God's moral attributes. Courage, justice, love, patience and the other ethical ideals do not have their own individual existence as individual and abstract entities; they come together in God's being.

This provides a mandate for seeking certain virtues. If God is caring and we are to be like God, we should become caring. If Jesus proclaims a kingdom that is different from all other kingdoms of this world, from this proclamation we will discover virtues that are consistent with God's hope for creation. Thus, to Plato's list of the cardinal virtues of temperance, courage, wisdom and justice we might add theological virtues like faith, hope and love, as Augustine did. For many, this gives depth to Christian ethics. God is more than a being who does good; he is good. Similarly, the goal for the Christian is not just a balance sheet that shows more good deeds than evil. We are to become virtuous people who reflect the nature of God.

Summary

Even though both Plato and Aristotle died more than two thousand years ago, many contemporary proponents of character education have adopted their core concepts. They view current social ills as the result of value systems in which all ideas are seen as equally valid. To correct these problems, advocates of character education call for a return to virtues such as those found in the classical writers. They agree with Plato and Aristotle that these moral qualities will not become part of a person's life by default. Simply discussing alternative viewpoints does not yield better people. Instead, certain character traits are superior and should be taught, both verbally and by example. Moreover, they argue that the rightness of these virtues will be evident to any rational person. For these modern virtue theorists, as for Plato and Aristotle, ethics is not simply a separate compartment among others in a human life. Everything comes down to the quality of one's character.

Positive Aspects of Virtue Ethics

Humans are multifaceted beings, and a comprehensive ethical system should provide guidance in all aspects of life. Virtue ethics does well on this point because character comes into play in the social, vocational, individual and spiritual sides of our lives. The person who is a citizen, a soldier, a Christian and a parent can find direction in moral virtue.

Virtue also adds a dimension that a pure rule-based or utilitarian approach struggles to include. Rules are rules and results are results, regardless of who is involved. However, the nature of our relationships or the specifics of a situation frequently become important factors. For example, while it may be virtuous to make difficult cutbacks in your lifestyle and take out a second mortgage on the house to help pay college tuition for your child, you may also think it would be foolish to do the same thing to put an unknown twenty-year-old Belgian student through school. Two different acts might technically qualify as murders, but a husband who kills his wife who was suffering greatly in the final stages of terminal cancer might be judged differently than a gang member who kills a child in a drive-by shooting.

In both cases our relationship to the people involved and the circumstances are relevant features. Character ethics allows us to balance these personal aspects of a decision with objective standards. On the one hand, right and wrong are not whatever we want them to be. Virtue is not the same thing as personal preference. On the other hand, we can still take into consideration unique obligations and responsibilities for family or friends.

An approach that looks to ethical ideals also seems to satisfy another intuition. While morality can be discussed in terms of right and wrong, these categories seem to be too constrictive for the way we see things in everyday life. There are degrees of goodness and badness. For example, many people feel that all abortion is wrong. Even so, some may not assign the same level of blame to a fourteen-year-old who gets an abortion after being raped by her uncle as they would assign to a thirty-one-year-old woman who is sexually promiscuous, uses no form of birth control and has just come in for her third abortion in five years. Since virtue ethics sees goodness on a continuum that points toward an ideal, it allows us to express the entire range of ethical evaluations.

Approaching morality from the direction of virtue also makes sense because it recognizes that a good act is not necessarily the same thing as a good person. Hitler may have occasionally acted with great compassion toward some individuals, but this does not make him a compassionate man. Moreover, a good person can act "out of character" and do something that goes contrary to his or her normal behavior. A single poor choice does not make a person bad. This approach frees us from limiting our judgments to a single event or action.

An additional advantage of virtue ethics is that it allows us to include a number of desirable qualities that seem difficult to absorb into a rule-based theory. For example, many people would agree that a good person is tactful, patient and generous. And while it sounds natural to encourage people to be tactful or generous, we lose something if we reduce these to rules. This is because rules only establish minimum levels of duty or obligation. Tact, patience and generosity, on the other hand, go beyond the moral minimum toward a positive ideal.

Another way of viewing the advantage of virtues over rules is that virtue provides a means of saying what is right about an act. Rule-breaking tells us when a wrong has been done. However, its opposite, keeping the rule, does not require that we see the rule-keeper as good. Instead, keeping rules is one's duty, an obligation. But is good only a matter of external behavior? For example, we could locate a group of individuals who have all complied fully with sexual harassment laws. However, within this group we might still recognize ethical differences ranging from those who harbor sexist attitudes to those fully committed to gender equality.

Rules focus on what we do not do, the actions we avoid. Virtue ethics, on the other hand, is more concerned about who we are, in a positive sense, and the types of good activities that flow from our character. It gets down into internal attitudes in a way that rules cannot. The language of virtue provides a vocabulary to express the value of good acts. Some things are much more than just a fulfillment of duty; they are virtuous.

Finally, character ethics seems to put the right spin on true heroism. It is impractical to believe that we can all become the next great running back in the NFL or a movie superstar. Moreover, achieving such goals does not necessarily lead to a good life. It is, however, within the grasp of each person to become virtuous, and this is a more constructive model for pointing the way to the good life. And if you ask virtuous people how they learned to live well, they will probably point not to the rich and famous but to close-to-home examples of people of character.

Potential Problems in Virtue Ethics

1. Does virtue ethics help us know what to do? While we have highlighted places where virtue ethics fills gaps left by deontological or utilitarian approaches, this does not necessarily mean that it is a sufficient replacement. Important questions can be raised as to whether this theory itself can stand alone. One reason for this doubt is that character ethics seems to give little concrete guidance in actual situations.

We can think of any number of cases in which people will agree on what dispositions are virtuous but will reach very different, even opposite, conclusions about what virtuous people ought to do. Imagine a conversation between two compassionate people. One will argue that compassion requires that we increase monetary support of those on welfare. As this individual defines compassion, a compassionate person wants welfare recipients to have better opportunities in housing, education and other areas of basic need. However, the other compassionate person may argue just the opposite. If we really care, she says, we will cut off welfare benefits, because welfare encourages people to become takers rather than givers. Instead of helping people through welfare, we teach dependency. Since dependency is a vice, compassion requires that we force people to become industrious and self-sufficient for their own benefit.

We do not resolve this disagreement by moving to a different virtue—to justice, for example. The first person may say that justice means that people should get what they deserve and that since humans deserve decent food, health services and housing, the just solution is to provide greater benefits for the poor. The second person, however, may say that getting what you deserve means getting what you earn. Since welfare represents unearned benefits, it is unjust.

Both of these individuals can be truly compassionate and just people and even have the same definitions of compassion and justice, yet still have sincere disagreements over what compassionate and just people should do. This has led some scholars to see virtue ethics as incomplete. Even when we agree which character traits are good, we still have to act. However, we have seen in these examples that virtue ethics does not help us untangle the question of what actions should follow from our dispositions. In fact, the same virtues lead these two people to mutually exclusive solutions. If virtue cannot tell us what acts should follow from good character, is something lacking?

2. Can virtues be used badly? According to character ethics, if a person acts in conformity with virtue, then the act is good. However, is it possible to act according to a virtue, or even a number of virtues, and do evil? For example, courage and generosity are mentioned as virtues in almost all lists we can find. But we would not say that it is good if a member of a white supremacy group planted and detonated a bomb in a synagogue, even if the white supremacist overcame the fear of discovery and punishment, and demonstrated great courage in perpetrating the violence. We would not extol the generosity of donors if their money financed the bombing.

In this case, courage and generosity, and any other virtue a person may display in completing this act (discipline, friendship, keeping promises, etc.), do not seem to be a sufficient guide for defining whether an act is good. On the contrary, regardless of the level of material sacrifice, courage, sense of duty or self-sacrifice involved in financing or carrying out this bombing, we would say this was a great evil. But if virtues are inherently good, then how could the bombing, if it involves virtuous character traits, be evil? This seems to point beyond the virtues to some additional standard of evaluating the ethical significance of particular acts.

3. Can virtue ethics answer the question, *Why be virtuous?* A good ethical theory should explain what is good about being good. Thus, virtue theory needs to explain why loyalty should be thought a virtue and disloyalty a vice. Both Aristotle and Plato argue that virtues in general are good because they allow us to live a good life. Therefore, if we are loyal, this character trait, along with others, will contribute to our overall fulfillment. However, this answer seems to lead us to a form of egoistic ethics because the ultimate goal is a good life: a life that benefits us. Virtue is not an end in itself. We must go outside virtue to discover the justification for such a life. It is, as Aristotle says, happiness. Thus, if the reason for goodness is that it will benefit us in some way, have we not simply adopted a variant of egoism?

Even if we abandon Plato and Aristotle's answer on why we should pursue virtue, it seems that character ethics turns out to be a version of some other ethical approach. For example, if we argue that we should be virtuous because people should conform to a rule or set of rules, we have adopted a variation of principle-based ethics. If virtue is defended on the basis that it results in good for many people (rather than just myself), we have opted for a form of utilitarianism. Once again, virtue does not seem to stand on its own. Instead, it ultimately hides behind something more basic than virtue itself as the foundation for ethics.

4. How do we handle conflicting virtues? While character ethics states that virtue is attained when a person adopts a number of positive attributes, it is also possible to think of cases in which virtues will be in conflict with each other. For example, two commonly mentioned virtues are honesty and loyalty, and virtue ethics would say that a good person will possess both. However, imagine you are in a situation where you must choose which character trait takes priority. You may know, for example, that a close friend has embezzled money from an organization. What will govern your actions—honesty or loyalty?

Virtue ethics seems helpful in answering the question of what to do when we have conflicting principles. Instead of ignoring one principle for the sake of the other, we focus on the type of moral attributes that a good person should develop. However, the same type of question then comes back to us in a different form. In the preceding example, we must decide which virtue will be exercised and which will be ignored. However, there seems to be nothing within virtue ethics to tell us whether honesty or loyalty should take priority when the two of them conflict.

5. Which virtues are virtuous? Plato speaks of temperance, courage, wisdom and justice as the cardinal virtues, while Augustine adds the theological virtues of faith, hope and love. Benjamin Franklin lists frugality and avoidance of "trifling conversation" as virtues. In short, not all catalogs of virtues are the same. Moreover, although some virtue lists include the same traits, the definitions of these traits may differ greatly from one person to the next.[11]

It may appear that such differences are minor quibbles over definitions or over which terms should go to the top of the list. However, there may be more to the disagreements than first meets the eye. For example, love appears on none of the Greek lists as a virtue; many Greeks thought love a dangerous emotion, something to be avoided whenever possible. However, for Christians, love is the ultimate moral virtue. Humility, which is almost always found on a Christian register of desirable qualities, is seen as a vice by the Greeks.

Moreover, Aristotle and Plato never imagined that the virtuous life was a possibility for the common person. Both thought that character education, which centered on contemplation, was beyond the grasp of ordinary citizens. For classical moralists

> virtue was the expression, not of a good heart, but of a good mind, such that a virtuous man is identified by his resourcefulness, his powers of achievement, his stature as a thinker and planner or, in a word, his rationality in the broadest sense. A man of virtue was to the ancients a man of special worth, and was to be contrasted, not with the vicious, as we would think of him, but with the worthless. Thus while our model of a person bereft of virtue would most likely be a criminal, the type of person most likely to occur in the ancients would be the slave, the "living tool," as Aristotle described him, the worthless person.[12]

The point is that differing ideas of virtues are more than just internal squabbles over which is the best of a shopping list of desirable qualities. These are serious disagreements concerning the basic questions of ethics—what is good, what is necessary for a person to be good and what type of person is good. It helps little to agree that character is of primary importance if we cannot resolve the question of what type of dispositions are good. When Jesus says, "Blessed are the meek," and Aristotle sees the meek person as one who, by definition, cannot be blessed, we are confronted by a fundamental disagreement about human nature and the goal of human existence. As chapter nine tells us, if Plato and Aristotle have not correctly understood the point of human life, they will also be wrong about the virtues necessary to reach the goal of the "good life."

Conclusion

Many ethicists (Christian and non-Christian) who reject virtue ethics as a whole nevertheless argue that virtue should be a component of any ethical theory one ultimately adopts.[13] What attracts them is the idea that ethics is about what kind of people we are, not just the kind of things we do. However, the common criticism, and the troublesome factor underlying almost every one of the problems noted in this chapter, is that virtue ethics seems to be incomplete in itself. It constantly looks beyond itself to fill in the gaps. How do we resolve the problem of the "courageous bigot" who bombs the synagogue? Does compassion lead us to increase or abolish welfare? Is there a way to get around the egoism that seems to be at the heart of Aristotle and Plato's quest for the good life? If virtues are to be integrated in the good person, why must we sometimes exercise one to the exclusion of others? Questions like these seem to indicate an incompleteness in these early versions of virtue ethics.

In addition, many Christians are troubled about classical formations of virtue theory because they define our ethical struggle as primarily a matter of the intellect. For Plato ignorance was the moral problem. For Aristotle the uneducated could not be virtuous. This seems to locate the solution to our ethical shortcomings in human rational capacities and leaves little room for God's grace, which is a necessary element in Christian ethical approaches. Moreover, while Christianity does not dismiss the relevance of reason in ethics, it often gives higher priority to other human capacities, such as our spiritual impulses, will or love. Stated otherwise, many Christians will argue that Plato and Aristotle misconstrue human nature as primarily cognitive. However, if rationality is not the goal of human existence but a tool to some higher human end, we will arrive at a different conception of the virtues.

That is where our next ethical system begins. It wants to maintain a central role for virtue. However, it also argues that Plato, Aristotle and, for that matter, most of the ethical systems in this book, go off the rails by assuming that ethics is primarily an intellectual task. More specifically, it questions whether we can assume a universal rationality that can provide the foundation for the ethical task.

9

THE MORAL OF THE STORY IS . . .

Narrative Ethics

IF YOU HAVE BEEN READING the last few chapters carefully, you may have detected a common theme in several of the ethical theories. In this pattern, which we will refer to as the Enlightenment or modernist model, we are told that certain virtues, principles or strategies should be adopted because they satisfy the demands of rationality. In short, getting ethics right is mostly a matter of getting our thinking right. Then, once our ideas are squared away, we simply apply these rational rules or techniques to ethical problems and out pops the most moral option.

In addition, modernists argue that their moral systems can be universalized. One need not live in a particular time and location, belong to one specific religion or be resident of a certain territory for a theory to be valid. In fact, the unique features of our background, things like religious beliefs or cultural traditions, are considered obstacles to rational thought. All particular convictions and commitments that are limited to our tribe or time must be set aside in order to arrive at universal, rational ethical conclusions.

In contrast, if one seeks counseling or psychological help with the goal of making some aspect of life better, we discover a different method. The first thing that happens is that the therapist will do a "history" or "narrative" that will focus precisely on the factors that are viewed as potential roadblocks for rational inquiry in modernism—pivotal life events, beliefs, family relationships, cultural background, religious commitments and similar factors. In this setting these particularities are not considered as peripheral but essential to our identity. Moreover, it acknowledges a connectedness to our life. We didn't just wake up this morning and become who we are now, with a set of beliefs, relationships and problems that may change completely when the alarm rings tomorrow morning. Our life is like a story whose present chapter cannot be understood apart from what we have experienced in previous chapters.

This stark contrast between the modernist approach to ethics and the therapeutic model forms the basis for what we will call narrative ethics. Narrative ethics is critical of the Enlightenment paradigm; it argues that, in the quest for a better ethical life, the Enlightenment paradigm eliminates all that makes life, *my* life, what it is. After all, we never meet generic, universal human beings. We meet individual persons. And if we want to really know who a specific individual is, we do not seek a description that could be applied equally to every other member of the species *homo sapiens*. Instead, we will want to know where this individual came from and where she or he has been. The cultural pressures, economic circumstances, close relationships, religious assumptions and educational experiences that molded this individual in a particular direction are important for developing a deep acquaintance. We will want to learn the pivotal influences, the important books and the timing of life-shaping encounters and events that gave this person's life its unique texture. In fact, it is not too much to say that we really don't know another person *until* we know his or her story. As Robert C. Roberts puts it, "The idea of a self as something to which its history is merely accidental does not do justice to the concept of a self with which we daily do business."[1]

A Story Within a Story

In addition to the observation that our lives bear more resemblance to a story than a neat but bloodless list of rational beliefs, narrative ethics argues that our lives are stories within a larger story. No one is born into a moral or social void. Instead, we come into a world of competing value systems, economic interests and national traditions, and these preexisting moral forces provide a context within which we live and make our choices. Thus, two people could live next door to each other but interpret the world in vastly different ways. After all, our world is not just a collection of objects and people. It also includes value judgments that define how we evaluate the worth and priority of these things and people in our lives.

Thus, if these two neighbors would both visit the hypothetical therapist at the beginning of the chapter, their divergent narratives would shape what they considered a problem or envisioned as a successful resolution. One might interpret a certain level of teenage independence as a serious revolt against parental authority, while the other would find it a normal and healthy stage of adolescent development. What one would view as signs of a healthy marriage might, to the other, be indicators of a relationship on the rocks. The point is that we are surrounded by broader stories. Depending on which narrative we own (or which narrative owns us), we will interpret the world differently. We could say, without too much overstatement, that in large part we live in different universes.

The role of the broader narratives in shaping our universe sheds light on why narrative ethics is critical of the Enlightenment's quest for purely rational approaches; namely, they are not all that rational. What is a clearly rational decision in one narrative context will often seem the epitome of irrationality in another. To illustrate, in the opening number of *Fiddler on the Roof,* Tevye tells the audience, "Because of our traditions, every one of us knows who he is and what God expects him to do." Later in the play Tevye disowns his third daughter, Chava, when she marries a non-Jewish Russian boy. If Tevye's decision is ripped from the context of his community and its traditions, his decision will seem irrational because he obviously loves his daughter deeply. However, if we look at this through the lens of Tevye's social and religious tradition, we may well see his choice as completely rational. Indeed, his community might single him out as an exemplar—one who displays moral courage in the face of a wrenching decision.

Ethics as If Life Matters

By drawing on this allusion to *Fiddler on the Roof,* I have actually engaged in the type of exercise commonly found within narrative ethics. Rather than applying abstract ethical rules to hypothetical situations, we have shifted our moral considerations from the ethereal realm of abstract reasoning into a concrete time, place and social framework that situates moral choices in the midst of relationships and value-laden narratives.

This close connection with life leads advocates of narrative ethics to highlight three particular advantages of this approach, which, to maintain the spirit of narrative ethics, I will illustrate by reference to narrative of Socrates' trial and death. First, narrative goes beyond intellect to touch us at the depths of our being. If you want to learn about courage and justice, Socrates' words about these virtues are certainly worth pondering. Still, more than twenty years of teaching about Socrates has convinced me that students learn much more about justice and courage by observing what he does during a trial where his life is on the line. While he talks about these virtues briefly and indirectly during and after the trial, the fact that he exemplifies them in concrete ways communicates in a more powerful way. When we are presented with profound ideas, we may or may not engage with them at a level that reaches our soul. However, when we see his example, it is hard not to place ourselves in the story, our own life at stake, and ask how we might handle the same circumstance.

A second aspect of narrative ethics on display in Socrates' story is the process by which we become the sort of people we want to be. The Enlightenment model's "think right, do right" method seems to chop life into a sequence of dilemmas in search of rational analysis and decision. However, this is out of sync with how we experience character development. Socrates did not walk into court and decide what sort of person he wanted to be that particular day. He had already "practiced" for the sort of situation in which life was in the balance by becoming a particular type of person who had developed certain virtues. As a result, those who knew him were not surprised by his words or actions during the trial and in his later conversations while he awaited his execution. There is continuity to his character. Over time, he had developed the sorts of dispositions that lent a high degree of predictability to future actions.

Finally, narrative ethics argues that stories have a ring of authenticity that we do not hear as clearly in cognitive approaches to ethics. Some readers will know that after Socrates is condemned to death at his trial, he is offered the opportunity to escape to a nearby city. Although he believes his sentence is unjust, he also argues that the laws of Athens are good and just. Therefore, he stays and allows himself to be executed rather than saving his life, because he does not want to undermine the young's respect for justice.

Many people will say that they have moral values that are so true and important that they would remain faithful to them even at the cost of their life. But talk is cheap. Until this verbal commitment is tested in real-life situations, we have good reason to be skeptical of how deeply ingrained a person's principles are. Socrates' statements about justice gain deep credibility because they are backed up by his willingness to face death for them.

To sum up, if narratives mirror the ways we engage moral questions most directly, experience character development and test the credibility of moral statements, advocates of narrative ethics argue that ethical method must include narrative in a fundamental way. As Martha Nussbaum puts it,

> Suppose one believes . . . that the most important truths about human psychology cannot be communicated or grasped by intellectual activity alone: powerful emotions have an irreducibly important cognitive role to play. If one states this view in a written form that expresses only intellectual activity and addresses itself only to the intellect of the reader . . . a question arises. Does the writer really believe what his or her words seem to state? If so, why has this form been selected above others, a form that itself implies a rather different view of what is important and what is dispensable?[2]

For this reason, narrative ethics looks to biography, literature and poetry as indispensable resources for moral development. The stories of others become mirrors in which we see exemplars of qualities we seek to develop in ourselves (or those we hope to avoid) and the processes and decisions that have shaped their character. Moreover, these narratives enable us to see more clearly the influence of a tradition or community that shapes and supports our values.

Within this process there is still an important role for the sort of philosophical analysis offered by more traditional forms of ethics. In fact, this sort of reflection is necessary to move from one specific situation in another's life to incorporation into our own moral inventory with its unique specificities. However, separating our analysis from a concrete story is a bit like trying to understand baseball by doing nothing but reading box scores and player stats. While these can illuminate certain aspects of the game, it is not the same as being in the stands and watching the infield shift to guard the third base line when a right-handed pull hitter comes up. And it is certainly nothing like being the third baseman when that hitter blasts a screaming line drive right at you.

Description and Prescription

To this point our description encompasses a very broad and diverse family of moral approaches. This makes it impossible to offer an evaluation that does justice to every variation of narrative ethics. To allow such an analysis, I will focus on one specific version of narrative ethics as outlined by Stanley Hauerwas. His approach falls into a category that I will call *prescriptive* narrative ethics. Prescriptive versions of narrative ethics argue that, although our world offers a vast array of competing narratives and traditions, only one narrative possesses sufficient truth to guide us properly. That narrative thus prescribes the standards to which we must conform our life.

Before we get to that, however, I want to note that others advocate a *descriptive* approach to narrative ethics. This variant also recognizes that our world presents a smorgasbord of narratives competing for our attention. However, it says that the task of ethics is not to make judgments about which narrative is true or false. In fact, it often argues that such evaluations make no sense in the absence of some sort of universally objective reason that can judge between these competing stories. The moral task is instead to acquaint oneself with a variety of narratives, empathetically enter into the situations and decisions portrayed within them, and find ways forward in one's own moral journey through the inspiration of those who act heroically. No one should or can embrace the values expressed in every narrative. It is, instead, the responsibility of the reader to choose from among these narratives, and even within specific narratives, the virtues they desire to develop.

Under the descriptive approach, ethics takes on a radically different role from what is typically conceived as its task. Since we cannot count on an objective, universal rationality to determine what is right, we rely instead on each individual, with his or her own individual reasons, for owning or rejecting particular virtues. Rather than searching for ethical truth, this model presupposes that there are innumerable stories that are potentially true and become actually true for us only if we choose them. While a particular story may motivate or inspire, whatever tradition one might follow ultimately depends on the subjective inclinations of the reader.

Because our subjective inclinations form the basis for truth, each person becomes the judge of ethics rather than being subject to its judgments. This makes the descriptive approach highly problematic from a Christian perspective because, like ethical egoism, it puts each individual in the "God position." However, as we soon will see, prescriptive versions allow us to incorporate other features of narrative ethics rather smoothly.

Christian Ethics as Narrative Ethics

According to Stanley Hauerwas, "Narrative is not secondary to our knowledge of God; there is no 'point' that can be separated from the story. The narratives through which we learn of God are the point. Stories are not substitute explanations that we can someday hope to supplant with more straightforward accounts."[3] From the beginning, he signals his belief that, at its heart, Christian ethics *is* a narrative ethics. The story of God's creative and redeeming work that stretches from God's adoption of Israel through the death and resurrection of Jesus cannot be reduced to a set of propositions or abstract rules without distorting the Christian message. Moreover, it is a "constituting story." Without this story there is no church. Because this is the case, we cannot separate Christian ethics from theology. This theology-ethics calls us to a new life that is defined by the story.

The Hauerwas quote also hints at why he is critical of modernist ethics and especially critical of those who attempt to frame Christian ethics within the assumptions of a universal rationality. As the Enlightenment's influence spread, faith traditions were considered localized and idiosyncratic at best, and superstitious or dangerous at worst. In this context Christian ethics increasingly looked like the guardian of a tradition, founded on blind faith and unable to withstand the rigors of rational inquiry. As a result many Christian ethicists succumbed to the pressure to reframe ethics in rationalistic terms, arguing that Christianity offers superior ethical ideas that are logically defensible, thus escaping the charge of particularity and obscurity.

For example, many such ethicists would identify the Ten Commandments as the heart of Christian ethics and then proceed to demonstrate the rationality of living according to these moral rules. However, Hauerwas says, "The Decalogue [Ten Commandments] is part of the covenant of God with Israel. Divorced from that covenant it makes no sense. God does indeed command obedience, but our God is the God who 'brought you out of the land of Egypt, out of the house of bondage' (Deut. 5:6)."[4] The exodus is not just historical information about a peripheral event leading up the "real deal"—the giving of the Ten Commandments, which provides a distillation of God's moral will for all people. Instead, the exodus creates a community who knows and is bound by covenant to a particular God with particular aims for his people. These commands can only be truly understood within the context of this covenant.

The exodus is a key episode in a story that brings Israel's calling to a climax in the death and resurrection of Jesus. It is in this story that salvation is found and our understanding of goodness follows the contours of a Christian theology about salvation. In short, Christianity does not have an ethics, as if ethics is like a condiment added on top of its doctrines; Christianity is an ethics. Thus Hauerwas rejects modernism's attempt to isolate ethics from the particularities of Christian theology. As he puts it, "The more we try to mine Scripture for a workable ethic, the more we are drawn to separate such an ethic from the understanding of salvation which makes such an ethic intelligible in the first place."[5]

The close connection Hauerwas draws between salvation and ethics offers another angle to understand his dislike of the Enlightenment model. The latter, which he sometimes refers to as "decisionism," is primarily about clearing up our foggy moral thinking with the aim of making right choices. In contrast, Christian morality is about being transformed into a new kind of people. This transformation is not primarily a better way of understanding, deciding or doing. Instead, Hauerwas says, "Ethics is first a way of *seeing* before it is a matter of *doing*. The ethical task is not to tell you what is right or wrong but rather to train you to see."[6]

This "seeing" is, again, not primarily cognitive but relational. More precisely, Hauerwas says, "We know ourselves truthfully only when we know ourselves in relation to God."[7] Moral knowledge is not mastery of ideas or moral tactics, but self-knowledge, an awareness that simultaneously "helps me place myself as a creature of a gracious God" and "exposes the unwelcome fact that I am a sinner."[8] Seeing the world in this way has two important ramifications. First, we are not autonomous beings set free to choose from among a spectrum of diverse narratives. Instead, we are creatures of a God who stakes a claim upon us and offers us salvation. Second, this perspective does not leave room for a morality that exists apart from theology. The Christian narrative is a moral claim about the nature of reality.

Scripture and the Church

Of course, it is within Scripture that we encounter the story of God's activity in history. However, Hauerwas quickly adds two important qualifiers about what it means to take the Bible as the source of Christian ethics. First, we know this story correctly only when we read the Bible as Scripture rather than as text. When we approach the Bible as text, we read it like we read any other writing, seeking to understand the cultural context from which it arises, the nuances of the vocabulary, how we should resolve apparent tensions within different sections and so on. This is all part of the process of making the proper interpretive judgments about the text. In contrast, Hauerwas says that "for Christian ethics, the Bible is not just a collection of texts but Scripture that makes normative claims on a community."[9] When we read the Bible as Scripture, it interprets and judges us. When we read it as text, we pass interpretive judgments upon the Bible. In this case it only becomes Scripture when it passes muster on some type of qualification external to the Bible.[10] However, the result is that whatever external resource we use to establish the Bible's authority has the last word on ethics, not the Bible itself.

If Scripture's authority is not grounded in its complete harmony, rationally defensible principles or some other quality, where does Scripture gain its authority? This brings us to Hauerwas's second qualification about Scripture. "Scripture is not an authority because it sets a standard of orthodoxy . . . but because the traditions of Scripture provide the means for our community to find new life."[11] Thus, when asked why the Bible should be treated as Scripture, Hauerwas says that it provides a story that allows us to live truthfully, a truthfulness that should be evident in the worship, habits and traditions of the narrative community.

This sort of answer concerning the authority of Scripture obviously will not be convincing to those who demand an argument that can stand up to rational evaluation. However, "the purpose of the church is not to prove that Christianity is true, but to demonstrate what the world is like if it is true."[12] The world's narratives look for hope and security in military power, economic clout, sexual fulfillment and other means. The church's mandate is to model how the world is actually a different place in view of the hope found in Christ's suffering and resurrection.

Stated otherwise, the task of the community is to introduce to others this new way of seeing reality. Its existence is to be a witness to God's story. "The church first serves the world by helping the world to know what it means to be the world. For without a 'contrast model' the world has no way to know or feel the oddness of its dependence on power for survival."[13] It is not the community's job to convince others of Christianity's truth by means of rational argument. Instead, "witness and argument are the work of the Holy Spirit."[14]

If the church is to be a faithful witness to God's story, it must be immersed in this narrative. The first means by which this occurs is worship, where we remember the story through preaching, sacrament and liturgy. However, this also occurs within a community that passes on what it means to live in a manner consistent with the narrative. This is not done by conformity to a set of well-defined rules. It is, instead, a set of skills learned by observation. First, this skill involves seeing reality in a new way. This requires practice because we are surrounded by other narratives that press their vision of reality and the good life on us.

Second, these skills should become virtues, dispositions to act in ways that witness to God's story. However, Hauerwas emphasizes that the virtues are not to be understood as generic dispositions that are found among all people in varying degrees. Christian virtues are shaped and defined by the story of God's interaction with the world. To illustrate, Aristotle would have found it incredible to designate hope as a virtue. However, for Christians who believe that Christ's resurrection has conquered death and that no force can overcome God's faithfulness to us, hope is not simply a personality trait possessed by sunny optimists. It is a fundamental virtue, one that all Christians must learn through residency in a community immersed in memory of the resurrection.

As a means of illustrating the particularity of the Christian virtue of hope, Hauerwas applies this concept to the issue of abortion. "The Christian approach is not one of deciding when life has begun, but hoping that it has. We hope that human life has begun! . . . [W]e are the kind of people who hope life has started, because we are ready to believe that this new life will enrich our community." Competing narratives may justify having children based on the belief that children are the hope for our future. However, Hauerwas, in view of the injustice and misery of our world that often claims children as its first victims, says that such a notion is absurd. Instead, he argues that "in a world that may well be about the killing of our children, having children is an extraordinary act of faith and hope. But as Christians our hope is from the God who urges us to welcome children."[15]

Summary

Narrative ethics maintains that because what makes us the persons we are is found in the particularities of life rather than impersonal logic, these elements must be incorporated at the ground level of ethical thought. After all, narrative binds my individual life into a coherent whole and places my life within a broader story that molds my values, convictions and aims. Without this narrative glue, "an emphasis on rule-determined obligations abstracted from the story makes our existence appear to be only 'one damn thing after another.'"[16]

While descriptive forms of narrative ethics believe that no single narrative is true for all, prescriptive variations, such as Hauerwas's, which we will evaluate shortly, argue that a single story reveals the truth and purpose of human existence. For Hauerwas, Jesus' death and resurrection draws into itself the earlier narrative of God's work in history to form a community, and those within this community learn to see themselves and the world truthfully. The mission of this new people is to live as a contrast model, as "resident aliens" in the midst of those who are dependent on their own resources, so that others will see the possibilities offered by the values of a radically different narrative.

The Positive Side of Hauerwas's Narrative Ethics

Many of you will be reading within a classroom context, and you probably will be tested on the theories presented in these chapters. Does this mean that those who get an F on the test are morally deficient individuals while A students are closing in on ethical perfection? Few people will draw such a conclusion, and I'm reasonably sure those who fail the test will have a different interpretation of their grade. The fact that most of us do not draw a direct line between our cognitive capacities and our ethical status helps us understand the appeal of a narrative approach. Hauerwas reminds us that the point of ethics is not getting all the answers right (which seems to be the primary concern in the Enlightenment model), but becoming better people.

Moreover, Hauerwas also helps us understand that we can only determine if we are heading down the road toward becoming better people when we have a measuring stick. "Better" implies a standard. For him, the Christian narrative about a life in the presence of a saving God provides the standard by which we measure our own life. For him, this gives Christians the status of colonizers, those with peculiar values and goals who live in the midst of those with very different moral views and aims. In this way he seeks to explode the popular myth that "all paths lead to the same destination." Because different narratives produced different types of people, Hauerwas argues that Christians should be so deeply informed and formed by the Christian story that others will see, by contrast, the poverty of their current story.

Potential Problems in Hauerwas's Narrative Ethics

As already noted, Hauerwas highlights some problematic aspects of Enlightenment ethics. The role of the critic who brings to light our easy assumptions and raises questions about "business as usual" is a valuable one. However, even though I have described his ethics as prescriptive, Hauerwas's prescriptions are frequently vague about important aspects of the alternative vision he offers. Ethical theories need to nail down the answers to key what, who, why and where questions, and I want to point out some places where his narrative approach leaves us with a number of lingering ambiguities about such questions.

1. Hauerwas creates ambiguity about what Christians ought to do in specific situations. Hauerwas clearly dislikes the decisionist model, which reduces ethics to an interconnected series of supposedly universal propositions or if-then strategies. Yet he is also firmly committed to an ethics that places us in concrete circumstances, and recognizes that these circumstances will require decisions. In such cases he argues that our response will emerge from a virtuous character formed by the Christian narrative.

While he seems rather confident about the power and precision of this narrative to send us on the right trajectories, application of this approach to specific moral issues raises questions. For example, Hauerwas argues that "nonviolence is not just one implication among others that can be drawn from our Christian beliefs; it is at the very heart of our understanding of God."[17] This leads him to the conclusion that Christians should be pacifists. This raises an obvious question: If pacifism is not just one viable option for Christians but is positioned at the center of Christian ethics, why have the vast majority within the church not come to a similar conclusion? If the Christian narrative is not precise enough on a matter as fundamental as whether war can ever be an option for believers, where does this leave us on other questions?

It is useful to remember that, for Hauerwas, narrative is intended to cultivate certain types of virtues in individuals. And in spite of the fact that he argues that the Christian story provides definition to our understanding of the virtues, we still encounter the same problem mentioned in chapter eight on virtue ethics. Knowing what type of people we ought to be still leaves considerable ambiguity about the actions that should result from our character.

2. Who is the narrative community Hauerwas speaks of? Hauerwas insists on the historical nature of the narrative community, stretching from the present all the way back to God's promise to Abraham. Within this Christian society we learn the skills necessary to live as God's people and become a witness to the world. Given this, it would seem that when we seek insight about or examples of these skills, we should be able to pause at any point along this history, poke our head in a church window and say, "Look, this is how it is done." We don't get much of that in Hauerwas. Instead, most of what he has to say about the church or individual Christians through history is critical.

This criticism becomes especially scathing when he refers to Christians who have construed ethics within Kantian or utilitarianism frameworks, as well as the approaches we will consider later in this book, such as divine command or natural law ethics.[18] However, these thinkers, who collectively represent the majority of Christian ethical musings over the past several centuries, are consistently portrayed as examples of all that is wrong with Christian ethics. Thus the narrative community that Hauerwas refers to as the training ground for passing on virtue does not appear to be the historical reality he insists on. Instead, it functions more as an ideal that is only rarely and sporadically manifested in actual history.

3. Where is the line between Scripture and the community? Hauerwas presents the Christian narrative as something one learns/absorbs over time, and this involves "unlearning" stories other than the Christian narrative that continue to exert an influence over us. In other words, in the actual world there is no place where this narrative is found in a pure, unalloyed state. We have not arrived at some perfect ethical destination but are always moving toward an ideal. The question is, then, how does the church judge itself to identify and root out alien influences? Hauerwas says that this learning is best done in the context of worship, in which we rehearse the narrative in preaching and sacrament. However, our worship itself reflects the distortions of other narratives. So where do we go to examine and correct the church itself?

The usual answer within Christian ethics is that we test it against Scripture. However, Hauerwas does not allow for this sort of clear delineation between Scripture and the narrative community. Scripture does not stand apart from the church's interpretation and enactment. However, what do we do if a particular Christian community's interpretation leads them to conclude that they are to engage in the ethnic cleansing of a region? If the biblical narrative has no independence from the narrative community's current self-understanding, we end up with a circular loop. What the biblical narrative says creates the community, and what the community says determines how the narrative should be interpreted. This circularity makes it difficult to see how one could ever challenge a belief that God calls the church to regional ethnic cleansing or any other interpretive position that arises within the community.

4. Why would anyone recognize the Christian story as a true story? A consistent theme throughout Hauerwas's ethics is that Christians should refrain from appealing to authorities outside Scripture and the narrative tradition to verify its validity. To do so involves reliance on competing narratives grounded in false views of God and reality. At the same time Hauerwas maintains that the task of the church is to be a witness that allows the world to understand the emptiness of its own narratives. Here's the problem. If one's view and evaluation of the world is so strongly molded by one's narrative, why should we expect to find anything within non-Christian narratives that would allow a non-Christian who observes this witness to conclude that it offers anything better? Instead, part of a competing narrative would seem to include the idea that it, not the Christian tradition, offers the best life.

As an example, let's return to Hauerwas's view that pacifism is an essential element of the Christian story. What happens, then, when Christian pacifists encounter those whose own narrative is one of universal conquest through force? Since each tradition comes with its own criteria for truth and goodness as standard equipment, how will the church's witness be viewed as anything other than sheer lunacy by those committed to a "universal conquest through force" narrative? Our question here is not whether Christians should be pacifists. Instead, the issue is how a person comes to recognize the truth of a narrative they do not currently believe.

Why would a person abandon a view once believed true for a new one that now appears to better describe reality? Untangling this question explains why Enlightenment ethics places so much emphasis on reason. If rationality is common to all, and we agree to be persuaded by logic alone, this provides a justification for modifying our ideas. However, Hauerwas is dead set against any such external authority, and insists that any conviction and recognition of truth that would occur within the "universal conquest through force" group will occur only through the witness of the Holy Spirit.

Even here, though, it would seem that unless the witness of the Holy Spirit simply rips us out of our existing narrative and forces us to see the world in a completely new way (which would be inconsistent with Hauerwas's insistence on the connectedness of life), we have to envision that all humans, regardless of their overarching narrative, possess something that allows them to recognize the truth as truth. In other words, it seems that the Holy Spirit's witness must resonate with something common to all human beings. However, Hauerwas places so much emphasis on the particularities of human existence, it is unclear what this common element might be.

Conclusion

There is much that is compelling and interesting about narrative approaches to ethics. Instead of starting in the abstract domains of an ideal rationality, it begins where we live. Not only is my life characterized, at least in large part, by the social, economic, ethnic, religious and relational particularities of my experience, it is also conditioned by my loyalties to larger narratives—ways of seeing the world that are in place before I come into being.

In addition, Hauerwas's idea of Christian ethics has features that nicely fit in with the aims of most believers. He appeals to our intuition that Christian morality is more than following rules and legalism. His insistence on grounding ethics in Scripture is consistent with Christian tradition, as is his belief that Christian ethics ought to transform our character and reorient how we see the world. Similarly, Scripture confirms Hauerwas's vision of a church that models a way of life that is so compelling that others will glimpse the truth of the gospel.

Despite all these positive aspects, Hauerwas, by critiquing the Enlightenment notion of universal rationality and focusing on the particularity of the Christian narrative, seems to leave no common thread in our humanity that explains why this narrative would be believed by anyone who does not already accept it. This does not mean that we have no option but to rehabilitate modernism's idea of rationality as the ethical foundation. There are perhaps other aspects of human existence that would allow us to bridge the gap between narratives and allow us to see the good and the true as good and true. Our next chapter examines the possibility that, instead of reason, we might look to love as shared moral turf that connects us to each other and to God.

10

ALL YOU NEED IS LOVE

Situation Ethics

WOULD YOU LIE TO SAVE YOUR CHILD'S LIFE? Is it permissible to kill if it is the only way to save the life of an innocent person? Can we justify stealing to keep someone from undeserved harm? A yes answer to any of these questions requires us to break some rule that most people consider basic to ethical behavior. If we are going to set aside such a rule, we ought to have a good reason for doing so. So what justifies disregarding an ethical norm? One answer that seems reasonable to many people is "love." For these people, you could say love covers a multitude of broken rules.

We might go a step further and ask what marks any act as good. Again, the answer for many will be the same: love. We do the right thing when we act in a loving manner. Good surely is not simply the result of adherence to laws. Telling the truth, respecting life or keeping our hands off others' possessions is how we express love for people. Can we then simplify ethics by combining everything under the one principle that explains the exceptions to the rules as well as the motives for our actions? If we seek a single standard to tell us whether an act is right or wrong, can we sum it up under the bumper sticker "All you need is love"?

The Ethics of Love

Love is a powerful force in our lives. Listen to the songs on the radio, pick up a novel or go to a movie. The topic, more often than not, is love. Life is worth living when we know we are loved and are able to give love. For Christians, love takes on a special role. The greatest of the commandments, as summarized by Jesus, is to "love the Lord your God" and "love your neighbor as yourself" (Mt 22:37, 39). Moreover, love is not just what we are commanded to do, it is who God is: "God is love" (1 Jn 4:16). Thus situation ethics (or situationism) boils down ethics to one guiding principle: that doing good is a matter of acting in love. It is not love plus honesty, chastity or anything else. All we need is love (rightly understood, of course).

Situation ethics is often seen as the direct opposite of Christian ethics. It is not uncommon to hear some Christians, when confronted by a decision they disapprove of, say, "That's just situation ethics." Is this evaluation correct? Is situationism the antithesis of a Christian approach? Joseph Fletcher, the most visible advocate of situation ethics, does not see it that way. He says his intent is not to offer an alternative to Christian ethics but to set out a model of Christian ethics. And he views situationism as the best means of doing this. In fact, he goes so far as to state that "Christian ethics is a situation ethic."

The fundamentals of situation ethics are summarized by Fletcher in a series of six propositions:

1. Only one thing is intrinsically good, namely, love: nothing else.
2. The ultimate norm of Christian decisions is love: nothing else.
3. Love and justice are the same, for justice is love distributed.
4. Love wills the neighbor's good whether we like him or not.
5. Only the end justifies the means: nothing else.
6. Decisions ought to be made situationally, not prescriptively.[1]

Situation Ethics and Agapē

Let's begin where Fletcher begins. His first proposition states that love is the only thing that is intrinsically good. As he explains it,

> *Christian* situation ethics has only one norm or principle or law (call it what you will) that is binding and unexceptionable, always good and right regardless of the circumstances. That is "love"—the *agapē* of the summary commandment to love God and the neighbor. Everything else without exception, all laws and rules and principles and ideals and norms, are only *contingent*, only valid *if they happen* to serve love in any situation.[2]

A couple of things should be noted in this quotation. First, one of the difficulties with constructing an ethical system on the principle of love is that it can have so many meanings. It can refer to romantic feelings, loyalty to friends, preference for fried chicken, sex, one's favorite color and numerous other things. Fletcher recognizes this problem and offers a definition that ties his first and fourth propositions together. The love upon which ethics should be built is what the New Testament calls *agapē*. Fletcher defines it as benevolence or goodwill, or as "giving love—non-reciprocal, neighbor-regarding—'neighbor' meaning 'everybody,' even an enemy (Lk 6:32-35)."[3] *Agapē* is to be distinguished from romantic/sexual love (*eros*) and friendship (*philia*).

There is nothing wrong with either of the latter two types of love in the right circumstances. It is just that *eros* and *philia* are too limited as a foundation for ethics. Both depend on mutuality: they require a two-way street. *Agapē*, on the other hand, does not rely on a response from the one loved. It does not even demand that we like the person who is loved. *Agapē* is love that is given regardless of what the one loved does. In addition, *agapē* is the only form of love that is not exclusive. It is an attitude we can hold toward everyone, unlike familial love, romantic love or friendship. Not only is it possible to have agapeic love toward all, but it also is commanded of all by God. While it makes no sense to command people to have romantic feelings (*eros*) or a bond of friendship with all (*philia*), we can act in a benevolent manner toward everyone. *Agapē* is a matter of will and reason, whereas *eros* and *philia* are primarily emotional.

A second aspect of situationism that should catch our eye is that no law, with the exception of love, is absolute. This is because, as the first proposition states, only love has inherent value. This leads naturally to Fletcher's second proposition: "The ultimate norm of Christian decisions is love: nothing else." If telling a lie to prevent a child's death is a loving act, we should lie. Lying in this case is not a choice between the lesser of two evils, but a positive good. Truth is not good in itself. It has no value except as a tool that helps us express love in most situations.

This is true for all other principles as well. If they do not allow us to act lovingly in a given circumstance, any rule (with the exception of love) can be suspended. This applies even to laws as basic to Christianity as the Ten Commandments. Referring to the Decalogue, Fletcher states, "Situation ethics has good reason to hold it as a duty in some situations to break them [the Ten Commandments], any or all of them. We would be better advised and better off to drop the legalist's love of law, and accept only the law of love."[4] Thus breaking a rule, regardless of whether it is a commandment against lying, stealing, adultery or any other, is not simply allowable but is ethically necessary and responsible if it allows us to act in love.

Rules do have a place in situation ethics—not to direct but to illuminate. Rules function as strategic guides; they are like "punt on fourth down" or "take a pitch when the count is three balls."[5] As Fletcher puts it, rules are "part of wise players' know-how." They are tools that can be used well or poorly. For example, even though punting on fourth down is almost always a good idea, it may not be the best choice if the clock is running down and you are behind by less than a touchdown. In other words, even a good strategy can create havoc if used improperly or in the wrong situation. Similarly, rules are destructive if used in an unloving way. Therefore, as Fletcher's second proposition states, "The ultimate norm of Christian decisions is love: nothing else."

Between Legalism and Antinomianism

Fletcher argues that this understanding of the relation between rules and love allows him to establish ethics in the middle ground between two extremes: legalism and antinomianism. Antinomian means "anti-law." This view says that no rules have general validity. Each decision must be made solely on the basis of the situation. Every moral choice is completely spontaneous. Antinomianism says no guideline or principle—not even love—can tell us whether an action is right or wrong.

The common misunderstanding is that this is what situation ethics promotes. Fletcher, however, strongly rejects antinomianism. The ethical life is not a lawless one. Instead, all decisions are to be judged according to one all-encompassing law: that of love. The mistake in antinomianism is that it throws out love along with the rest of the law. Therefore, like Paul, who condemns a group of antinomians in Corinth

(1 Cor 6:12-20) who mistook Paul's condemnation of the law as a rejection of all moral guidelines and lapsed into a "do what you want" attitude toward ethics, Fletcher also disputes antinomianism.

At the other end of the ethical spectrum is legalism. It is this particular point of view toward which most of Fletcher's criticism is directed because this is where he thinks Christians are more likely to err. Legalism comes from the word *law*. It is the insistence that predetermined laws are to be put into action when they are relevant to the situation at hand. No exceptions. In order to know what to do in a given situation, you simply find the right rule and follow it.

The problem with legalism, according to situationism, is that it depersonalizes. We all know people who are hung up on rules. They are good at being right, but not very good at being good. They know the letter of the law, but have forgotten the purpose of the law. Fletcher says this happens because legalism's zeal is directed toward the law, not people. In its place, situation ethics seeks a "personalism." Love ensures that ethics is personalized because it makes no sense to talk about impersonal love. Love is, by definition, personal. It demands that we put people at the center of our concern. We should be zealous, but zealous for human good. Things such as laws are not to be loved, since they have no inherent value. Because people do have value, they are to be the objects of love.

Fletcher finds a theological basis for this in Scripture. God is a personal being who creates us in his image. Persons—flesh-and-blood human beings—are to be our primary concern in ethics. Jesus personalizes the law when he plucks wheat on the sabbath. This act was a technical violation of the law prohibiting work on the sabbath. However, Jesus justifies this breach of the law by stating, "The Sabbath was made for man, not man for the Sabbath" (Mk 2:27). It is not the law that is important; people are important. Therefore, Fletcher rejects any form of legalistic ethics.

How Love Works

It is difficult to find a Christian ethicist who will disagree with giving love a major role. However, most will include at least one other virtue—

justice—to the list of absolutes. Fletcher disagrees with separating these two virtues and states, instead, in proposition three: "Love and justice are the same, for justice is love distributed." Stated otherwise: "Justice is Christian love using its head, calculating its duties, obligations, opportunities, resources."[6] This ties in with defining love as *agapē*. *Agapē* is not sentimental and softheaded. It is not primarily a feeling. We need more than impulses or gut reactions to ensure that people get what they deserve. To discover the loving response, we need to think, plan and make rational judgments. Therefore, Fletcher does not shrink from describing love as "calculating." It adds up the costs for all involved.

Love also adds up the costs with the end in view. The fifth foundational proposition of Fletcher's ethics—"Only the end justifies the means: nothing else"—indicates his acceptance of consequentialism. Good is determined by the results we obtain. Fletcher defends consequentialism by stating, "'If the end does not justify the means, what does?' The answer is, obviously, 'Nothing!'"[7] Because love is the only thing that is good in itself, it is the result we should seek. Any means that get us there are allowable, as long as the goal is love. Fletcher cites with approval the example of a frontier woman who kills her crying baby with her own hands to keep Native Americans from discovering and killing an entire group of people trying to get to a fort. Killing for a loving purpose, even if it is your child, is justified because only love is intrinsically good. Love, the one absolute, justifies anything.

In his final proposition—"Decisions ought to be made situationally, not prescriptively"—Fletcher argues that abstract ethical questions are unanswerable. It makes no sense to ask if abortion is permissible. It may or may not be. Everything depends on the situation. We do not have a real question without a concrete situation. Each case is different, and we cannot properly pronounce a verdict until we know all the variables. Ethics can be done only on a casuistic (case study) basis. Rules are not enough. We need to know the facts of the case—the who, what, when, where and why factors—to know what a loving solution is.

This indicates that to some extent love is not enough by itself. Even when we know that we ought to love in all situations, we still need to know the details of the situation before we give an ethical answer. This is because, Fletcher argues, love is not a substantive; it does not have predefined factual content. It is not a property or characteristic. Love is, instead, what Fletcher calls a "formal" principle. It refers to the motive by which we act ("act in a loving way") without prescribing beforehand what act is loving. Love tells us how we ought to go about doing something without telling us what to do. The content of love—the "what"—arises only as we come to understand the concrete demands of the situation. The principle of love is absolute, but the application of the principle is relative to the situation. As Fletcher puts it, the answer is found in "love plus the situation."

Summary

Some people are able to stay beyond the reach of some of the big questions of the day—divorce, cloning, homosexuality, euthanasia and others—but as time goes on fewer of us can escape dealing with these issues in our own lives or the lives of those we care about. And when these issues finally hit home, an interesting phenomenon sometimes happens. We find that answers we once held with confidence no longer seem adequate now that we know people who face tough decisions. No longer can we depersonalize the problem and handle it as a mental puzzle. Now we see human faces embroiled in struggle, and those faces belong to people we love.

Situation ethics wants that sense of attachment in moral decision making. It does not ask us to adopt a wishy-washy version of love that excuses anything someone may want to do, but situationism does remind us that people, not rules, are what make ethics so important. Legalism demands that we stand back from the situation, but when we love the people who wrestle with complex issues, it seems more appropriate to stand close. In such times Fletcher argues that only love counts. And he notches up the responsibility level for Christians by reminding us that love is the proper response, not only for those with whom we have a special relationship but for all people.

The Positive Side of Situation Ethics

Situation ethics has been greatly maligned in many Christian circles.

Quite bluntly, much of the criticism grows out of ignorance of what Fletcher really says. If approached with an open mind, situation ethics has much to commend it. First, it does have an absolute foundation on which to build. All other norms are relative, but they are relative to one absolute: love.[8] Therefore, situationism cannot be rightly criticized as a completely relativistic view, which many have sought to do. Fletcher does not promote an "anything goes" ethics as many have supposed. When we act in a loving manner, certain options cannot be seen as ethical. Love will not tolerate irresponsibility. Moreover, we cannot adopt an indifferent "live and let live" approach. Indifference is, in Fletcher's view, the opposite of love.

Second, Fletcher builds his one absolute on the proper basis. From a Christian perspective, any system of morality that does not begin from the nature and character of God is off to a false start. Situation ethics does not arbitrarily select love from a list of possible ultimates. It begins by asking who God is. Since it is difficult to think of anything more basic to God's identity than love, Christian situationism appears to begin at the right point.

A third helpful element of situation ethics is its rejection of legalism. When rules are idolized and become the "tail that wags the dog," people get hurt. Situationism avoids this by replacing love of law with love for people. This is biblical in that it stresses our responsibility for others and defines those "others" inclusively; we are to love everyone. Situationism's personalistic approach also helps us recognize the importance of circumstances in ethical evaluation. Passing yourself off as a highway patrol officer in a prank call to your sister is different from fudging the numbers on a tax return. Technically, both involve dishonesty, but we do not judge them the same because we recognize that the two situations are different. Situationism incorporates what we all do instinctively when it acknowledges the importance of the context and circumstances.

A final positive element in Fletcher is that he provides a means of avoiding conflicts between ethical rules. Many people assume that Christian ethics consists of a set of rules from God. Because the source—God—is absolute, the rules are absolute as well. Under such a rule-based system, ethical decisions are simple. You find the right law and use it. Is your situation one in which you must choose whether to lie or tell the truth? Only one rule is involved; you follow it and that's that.

But things get murky sometimes. What will you do when you have promised to keep a secret but discover that doing so will allow a false accusation to do great damage to a person's reputation? We are stuck between two rules: "Keep your promises" and "Honor truth." If the rules are viewed as equal absolutes that are always to be obeyed, you have a no-win situation. Since situationism has only one rule that applies in every situation, there is never a conflict. Therefore, borderline cases do not require that we eliminate an absolute, because love alone is valid in every situation.

Potential Problems in Situation Ethics

There is so much that is good about love because it takes us directly to the heart of God. It certainly cannot be left out of any attempt at a Christian ethics. In addition, Fletcher keeps love on a solid foundation by avoiding the emotionalism and sentimentality often associated with the term. Instead, he sees love as intensely practical and down-to-earth. It does not give people what they want but considers what is best for their overall well-being. This makes it difficult to critique situationism without coming off as attacking love. However, most of the difficulties with situationism are not found in what it includes but in what it omits.

1. What is included in the "situation"? One significant omission in situation ethics is a clear definition for the term *situation*. Fletcher says that we cannot make ethical decisions in the abstract (proposition 6). We need a case, a concrete situation. Therefore until we know what is included in a situation, we are not in a position to make our decision.

However, behind this approach there lurks a problem, as illustrated by one of Fletcher's own cases. He states, "A young unmarried couple might decide, if they make their decisions Christianly, to have intercourse (e.g., by getting pregnant to force a selfish parent to relent his overbearing resistance to their marriage)."[9] Do we now have a situation in which we can use Fletcher's formula of "love plus the situation" in order to determine the loving action? At a minimum the definition of a situation must tell us who is included in the situation and what time period is in view. Who, then, is involved in the situation in the case? Does it embrace only the two people trying to overcome a parent's objection? Or should we include other players such as the reluctant parent, others in the inner circle of family and friends, the child conceived so that two people can be married, the broader circle of acquaintances and community? If *agapē* defines our "neighbors" inclusively (as Fletcher argues), do we also have to consider whether this expresses love to society as a whole? What about God? Is our love for him included in the situation?

Similarly, do we take into account only how this decision affects people at the time of their decision to engage in intercourse? Are we to include the consequences over the next week? The next five years? A lifetime? If we are more than just physical beings, do such decisions have significance in the context of eternity? In short, without a clear understanding of what is meant by a "situation," we cannot put situationism into practice. For this system to be workable, we must know who will be touched by any particular decision (which is impossible), how it will affect them (also impossible when we do not know who is affected) and at what time the results are to be evaluated (which situationism does not tell us).

2. What is included in "love"? A second significant omission is the absence of a definition for *love*. Although love is the center of his ethics, Fletcher does not tell us what love is. He does have something to say about what love is not, but this is not the same as providing a positive definition. In situationism, love is not assigned a factual content but is a "formal principle" that tells us the goal we are to seek and the way we are to pursue it. The problem with this is that even when we are told to do the loving thing, there is no way to determine what the "loving thing" is. Given Fletcher's definition of love (or lack of definition), would it ever be possible to say any decision was wrong?

It is not difficult to envision two people, both situationists, coming to an impasse on almost any ethical case, even when they agree on the facts of the situation and that love is the only absolute. Returning to Fletcher's example of the young couple, we can envision two situationists in sharp disagreement about the proper way to express love. The young man could argue that under the circumstances it does not serve the purpose of love to have two people willing to commit themselves to each other for life kept apart by a parent whose objections seem irrational. Thus the loving course for this situationist may be to approve of premarital intercourse to pave the way for the marriage. The young woman might argue that for a number of reasons it is unloving to engage in premarital intercourse to force a mother's or father's blessing on a marriage. The young woman may see this use of sex as an unloving manipulation of her father, who would not have approved the marriage freely. Or she may see it as a case in which a child is conceived only as a means to an end. The question for situationism is this: How do we decide who is right?

Without any propositional content for love, we are left wondering what sorts of acts are loving acts, even if we agree with a situationist approach to ethical decision making. We have only a circular definition in which love equals "the most loving thing to do." James Gustafson expresses the difficulty in this way: "'Love,' like 'situation,' is a word that runs through Fletcher's book like a greased pig. . . . Nowhere does Fletcher indicate in a systematic way his various uses of it. It refers to everything he wants it to refer to."[10] The problem with a word that can mean everything is that it ultimately means nothing. And for Fletcher love has no predetermined limits by which we can discern the difference between loving and unloving acts. Therefore, when situationists tell people to love without telling them what love is, are they really saying anything?

3. Is every rule-based ethics legalistic? Situationism argues that love and law cannot stand together. The only absolute is love. So when faced with the decision about picking grain on the sabbath, Fletcher concludes that "Jesus was ready without hesitation to ignore the obligations of sabbath observance, to do forbidden work on the seventh day."[11] He interprets this to mean that we must choose either love or law—and Jesus chose love.

We can agree with Fletcher that Jesus condemns legalism. There is also no doubt that rule-based ethics can be used legalistically. However, this does not mean law is irrelevant, nor does it make Jesus a situationist. The error is in Fletcher's interpretation of this event, in which he states that Jesus ignores the sabbath law. This does not seem to be the case, however, because this law had continuing significance for Jesus. It was not reduced to a strategy. He does not challenge the continuing relevance of sabbath law. Instead, what Jesus seems to challenge is a particular application of this law. For Jesus to deny that sabbath law is the primary consideration in this circumstance is different from arguing that he saw the law itself as irrelevant.

Fletcher seems to assume that all rule-based ethical approaches are legalistic because they do not consider the situation. However, there is no reason to believe that this has to be true. We need to analyze the situation to know how and when rules are to be used. The situation is important because not all laws apply to every set of circumstances, and those that are relevant may not apply equally. I may have promised to go on a hike with a friend but decide to cancel when my wife calls with car trouble. This does not require that I conclude that honoring my promises can be reduced to the role of a guideline, as Fletcher advocates. Suspending a particular rule for good reason is different from eliminating its normative value. If we separate the question of whether law itself is valid from the question of whether a particular use of a certain law is valid, we do not need to conclude that the occasional need to choose one law over another reduces all rules to guidelines.

4. Is situation ethics selective? No Christian ethicist disagrees with Fletcher because he includes love in his ethics. However, many do object when Fletcher narrows everything down to love because he seems to be arbitrarily selective in what he takes from Scripture. Fletcher frequently appeals to Jesus' summary of the law ("love the Lord your God" and "love your neighbor as yourself") to argue that love is the only standard. However, this ignores a very basic question. If all other ethical rules are relative, why do they continue to appear in the New Testament even after Jesus' summary of the law? Not only do we find ethical rules, but there is nothing in the contexts to suggest that these are, as Fletcher puts it, only strategies on the level of "punt on fourth down" or "take a pitch when the count is three balls." If we are going to appeal to

Scripture as the basis of our ethics, as Fletcher does, we cannot eliminate the parts that do not support our theories.

It also seems that situation ethics is selective in how it understands
Jesus' summary. In all the cases he cites, Fletcher discusses what it
means to love our neighbor, but he ignores the question of how we
know when a decision manifests love for God. This is not to imply that
what is a loving response to our neighbor will differ from an act that
expresses love for God. However, if we begin from our perception of a
neighbor's need and his or her view of what a loving response is, we can
become subjectivistic in our concept of love. Understanding what it
means to love God should redirect our attention to Scripture as a whole.
And Scripture has a lot to say about what it means to love God.

5. Does situationism fail to take sin seriously enough? For Fletcher
the only thing that distinguishes Christian situationism from non-
Christian situationism is that the former is "responsive love." This is
love that grows out of our thankfulness for what God has done for us.
"It [Christian situationism] is distinct from other moralities only because of its reason for righteousness."[12]

This is true as far as it goes, but it doesn't go far enough. Fletcher
fails to consider the effects of sin on our moral capacities, and this
omission suggests some questionable assumptions in his view of human
nature. First, is the type of love that situationism demands possible
apart from God's grace? Christian thought has traditionally empha-
sized that *agapē,* the centerpiece of situation ethics, is a gift from God,
not the result of unaided human effort. However, Fletcher clearly holds
that *agapē* is available to everyone and that sin has no effect on our
capacity to love "agapeistically." Second, one of the problems with strip-
ping love of any definition is that it is human nature after the Fall to
rationalize whatever we want to do as loving. Can we trust ourselves to
be honest about whether our motive for a decision is love? When love
remains undefined, there are no external checks to our own motives.
Finally, given the effects of sin in the world, is it possible for us to know
which acts manifest love? Fletcher never doubts that we have this capacity. However, his faith in our ability to determine how to rightly
express love does not appear to be shared by Scripture. Otherwise, why

does Scripture spend so much time telling us what does and does not count as proper conduct? In short, situationism seems to have far too much confidence in human nature apart from God's grace.

Conclusion

If we lived in a perfect world filled with perfect people, Fletcher's belief that love is the sole standard of right and wrong would be worth a long look. "All you need is love" would be true because it would be all we desire. "All you need is love" would be a workable system in a world where unloving impulses were never a part of our decisions. However, we live in much less than a perfect world, and no individual is motivated by love alone. In our fallen circumstances, therefore, it is necessary to ask the question, What does love need? What is necessary for God's love to get through to a flawed and sinful creation?

Most Christian ethicists do not advocate legalism but believe that love needs law. It is the problem of defining love that prompts them to make a place for ethical principles. In view of our sinfulness, can we understand love unless it has unmovable flags that tell us when we have stepped beyond its borders? It is true that laws do not turn people into lovers of God or neighbors. However, without law as a means of telling us when we have crossed the boundaries of love, we are left with only our flawed abilities and inclination to evil as a guide. Rules help us define love by telling us what is not loving activity.

Our struggle with love is not simply an ethical problem; it is a spiritual problem as well. The reason we do not love sufficiently is not just that we have mistaken notions about what it is (although we have plenty of these) but also that we encounter spiritual obstacles. The result of sin is that even when we know what love is, we are often incapable of acting on it. Since it makes no allowance for sinfulness, situationism's ideal—all you need is love—is not adequate by itself.

DOING WHAT COMES NATURALLY

Natural Law Ethics

THE REPORTS HAVE ALL BEEN filled out, and the police car has just pulled away. There you stand in the driveway, broom in hand, looking through a shattered window at a blank space in your dashboard where a stereo used to be. How do you feel? I can guess. You feel frustrated, angry and violated. It doesn't take a genius to anticipate someone's feelings in this situation; all it takes is a human being. You are just "doing what comes naturally" when you feel violated by theft.

Loss of property is not the only thing that gives rise to these feelings. The threat of bodily harm, being lied to, sexual infidelity and a number of other acts generally held to be moral evils do the same thing to us. Why is it natural to react in certain ways to being wronged? Thomas Aquinas, a medieval theologian, provides a possible answer. He says the world and the humans who inhabit it are made to work in a particular way. When things go wrong, certain "warning lights" come on. Anger and the feeling that you have been violated after a burglary are moral flashers, signaling that something is not right. Like gauges running in the red, they also tell us that something will break down if operations do not come back to match the purpose of the equipment.

This is a brief summary of an approach known as natural law ethics. *Natural*, in this case, refers to how things ought to be, not how they are. When something functions the way it was designed to work, it is functioning naturally. Natural, therefore, is the equivalent of ideal, right or good. Thus a sense of well-being lets us know that things are as they should be—natural. Similarly, feelings of disgust or guilt tell us that things are out of kilter.

The "law" part of natural law ethics tells us that there is consistency to the way the world ought to work. Just as we speak of the constancy of gravity as a law, so can we speak of the wrongness of stealing car stereos as law. Theft will be no less wrong tomorrow than it is today. Moral law is universal and consistent.

A Connected Universe

To get some idea of how Aquinas arrived at his natural law view of ethics, we have to begin with how the universe works and why it works that way. Let's start with the how question. The world is an incredibly fascinating and mysterious place. Because we are right in the middle of it, we often miss its wonder. However, even a casual observer will be struck from time to time by the realization that there is a unity to the universe.

A lot of things have to come together in precise ways just for us to exist. In addition, most of the processes that have to interconnect for life to happen and be sustained are mindless. The sun does not have a brain that calculates how far it must be from the earth to maintain a proper temperature range for human life. The earth has no mental awareness that a certain type of atmosphere of a particular depth is necessary for life. My blood cells do not consciously transport the oxygen necessary for the survival of other cells in my body. Yet these three seemingly disparate systems, made up of smaller systems that must themselves work together in intricate ways, combine with a great number of other structures in this world to make life possible.

Science can describe how these systems work because the processes make sense to us—they are rational. But this points out another thing we take for granted. Why are we able to understand the logic of the universe? It is perfectly possible to think of two systems that each have their own internal logic but are unable to "read" the other. For example, if someone would speak to me in Cantonese, it would sound like gibberish to me. That does not mean that the Cantonese language is gibberish. It has its own logical intonations, syntax, vocabulary and alphabet. However, since I am not trained in the Cantonese language, I cannot detect its logic.

This is not the case with our attempts to understand the world, however. The "language system" our minds use to process information seems to match, in some way, the language of the natural world so that the data received is understood. Without some form of compatibility between the logical structure of our mind and the logic of the universe, it would be impossible for us to know anything about the world outside our mind. How this compatibility works is an open and difficult question, but the assumption that our ideas correlate with what is "out there" is a common intuition.

Questions about the operations of the universe inevitably lead to why questions. Why is there rationality in the movements of a mindless universe? Why do these movements interlink in their operations, and why can we describe, to some degree, how it works? When we start asking more than descriptive questions and begin looking for ultimate explanations, we need to bring God into the picture, says Aquinas. He argues that a proper understanding of cause and effect requires God as the foundation. At the base of scientific method is the concept of cause and effect. Every effect needs a cause, for nothing just happens of its own accord. We assume that prior actions stand behind and explain events of the present. Moreover, effects tell us something about their causes. A good detective can often reconstruct with great accuracy a crime that no one witnessed. By looking at different parts of a crime scene—fingerprints, gunpowder residue, ballistics, DNA and other factors—much can be learned about who committed the crime.

The same is true for the universe. Everything that comes into being needs a cause to bring it about. Therefore, the universe, since it is not eternal, requires such a cause. Aquinas argues that God is the cause of the universe. On this view, careful consideration of the universe (the effect) will provide information about both the existence and the nature of God (the cause) if we investigate carefully and reason correctly. And we can correctly interpret the data because our minds are built by God to process this information. In a sense, just as a criminal leaves fingerprints at a crime scene, God leaves his fingerprints on the world. Unlike the criminal, God wants our investigation to lead to him.

What's "Natural" About Natural Law?

What I have described is often labeled "natural theology." This is the idea that nature, both physical and human, leads us to correct ideas about God. If we correctly read the "fingerprints" to learn how nature works, in Aquinas's view, the answer to why things are as they are will be God. Thus the "natural" in "natural law" should not be understood as if the laws embedded in nature come from nature itself. Instead these laws originate in God. They are God's laws for nature. Natural theology is built on what is called "general revelation." General revelation is the doctrine that God reveals certain things about himself to all people. Those who do their detective work properly can work back through the chain of cause and effect to arrive at truths about God.

Natural law ethics is the part of natural theology that tells us how God wants us to live here and now. Aquinas says nature reveals two ethically important truths about God. First, the logic of the world tells us that God is rational. The rationality of God is reflected in the consistency and structure of nature. Our own rationality also points to God's rationality. After all, humankind's capacity for reasoning did not just happen. It is an effect that must be explained by a cause. Second, the world is full of just the things humans need. Physical things like food, water and oxygen have a use or purpose, even though these objects are not aware of their purpose. Their presence is not just a lucky fluke. To Aquinas, it demonstrates that God has intentions for his creation.

God also has intentions for us, which is what natural law ethics is all about. To live according to natural law is to live by God's intention. Aquinas says ethical direction can be found in what is common to all humans, what we call human nature. In short, "doing what comes naturally" (if understood properly) is good. Thus, we look to inclinations that are common to all people. If we follow these common dispositions, we act as God intends. As Aquinas tells us, "All those things to which man has a natural inclination, are naturally apprehended by reason as being good."[1]

Our moral inclinations are not hard to figure out because humans have a moral sense and conscience. Certain acts carry with them rather predictable results. Doing right gives us the satisfaction of a clear conscience. We naturally feel down when we are wronged. Following from his view of cause and effect, then, Aquinas says that if we do what is good, it will lead to happiness. Happiness results from moral goodness, and since we desire happiness, we have a predisposition toward goodness.[2] Of course, Aquinas will have more to say about the proper understanding of happiness later.

Some human impulses, such as self-preservation, are found throughout nature. Even a brainless plant is programmed for survival. Other inclinations, such as the drive to procreate, we hold in common with the animal world. Other drives are distinctly human, such as the need for friendship and civilized society. The highest of our natural inclinations, however, is rationality. "To the natural law belongs those things to which a man is inclined naturally," says Aquinas. "And among these it is proper to man to be inclined to act according to reason."[3] For Aquinas, it is of prime importance that humans are, by nature, rational beings. Reason allows people to discern good and evil, making us ethical beings. Rationality pushes us to understand how the world works and gives us the possibility of acting in ways that fit the patterns of nature. Reason is the apex of human capacities; reason should, therefore, guide human action.

"Doing what comes naturally" sounds dangerous because in modern parlance it usually means that we can follow our impulses, whatever they may be. However, Aquinas is not saying, for example, that merely because humanity naturally seeks to survive, we therefore can kill any being that threatens us. Or that because human beings naturally seek to propagate the species, we therefore can attempt to procreate whenever the urge strikes. First, we are to follow our natural desires rationally. Reason puts limits on procreation because we acknowledge social, moral and spiritual obligations to our offspring, and these obligations cannot be fulfilled unless the boundaries are recognized and followed.

Reason also trains us to want what is good for us. The fact that every person has a conscience is evidence to Aquinas that humanity is inclined toward goodness. However, Aquinas recognizes that conscience does not work the same for everyone. People taught from childhood that dancing is wrong may have troubled consciences if they go dancing. Others may get no message at all from their conscience when they do the same thing. The conscience, it so happens, must be trained. New desires or awareness of guilt may be born when we subject our actions to reason. Thus, says Aquinas, "many things are done virtuously, to which nature does not incline at first, but which, through the inquiry of reason, have been found by man to be conducive to well-living."[4] Reason, when it works correctly, educates the conscience.

Second, we need to remember that our inclinations are a package deal. Human beings are more than just physical beings, so an unbridled pursuit of physical inclinations such as self-preservation or procreation will interfere with social and spiritual desires. For example, killing people simply because they have the ability to kill us puts a damper on our social lives and thus interferes with natural social dispositions.

Finally, while all desires are from the same source, not all have the same value. There is a hierarchy of inclinations. When we fulfill physical desires, the benefit is generally short-lived. A good meal only takes us so far. We can go a little longer on social fulfillment. Moral and rational goodness gives us more mileage yet. Those things which are less perfect bring less happiness. Since reason is the natural capacity that makes us most like God, moral fulfillment is found in acting rationally. In short, we follow natural law most closely when we do what appeals to the highest element of human nature. Inclinations must be properly ordered so that fulfilling lower desires supports the higher.

God intends that we "be all that we can be." We are designed so that human nature points us toward what we should do. When we live in sync with higher inclinations, the result is a deep and profound happiness. Thus natural law may be called a self-realization approach to ethics, but only if we understand that self-realization cannot be separated from God's intent. We do not set the terms for human happiness. God does, and he communicates these terms to us through our nature and inclinations of humanity.

Conversely, evil results from doing that which is naturally damaging to us. It consists of acting in ways that are unfulfilling, as we choose the lower over the higher. Seeking fulfillment is not optional; it is part of who we are. However, we can seek fulfillment in the wrong way. The person who steals stereos from cars does so to find happiness. The inclination to find happiness is itself not wrong, but it is unsuccessful in the end if that is the only horizon of our search, because it puts physical desire above the social, moral and spiritual inclinations. When we try to fulfill the lower needs to the exclusion of the higher, we have embarked on a course that is irrational and unfulfillable.

The "Law" in Natural Law

Aquinas conceives of law as a set of concentric circles. The more general laws are on the outside; inside are the more specific laws. The primary principle of natural law is that "good should be done and evil avoided."[5] This is an unqualified good that should always be followed. As you can see, this principle is very broad. It does not give much practical guidance for actual cases.

Natural law becomes more specific as we move toward secondary principles. Aquinas includes in the list laws such as those enshrined in the Ten Commandments. Aquinas argues that all people know these principles naturally. Indeed, a good argument for this can be made by reviewing quickly the ethical principles of different cultures and times, for the content of the Ten Commandments is found in the laws of every society. We see that content reflected even in the lives of people who do not live according to these laws. Even compulsive liars want you to tell them the truth. The most cold-hearted killers seek to preserve their own lives. This desire for truth and life is evidence that the natural law lives on, even in the worst of us. And when we are living as we should, which is the meaning of *natural* for Aquinas, these principles are clear and reasonable. However, our knowledge of them can be distorted by irrationality.

Like the primary principles, these secondary laws cannot be changed; they are part of the order of creation. However, laws at this level are not unqualified. Aquinas illustrates this with the rule that "goods entrusted to another should be restored to their owner." The rule itself is always valid, but we should not always act on it. Aquinas says,

> Now this is true for the majority of cases: but it may happen in a particular case that it would be injurious, and therefore unreasonable, to restore goods held in trust; for instance if they are claimed for the pur-

pose of fighting against one's country. And this principle will be found to fail the more, according as we descend further into detail. . . . The greater the number of conditions added, the greater the number of ways in which the principle may fail.[6]

Thus Aquinas acknowledges that even a secondary law like "goods entrusted to another should be restored to their owner" needs more explication as we move to more specific questions. As we get greater detail about the circumstances in which we must apply the rule, we should be prepared to deal with more ambiguity. This is because reason is not infallible. It is possible for people to be mistaken about the proper application of natural law, even while they have a clear knowledge of its central principles.

We might want something more airtight than what Aquinas gives us, but ambiguity does not render laws useless. You may not realize it, but the basic documents of the United States are built on natural law assumptions. For example, the Declaration of Independence sets out three rights that are "self-evident" and given by God—the right to life, freedom and the pursuit of happiness (or, for those who are single, the happiness of pursuit). These rights function as general equivalents to Aquinas's primary principle of "do good and avoid evil," which he also considers self-evident and of divine origin. Constitutionally, all laws for society should derive from these broad self-evident rights and should never contradict them, just as secondary laws are the fleshing out of "do good and avoid evil" in natural law.

Interpreting and applying these three constitutional rights to specific issues are difficult tasks and often cause for much debate. Even the brightest constitutional experts on the Supreme Court often are split on questions of proper interpretation. Similarly, Aquinas warns that we should expect disagreement and murkiness when we get into the details of applying the principles of natural law. The point is that the ambiguity of the U.S. Constitution does not make it unworkable. Likewise, Aquinas does not believe that ambiguity is a death blow to natural law ethics.

Aquinas attempts to balance two elements simultaneously. On the one hand, he wants to identify why all people have moral responsibility, which he does by arguing that God's moral laws are known to all, even if some do not realize that God is the source. On the other hand, he gives us some means of understanding why it is possible for people who have this knowledge of the law to disagree on its proper application in specific cases. Reason is not a perfect guide and is overridden often by a sinful will.

Other Levels of Law

Just as Aquinas conceives of natural law as a hierarchy of different laws with the more specific included in the general, he sees a hierarchy of different types of law. Below natural law, and therefore a part of natural law, is what is generally called "positive law." One of the precepts of natural law is that humans are social beings by nature. We are inclined toward corporate life because society is necessary for our moral, intellectual and spiritual development.[7] In other words, it is not possible to "be all that we can be" as lone rangers.

Society has a twofold purpose. First, Aquinas tells us that "man has a natural aptitude for virtue; but the perfection of virtue must be acquired by man by some kind of training."[8] Society steers the "natural aptitude for virtue" down the right channels. Second, moral development is hampered by anarchy, evil and injury. Thus society has a responsibility to restrain evil so people can concentrate on their higher needs. The purpose of positive law and its twin duties of training and restraining is to create a proper environment for moral development. This means that positive law does not itself make us good; it only provides a context in which good may flourish.

The fact that positive law only sets the stage for natural law means that natural law is higher. This has two implications. First, because the lower is always contained in the higher, society is not free to enact any law it wants. Any human law that conflicts with natural law is invalid. Second, since positive law is more narrowly focused, not all moral laws should find their way into civil law. It is possible for some things to be legal by the standards of positive law but still be immoral. For instance, lying violates natural law, but we do not make all forms of lying subject to civil penalty. However, society does have a responsibility to restrain forms of lying (such as libel or slander) that are especially injurious to people.

Natural Law and the Gospel

I have said little to indicate why Aquinas's version of natural law ethics should be considered a Christian approach. He does use God to explain our ethical sensibilities, but this is not exclusively Christian. There is another important piece of this theory outstanding. For Aquinas, natural law is insufficient by itself because it does not satisfy the highest human aspiration of all. He says that all people seek salvation. Our ultimate aspiration is perfect and eternal happiness or beatitude. This is found in seeing God, what Aquinas calls the Beatific Vision.[9]

This goal is beyond the reach of any human capacity and thus requires means other than natural law to attain. "But since man is ordained to an end of eternal happiness, which is inproportionate to man's natural faculty, . . . it was necessary that, besides the natural and the human law, man should be directed to his end by a law given by God."[10] This "law from God" is what Aquinas calls divine law. Divine law, because it deals with that which is above nature, is a higher level of law. Just as natural law is higher than positive law but contains all true positive law, natural law is contained within the divine law and completed by it. Divine law is the gospel in the fullest sense. It tells us not only that God exists and what is moral, but also what is required for us to see God and thus fulfill our highest inclination.

For Christianity, the way of salvation is found only in Scripture's witness to Christ. This takes us beyond general revelation to what is called special revelation. We cannot learn that Jesus died for our sins from gazing at the mountains, inspecting the starry heavens or watching a sunset over the ocean. This is known through Scripture.

Since divine law is above nature and thus above reason, it must be accepted by faith. However, just as natural law is contained within the gospel, faith does not contradict reason but goes beyond it. Salvation is supernatural, above nature and reason. Thus, while natural law is good, it is incomplete. Being good by natural law standards does not bring salvation, but Aquinas reminds us that, since natural law is contained in the gospel, we are not saved without moral goodness.

Summary

Aquinas's natural law approach helps us makes sense of a question that often puzzles Christians. If right and wrong come from God, why do many non-Christians have moral principles similar to those in Christianity? Aquinas says similarities are to be expected. All inhabit the same world and process information from it through the same rational faculties. Therefore, Christians and non-Christians alike should reach the same conclusions about morality, even if non-Christians do not recognize the source (although Aquinas argues that correct use of reason would reveal this as well).

At the same time, Aquinas does not make moral goodness the equivalent of salvation. While God is present in such a way that we can see him partially in nature, ultimate salvation involves a destination beyond and above nature. This requires Christ (not just creation), faith (not just reason) and Scripture (not just general revelation).

The Positive Side of Natural Law

If Christian ethics begins with the nature of God, we may want to ask what we would expect from God, given what Christianity says about him. Several ideas seem to follow from this. For example, we would anticipate that God desires that all people know something of his existence and his expectations of us, that God would construct humanity so our aspirations move us toward his goals, and that natural life would be integrated with spiritual life. Natural law ethics is a way to bring these expectations together.

First, the concept of general revelation can explain why people of different religious persuasions, or perhaps no religious affiliation at all, frequently have a keen sense of right and wrong, and live highly moral lives. I have little use for most radio talk shows, but one I listen to occasionally is hosted by a Jewish man who has terrific ethical insight. This would not shock Aquinas at all. Reason is not the exclusive domain of Christians. Even though these two individuals would have theological differences, Aquinas would say that this Jewish talk-show host has tapped into the revelation God makes available to all through nature.

If natural law theory is correct, we do not have to argue the case for Christian ethics from foundations that are foreign to non-Christians. A person need not already believe in God or Scripture, or submit to the teachings of the church. They just have to be able to observe and reflect. Moreover, careful observation can be a powerful foundation for morality. The ethical principles Aquinas asserts are just plain old common sense. Everybody benefits from a world where people are truthful, refrain from causing physical injury, return goods held in trust and submit to some form of social order. General revelation explains why this is so.

Second, if we believe that God wants people to learn about him, we would expect that he would reveal himself, not just in the world but also through the divine gift of human reason. We would think it odd to encourage talented scientists to develop their skills in their respective fields but then to turn off their brains when it comes to ethics and religion. Yet Christians have often advocated such a compartmentalization of life, as if reason is proper for everyday reality but is somehow destructive of faith. Aquinas would argue that if reason is good in the pursuit of science, it is even better in the pursuit of a higher aspiration: moral goodness.

A good God wants us to do what is best for us and would shape us to desire what is best for us. After all, Scripture tells us that we are to love our neighbor as ourselves, not instead of ourselves. Natural law helps us see what is good about self-interest and to understand what human drives and inclinations are really all about. It clarifies self-interest by defining it in terms of our search for God. It seems logical that if God exists, and humanity was created to live in fellowship with God, then our deepest aspirations would be satisfied in knowing him.

Natural law also offers insight on how to balance our various aspirations. Our final goal is not a full stomach, but this does not make fulfillment of physical needs evil. It is difficult to pursue intellectual, moral and spiritual excellence when we are hungry. Thus, physical gratification is good when it allows us to follow higher aspirations. Likewise, as much as we like to complain about social structures and institutions, we recognize that they have a positive role. But we also recognize that even good social structures do not satisfy our deepest longings.

We have aspirations on all levels of life—physical, social, intellectual, moral and spiritual—and these are all necessary and good. Natural law ethics tells us that all our inclinations contribute to our total well-being. We do not have to hate our physical inclinations and social desires. We just need to put them in the proper order.

Natural law ethics is not a theory that can be believed only through sheer willpower. Rather, it begins with the common experiences of people—our moral sensibilities, the sense of obligation to family and society, physical inclinations and our search for the divine. However, natural law theory does not just stop with a simple description of natural operations; it goes on to address the question of why the world is as it is. Why do people form families and societies? Why does morality make sense? And why are people the kind of beings who ask why? Natural law explains how science and theology are related. They are not enemies. Instead, science, in its description of natural processes, leads us to theology, which explains the purpose of natural processes.

God created nature so the proper cause brings about a positive effect. Divine involvement in this world, when seen from Aquinas's perspective, fits with what we experience. At the same time, natural law ethics maintains what is distinctive about Christianity. Being good is not good enough. We cannot achieve salvation by our own doing, no matter how good or rational we are. Thus, the basics of Christianity—Christ, faith and Scripture—are not disposable but are essential for salvation.

Potential Problems in Natural Law Ethics

1. Can we get from facts to values? While many people are attracted to natural law because it bases ethics in the facts of nature, there is a danger in this. The problem is whether we can make the leap from a statement of fact to a statement of ethics. As David Hume puts it,

In every system of morality, which I have hitherto met with, I have always remark'd, that the author proceeds for some time in the ordinary way of reasoning, and establishes the being of a God, or makes observations concerning human affairs; when of a sudden I am surpriz'd to find, that instead of the usual copulations of propositions, *is*, and *is not*, I meet with no proposition that is not connected with an *ought* or an *ought not*. This change is imperceptible; but is, however, of the last consequence. For as this *ought* or *ought not*, expresses some new relation of affirmation, it is necessary that it should be observ'd and explain'd; and at the same time that a reason should be given, for what seems altogether inconceivable, how this new relation can be a deduction from others; which are entirely different from it.[11]

The essence of this criticism is that factual claims are different from ethical claims. When we shift from one to the other, we need to show why the transition is justified.

Natural law theory is particularly vulnerable to this criticism because it does not just say that matters of fact must be brought into the ethical discussion, but it also says that ethics is derived exclusively from understanding the facts of the world. Hume has no problem asserting, with natural law, that it is a fact that we naturally seek God, form societies and seek to survive (as long as these claims can be derived from the data). What he objects to is the jump from these facts to the conclusion that we ought to do these things. To say that we do worship is different than saying that we should worship.

The gap between is and ought can be spanned only by bringing in something from outside the realm of fact. The difficulty is that this takes us outside natural law, which maintains that all we need to know about ethics comes from within nature. But, as David Little tells us, natural law assumes that we can justify the shift from a "set of descriptive generalizations regarding how men do act, to a set of prescriptions regarding how they ought to act."[12] Unless such a justification is possible, natural law theory is on shaky ground.

2. Can reason get us to divine truth? At the core of natural law ethics is the belief that reason, properly employed, will direct us to truths about God. These truths are available not just to Christians but to anyone who correctly interprets the processes of nature. However, what does it mean to say that a non-Christian knows something about God? Do concepts of God formed outside the realm of salvation prepare us for a more complete view of God? Karl Barth answers in this way:

> What is "God" to the natural man [the non-Christian], and what he also certainly calls his "God," is a false god. This false god is known by him and is therefore knowable to him. But as a false god it will not lead him in any sense to a knowledge of the real God. It will not in any way prepare him for it. On the contrary, it will keep him from it. Its knowledge and knowability will make him an enemy of the real God.[13]

Here Barth acknowledges that people do search for God and form ideas of who God is. What he questions is whether these attempts are successful. Barth clearly concludes that they tell us nothing about God. In fact, he sees a danger in what Aquinas proposes. Whatever is found through human reason will be a human invention, something compatible with our own abilities. We do not discover God; we create a god. And what we have created becomes an idol, an object of worship. And because we are busy worshiping the god created with our reason, we close ourselves off to the real God.

Christianity, like natural law, affirms a God who creates and governs nature through his laws, but Christianity does not stop there. The god of natural law is only a watchmaker who creates the product, winds it up and lets it go. People may be able to come up with the idea of such a god on their own by carefully observing the watch. This view of deity, however, falls far short of the God of Christianity, who redeems nature from its fallen state. The distant watchmaker is very unlike the God who comes to earth in human form. But natural law cannot get us to a Savior who dies for human sin. This is Barth's point: If we only know god the watchmaker, we really do not know God the Redeemer.

3. Does natural law overlook sin? This criticism is closely linked to the previous one. Whereas earlier we questioned whether God as Creator can be separated from God the Redeemer, here the issue is whether moral goodness can be separated from salvation. When Aquinas distinguishes between natural law and divine law, the result, as L. Thiry tells us, is that "one can be a good man without being a Christian, but one cannot be a good Christian without being a good man."[14] Natural law makes a person morally good, but not Christian. The message of Christianity is found only beyond nature in divine law. But does the idea of moral goodness apart from salvation make sense?

With Aquinas's view of law as a hierarchy in which people fulfill the lower to get to the higher, Christianity becomes something that one can "grow into" from the earlier stage of being morally good. Goodness, found through natural law, is the step that leads to salvation, found in divine law. Salvation thus becomes an addition to goodness.

However, what distinguishes Christian ethics from other forms of ethics may be more important than what unites them. In most ethical approaches, being good is the result of successfully following the demands of ethics. However, in Christianity, goodness seems to be more the result of what God has done in and for us. Our own attempts at goodness never measure up and may even keep us from recognizing the need for salvation. In other words, human efforts at being good and winning salvation are the problem. Thus, if natural law ethics gives us morality without salvation, does it make us good by Christian standards?

4. Is natural law clear enough? We learned earlier that natural law ethics does not intend to deliver a catalog of crystal-clear rules that apply automatically to every situation. It does claim, however, that all people have some knowledge of what is necessary to live life as God intended, even though human frailty can interfere with a person's ability to always know how to use that knowledge wisely. This is all well and good, because a certain level of uncertainty is present in every ethical theory. Still, a good process will give some concrete guidance in moral decisions. If Aquinas is correct that natural law allows us to "be all that we can be," we need some level of specificity.

For example, we might want to ask what position on contraception results from using natural law in decision making. The Roman Catholic Church, which relies on natural law as the basis of its moral theology, argues that artificial birth-control methods should be prohibited. Since conception is the natural result of intercourse, avoiding pregnancy by artificial means is deemed unnatural and thus immoral. In an encyclical Pope John Paul II made clear that he considered contraception to be intrinsically evil: because "of its very nature [it] contradicts the moral order and . . . must therefore be judged unworthy of man."[15]

The problem is to determine what moral message nature is trying to send us. It is clear that reproduction and intercourse go together, but it is not clear to everyone that using contraceptive methods is "unnatural." In fact, if natural inclinations are to be rationally directed, one can argue just the opposite: that seeking to postpone or avoid pregnancy through contraception is rational. John Jefferson Davis implies this when he states,

> Man's calling is not simply to let "nature take its course," but to *consciously* redirect nature toward the fulfillment of the divine plan. Just as God himself created the human race and re-created a fallen humanity according to a conscious plan, so it would follow that man, as God's vice regent on earth, should imitate God by exercising his procreative gifts according to a conscious plan.[16]

Natural law advocates come out on both sides of the question of artificial birth control, as well as most of the other important debates of today (e.g., capital punishment and euthanasia). Since this is the case, it is fair to ask whether natural law is a useful theory. If the decision-making process in natural law ethics cannot give clear direction on an issue as central as contraception, does it accomplish what an ethical theory should accomplish? How much ambiguity is too much?

5. How do we separate nature from nurture? The linchpin of natural law theory is that all people have certain attributes in common: there is something that can be called "human nature." However, it may be very difficult to determine which behaviors are human nature and which seem natural only because they conform to what we have always seen. For instance, a young woman in one culture may find flirting to be a natural part of communication with the opposite sex. In another culture, a young woman of the same age may be embarrassed to even think of speaking with an unmarried male. Both may find their responses to be "natural."

The same question may be raised in another way. Aquinas views the idea of family and the raising of children as part of natural law. But this brings up a question that is a hot topic today: What is a family? Do only dad and mom and children count as a family? Is a "family" no longer "natural" if it is missing any of these three ingredients? What about homosexual partners? What about an extended family with many relatives involved in child rearing? What if the parents turn the children over to a nanny or send them to boarding school for the greater part of their childhood?

Some people would see some or all of these as proper definitions of family, and their answer will often reflect what they are used to seeing. However, for Aquinas, natural is not just a matter of preference but a matter of morality. But how do we separate family configurations into categories of natural (moral) and unnatural (immoral) when it is difficult, if not impossible, to distinguish which responses come from nature and which grow out of nurture? How do we separate human nature from cultural training?

Conclusion

Natural law has a lot going for it. It is a common human experience to draw conclusions about unseen causes by looking at what the causes left behind. Thus, it seems to follow that God, though unseen by us, would put something of his character into what he has created. If God is good and cares for humanity, we should not be surprised if God decided to make nature an owner's manual for ethics. If we read the manual correctly and "do what comes naturally," all will be well.

But Aquinas includes another aspect of God's plan that does not come through nature: divine law. This is necessary because a God who transcends nature cannot be known fully through the created order. This leads proponents of our next ethical theory to say that natural law ethics begins at the wrong place. If God is beyond nature and reason cannot know him fully, why not start where God is revealed most clearly—in divine law?

12

GOD SAID IT,
I BELIEVE IT,
THAT SETTLES IT

Divine Command Theory

"GOD SAID SO." We have probably all heard this phrase used to support an ethical position, and it gives rise to two opposite responses. For some, there is a great deal of security in this claim. What is more dependable than God's Word? How can human reasoning, which never seems to get us to an agreeable conclusion anyway, stand up against what God commands? Isn't faith in what God says the key to knowing what is right and wrong?

But not everyone finds "God said so" to be a very helpful way to seal ethical debates. Of course it gets you nowhere with someone who does not believe God exists. A nonexistent God does not say anything. It is also clear that not everyone is in agreement about which god is worth listening to. In such cases, invoking your god's commands does not solve the problem: the other person in the debate has a different god. The discussion just gets pushed back to the question of "which god is God."

To some it looks as if the people who use this line are just too lazy or scared to engage in real debate, and God becomes the barricade they hide behind. Still others find it a simplistic escape from complex questions, the last-ditch justification of someone caught in a position they refuse to surrender but cannot defend.

A negative response to "God said so" is not limited to those who do not share the speaker's religious convictions. Even a believer can feel that "God said it" is used like a verbal trump card, making it appear that anyone who disagrees is not arguing with the person who throws it on the table but with God himself. In such cases this approach comes off more as a cheap ad hominem attack on a person's faith than an honest discussion of the issue at hand.

Divine command theory, sometimes called theological voluntarism, can be expressed by the bumper sticker "God said it, I believe it, that settles it."[1] At its core is the belief that God is the source of moral truth and communicates his will to humanity via commands ("God said it"). Our choice is to go our own way or to follow ("I believe it"). If right and wrong comes from God, nothing else matters. Opposing views of friends, parents, public opinion or experts in any field take a back seat. When we are confident that God said it, and we are committed to God, "that settles it." Why should any amount of debate change our minds?

Human Limitation—Dependent, Sinful and Mentally Inadequate

Advocates of divine command ethics (or voluntarism) recognize that some of the objections to the "God said so" approach are practical in nature. They come about because the approach is used wrongly. However, this should not count against the system itself; any set of ideas can be abused. On the other hand, sometimes the negative response arises from differences in worldviews. At a minimum, "God said so" assumes a certain kind of universe: one in which there is a God who made the rules about right and wrong, and the duty of people is to obey those rules.

Voluntarists argue that these two assumptions, understood correctly, offer insight into two of the big questions of life. The first question is, Who is God? In Christianity, when we talk about God, we are talking about the infinite, all-knowing, all-powerful, unlimited Creator and Savior of the universe. Nothing less. A God like that cannot be relegated to the "take it or leave it" category. If this is true, the second question—Who am I?—cannot be answered in isolation from the first. We are finite, limited creatures whose very existence hangs on God's will. Not a single breath, muscle twitch, blink or thought occurs without God allowing it to be.

If contemplating God's power and immensity isn't enough to put us in touch with our finitude, we should also remember that God is a being with a moral character. This puts us in an even more precarious position because, while God is perfect in goodness and justice, we are not anywhere close to moral perfection. We are not just morally imperfect, we also are guilty of sin against God. Sin "against God" should be understood in two ways. First, divine command advocates say that it means sin as measured against God, who is the standard of what is good and right. Second, it is sin understood as rebellion against the God who has the right to our loyalty and obedience. The prodigal son recognizes this. When he comes back home, he confesses, "I have sinned against heaven [i.e., God] and before you" (Lk 15:21; compare Ps 51:4; Lk 15:18 RSV). It is true that his earthly father has been wronged, but doing wrong by others also puts us at odds with God. The prodigal's wandering has a deeper dimension to it because God's desire that we honor our parents has been put aside.

There's one more thing. Human intellect, as powerful as it may seem from our point of view, is limited in its ability to comprehend the way and will of God. Many divine command theorists point to the last few chapters of the book of Job. After Job and his comforters have done their best to figure out how Job landed in such a rotten situation, God speaks to him from the whirlwind:

> Where were you when I laid the foundation of the earth!
> Tell *Me*, if you have understanding,
> Who set its measurements, since you know?
> Or who stretched the line on it?
> On what were its bases sunk?
> Or who laid its cornerstone,
> When the morning stars sang together,
> And all the sons of God shouted for joy? (Job 38:4-7 NASB)

This goes on for four chapters. Job is bombarded by God with unanswerable questions about the whys and wherefores of the universe. When the questions finally end, Job has a pretty good grasp of his intellectual inadequacy, and his only response is this:

I know that You can do all things,
And that no purpose of Yours can be thwarted.
"Who is this that hides counsel without knowledge?"
Therefore I have declared that which I did not understand,
Things too wonderful for me, which I did not know.
"Hear, now, and I will speak;
I will ask of You, and You instruct me."
I have heard of You by the hearing of the ear;
But now my eye sees You;
Therefore I retract,
And I repent in dust and ashes. (Job 42:2-6 NASB)

Job has taken a pretty good thrashing here, but we miss the point completely if we read this as God bullying a hapless man who has suffered awful misfortunes. Job has been "put in his place," but this is good because it puts him in touch with reality. Divine command ethics stresses that only when we acknowledge the reality of our dependence, our sinfulness and the inability of human reason to grasp God's ways can we be in a position to move forward. God's rightful authority over humanity is the foundation of ethics.

Because all of this looks like basic Christian orthodoxy, we can see the appeal of divine command ethics to many Christians. From the foundation of God's power, moral superiority and all-surpassing knowledge, voluntarism builds its ethics, which can be summarized in the following three propositions:

1. Our creaturely nature obligates us to rules that are part of the created order. God, who is not a created being, is not bound by these rules.

2. Good and evil do not exist independently of God. Instead, they are created by God just as surely as we are.

3. While there may be a logic to God's action and decrees, it is presumptuous for humans to believe that our finite minds can discover it.

Goodness and Creation

The first proposition starts with the assertion that we are not absolutely free (which is different from being free). Some limitations are self-imposed, but boundaries also are imposed on us from outside. We cannot draw a picture in five dimensions, be in Oklahoma and Ghana at the same time, or flap our arms fast enough to fly to Milwaukee. We have to live with these and other restrictions whether we want to or not. It is not a matter of choice.

Divine command proponents see such limits as necessary reminders of who we are. Absolute freedom is beyond our grasp precisely because we are creaturely beings. In contrast, God is not bound by such strictures because he is not part of the created order. There are no rules for God. The answer to the question, Where does a six-hundred-pound gorilla sit? is, of course, anywhere it wants. God is the six-hundred-pound gorilla of the universe. There is nothing or no one that can dictate what God can do. In other words, God is what we are not: absolutely free.

This becomes ethically relevant because if there are no restrictions on what God can do, there are also no limitations on what God can decree to be good or evil. This ties the first proposition (God's freedom) to the second (right and wrong are created). Things are not good or evil independently of God's will; otherwise we impose a standard that God has to abide by to issue good commands. God would have no choice about what is good, because goodness would have its own existence.

Instead, theological voluntarism argues that we need to be clear about what it means to say that God is the Creator of all things. His creative work encompasses not only the mountains, the stars and other physical objects. It even includes more than the laws that govern the actions of these things. God creates all things other than himself; there are no preexisting givens. Thus God also creates right and wrong. The standards of goodness are just as dependent on God's will and creative activity as human life is. Good is not something that God discovers and conforms to; God creates good. Duns Scotus puts it this way: "The divine will, which is the first rule of all works and of all acts, and the activity of the divine will, of which the first rule consists, is the first principle of righteousness. For from the fact that something is suitable to the divine will, it is right, and whatever action God could perform, is right absolutely."[2] To put it simply, if God says it is right, it is right.

God's Logic and Human Understanding

Both divine command theory and natural law ethicists believe that we do know something about God's moral demands. The relevant question is how we know, for it marks a major dividing line between the two groups. Both systems recognize the power gap between God and humanity. In spite of our inability to do what God does, however, natural law theory is confident that human reason can, at least in part, discover God's moral will through general revelation. Divine command ethics rejects general revelation on two fronts.

First, it argues that natural law advocates fail to note the intellectual gap between God and humanity when they assert that we can discern God's moral character through human reason. General revelation assumes that we can unravel God's logic and read God's moral will from the natural world. But is it not true that God is "wholly other"? Does not his absolute freedom and perfection mean that he belongs to a completely different category of existence—that God is supernatural? The otherness of God prompts Richard Mouw to remind us that

> it is not always easy to ascertain what God's own thoughts might be when it comes to the issues of moral justification. There is an important element of mystery and awe that characterizes a healthy relationship to the God of the Bible; the distance between moral decision making and worship is not always very great in the Christian life. There are good Christian reasons for nurturing a resistance to attempts to "psyche God out" in too much detail in dealing with the issues of ethical theory.[3]

Divine command ethics says that it is arrogant to believe that our puny little minds will do any better than Job's at comprehending the secrets of the universe. If God's way of existing is above our own, then human reason, a tool used to discern the natural world, surely cannot know anything of God's existence.

A second basis for rejecting general revelation goes back to human sinfulness: there is a moral chasm between God and humanity. Imagine being led into a totally dark room and being asked to describe the colors of the objects in the room. If the darkness is complete, your task is impossible. This does not mean that the objects have no color; you are just unable to see them. In a similar way, while God may indeed leave traces of his moral will in creation, divine command theory asserts that our sin has blinded us to it. We cannot discover the good, because sin has infected our rational capacities. God may well have invested himself in the world in such a way that his will is present, but we are unable to see it because of a problem of our own making: our sinfulness.

This explains the third proposition. Our minds are not up to the task of understanding God's ways. The purpose of discussing the impotence of human reason is not to undercut the idea that God speaks to us. Instead, what divine command theory rejects is that God speaks to us through nature. How we know God's moral will cannot, in the minds of divine command ethicists, be answered by appeal to general revelation. We can rely only on special revelation. What God expects from us comes through his commands in Scripture.

While reason is rejected as a tool for discovering right and wrong, it is not dismissed entirely. We just need to use it for the proper jobs. According to many advocates of voluntarism, the world consists of two types of realities known by two different means. Reason is adapted to deciphering the natural world. We must apply rationality to determine how much reinforcement to put in the foundation of a four-story building or to discern the most cost-efficient way to make shoes. These are problems of nature, and the human mind, a tool fit for nature, resolves these puzzles. Access to supernatural realities, on the other hand, is gained through faith. Thus to know God's moral will, which is not part of nature, we accept his dictates as revealed through Scripture. Reason and faith are two ways of knowing, and each is to be used in its proper "world."

Trust and Obey

Since we are not saved by understanding, it is not necessary that we understand why God calls us to do certain things. As Mouw says, our relationship with God includes mystery and awe. This is where faith comes in. When we recognize that God has a right to demand anything he desires and that he has made his demands known in Scripture, our duty is to believe and conform to his will. The old hymn may say it best:

> Trust and obey,
> for there's no other way
> to be happy in Jesus,
> but to trust and obey.[4]

The emphasis on faith and obedience reveals a central theme in voluntarism's concept of humanity. The most important thing about humans is not that we are rational beings (so natural law theory). Instead, what is significant is that we have a will: we can choose. The will, not reason, is our point of contact with God. We do not share the same range of choices that God has. What is proper for humans to choose is limited by God's commands, while God's choices are unlimited. We do share with God that we can choose. When God decrees what is right, the proper choice for humans is to obey his decrees.

Divine command theory finds this to be closer to Scripture's concept of faith than what is taught by natural law. If knowledge of God's moral laws comes through reason, as natural law ethics says, this seems to reduce faith to mental assent. Having faith means only that we have concluded that certain things are true. By connecting faith with the will, however, voluntarists argue that faith becomes a matter of action. It involves willing and obeying what God has commanded.

Summary

To some, divine command ethics sounds heavy-handed and hierarchical. In its crudest form it plays like a "sit down, shut up and do as I say" approach to ethics. In a more nuanced but still harsh evaluation, this ethical perspective has been described by P. H. Nowell-Smith as "infantile morality." He argues that, except for rare instances, it is unacceptable to issue commands to adults without explanation. Expecting obedience from children is a different matter because they are unable to comprehend the logic behind everything a good parent wants them to do. However, Nowell-Smith argues that once people have the maturity, experience and rational capacities of adults, laws should not be imposed on them by others, including God. This treats rational beings like children, which explains why Nowell-Smith says divine command ethics is an "infantile morality."[5] Mouw agrees that it is improper to issue to an equal commands that require unquestioning obedience, but he argues that our relationship with God is different.

In order for Nowell-Smith's account to work, then, he must argue that there should come a time when the Christian begins to see God as someone who operates on an "equal footing" with human beings; the "respect felt by the small for the great" must disappear from the relationship between God and adult humans. Mouw responds, "But once we put the matter in this way, it hardly seems worthy of serious consideration. . . . It would seem quite unreasonable to expect Christian believers to treat God as an equal when, according to the best accounts of what the deity is like, God is obviously superior to any human being."[6]

Divine command theory reminds us that we never measure up to God. In comparison to God we are always children in our intellect, moral accomplishment and capacity to exist independent of his being. Therefore God has a right to demand obedience. However, as Mouw emphasizes, there is more to God's moral demands than brute superiority. God's authority is also rooted in his redemptive relationship with humanity. "The God who commands is the same one who has, in the person of Jesus, entered into a human frame of reference. The Creator became Redeemer, stooping to become like one of us. When God commands, he does so with an intimate knowledge of our condition, having suffered in the same ways that we suffer."[7]

Positive Aspects in Divine Command Theory

One of the positives in divine command ethics is that it fills in certain theological gaps left open by other systems. Many problems in people's theology come about not because people believe false doctrine but because they fail to balance sound doctrine with other truths. This seems to be the case when it comes to finding that healthy symmetry between God's magnitude and sovereignty (transcendence) and his closeness and intimacy with his world (immanence). The trend in recent years has been to stress the latter, the "user-friendly" side of God. However, this can lead to a false understanding of God's nature unless balanced against God's transcendence. C. S. Lewis reminds us of this in *The Lion, the Witch and the Wardrobe*. Before the children meet Aslan, the lion who is the Christ-figure, they question Mr. and Mrs. Beaver about him. "Then he isn't safe?" Lucy wants to know. "Safe?" says Mr. Beaver. "Don't you hear what Mrs. Beaver tells you? Who said anything about safe? 'Course he isn't safe. But he's good. He's the King, I tell you."[8]

In the same way, divine command ethics reminds us of God's magnitude. God is not "safe" in the sense that he is anything we want him to be. The sovereign God does not stay out of our lives until we want him. Divine command theory tells us that, as King, God not only has authority but also asserts that authority in his moral imperatives. This provides a natural link between God's nature and moral goodness. If God is sovereign, it seems logical that his will dictates what is right. In fact, the way voluntarism works it out, we cannot begin the discussion of right and wrong until we talk about the nature of God.

Divine command theory also helps us avoid theological imbalance on the relation of human sinfulness and human value. Sinfulness is not a popular subject today because it seems to interfere with affirmations of self-esteem and the goodness of people. Self-esteem is incorporated into the curriculum of many school systems in an attempt to encourage children to have positive feelings about themselves. The criminal justice system often sends the message that there are no bad people, that in fact "bad people" are really good people who have been directed by bad circumstances to do bad things. This has also found its way into churches. Human sinfulness may get a quick mention from the pulpit, but the fact of sin is soon eclipsed by an emphasis on the good side of being human.

But we have seen some of the problems that occur when ethical systems leave sin out of the moral equation. Although we do not really enjoy being reminded of our sinfulness, it helps explain a lot of things. For example, if our whole being, reason included, is implicated in sin, this might explain why we cannot agree on what is right and wrong. It may also supply a rationale for why the created world does not effectively tell all people what they need to know about ethical matters.

Divine command ethics also helps us maintain the centrality of Scripture. The answer to what role Scripture plays in our moral decision making is straightforward. The Bible contains God's commands, which tell us what is good and bad. It is our duty, therefore, to know and obey these commands. For many, this approach is a way to flesh out their faith. Quite often, faith can be a nebulous concept with little definition. But divine command theory connects faith to God's commands in a concrete way. Since these directives are our sole basis for moral knowledge, faith is the sole means to moral truth. Moreover, faith is more than mental assent. It carries with it an obligation to obey these commands.

Potential Problems for Divine Command Theory

1. Could God command cruelty? Many of the criticisms directed at divine command ethics form around the question of what God can or will do. The classic statement of the dilemma is found in Plato's dialogue titled *Euthyphro*. In this dialogue, Euthyphro asks Socrates, "What is holiness?" As Socrates usually does, he tosses the question back to Euthyphro, who comes up with a number of answers that Socrates immediately shoots full of holes. Finally, Euthyphro defines piety as "that which is loved by the gods" (remember, the Greeks believed in multiple gods). Of course, Socrates has another question: "Is what is holy holy because the gods approve it, or do they approve it because it is holy?"[9]

Like Euthyphro, you may not see the dilemma right away, but it may become clearer if we eliminate the polytheistic assumptions of Socrates and change the term *holy* to *right*. The question now looks like this: Does God command us to do what is right because it is right, or is something right because God commands it? Two possibilities are present here. As Mouw puts it, God's commands can be seen as either "right-indicating" (pointers to rightness) or "right-making" (creators of rightness).[10]

This is really a question of whether God is a Supreme Court justice or a legislator. The justice knows the statutes and can point out what we must do to stay within the boundaries of the law, but the law itself is independent of the justice. The legislator, by contrast, does not just interpret law; the legislator creates law. The law does not exist until the lawmaker legislates. Which gives us a better picture of God? Because voluntarists stress God's freedom, will and sovereignty, they see God as legislator. He is not tied to the dictates of some standard he did not create. Instead, right is right because God legislates it. God's declaration that certain actions are good is "right-making."

Viewing God as the ultimate legislator avoids limiting God's freedom and power, but it may create another problem. If God is so radically free and powerful, could he make a world in which torture is good? If God's say-so makes it right and there are no restrictions on God, could he decide that child abuse is virtuous? Affirming this option is frightening to us, because there is a natural inclination to believe that a command that we ought to abuse children would be morally repugnant, even if it came from God. But we need to notice what this implies. It assumes a standard of goodness that is independent of God. Otherwise, we would have nothing by which to measure God's commands.

Asking whether God could make child abuse a good act may seem like just another one of those mind games that philosophers like to play. Surely no Christian would ever think that God would decree such a thing, so why even discuss the possibility? The main reason is that this theory asserts that right is right because God commands it to be and that there are no limits on what God can do. The only way to know if this assertion is true is to test it, so the question whether God could command torture or some similarly horrendous act is a fair test case.

One work-around proposed by some proponents of divine command theory is that we need to properly understand what it means to say that God is free or without limits. God is free, but not arbitrary. There is no possibility of saying anything comprehensible about an arbitrary God. Without constants, there would be no attributes that could be ascribed to him. How can we describe someone without attributes? Thus some defenders say that God does have a character and, since this is the case, there are certain things he will not do. For instance, if God is a loving being, he will not act out of character and command something that is unloving, such as cruelty to children.

2. Does good exist independently of God? Some critics have argued that to appeal to a divine characteristic, such as love, to tell us what God will not do seems to put God back in the role of Supreme Court justice—"God commands us to do what is right because it is right." Arguing that God would not command us to torture children assumes that loving acts are good and unloving acts are evil. However, this also sets up love as a standard by which even God is judged: if God commanded that we torture people, then he would be evil.

Of course your response might very well be that God would not ever do anything unloving, because he is a loving God. You might argue that God will not command unloving acts because it is impossible for him to do something contrary to his nature. But what happens to the absolute freedom of God in this case? Have we not now said that there is something God cannot do?

The other potential explanation for why God would not do unloving things is that such acts are possible but that a good God would not do them. Notice, however, that God is still limited here: it is not possible for him to do something unloving and at the same time be a good God. Thus there is a standard other than God's will that determines the goodness of God's actions. In this option God becomes the legal expert who knows what is good. He no longer is the God of voluntarism who creates good by his command.

3. Can we discount the role of reason? Because of the fallibility of human reason, many find reliance on God's imperatives comforting. Divine command ethics taps into this with its emphasis on faith and rejection of reason as ethically authoritative. However, this tends to present faith and reason as an either-or choice. Either we live by faith or we live by reason. However, putting faith and reason at opposite poles, as divine command often does, may be too simplistic and could create unanticipated difficulties.

One problem is that faith without reason becomes blind faith. I think it is safe to say that everyone has a faith and lives by faith, though not all faiths are religious in their orientation. To "have a faith" refers to a body of beliefs or a worldview that one holds to be true. To "live by faith" speaks of our personal commitment to act on a set of beliefs. Thus egoists make self-interest their ultimate concern, Kantians put their faith in autonomous reason, and utilitarians believe happiness for the majority is the goal of ethics. Each of these approaches has core beliefs, and its followers order their lives by these doctrines: they live by their faith. Each faith system also gives reasons it believes its faith is superior.

The last point is significant because divine command theory does the same thing. Why should anyone accept it? Proponents argue that if we take seriously the sovereignty of God, then it is reasonable that he has the authority to set the moral requirements for creation. So far so good. The next step, if we take seriously the fallenness of humans (reason included) and the intellectual gap between God and humans, is that it seems reasonable to distrust reason and rely on faith alone. This step is a problem, however, because it uses a reasonable argument to convince us of the worthlessness of human reason. But why should we trust reasonable arguments for accepting divine command ethics if reason cannot be trusted to get us to truths about God? This seems inconsistent. If we are going to dismiss the authority of reason for ethics, we cannot legitimately use it to establish the validity of divine command ethics. However, without using reason, there is no justification for believing this system. We are left with blind faith.

4. How do we interpret commands? Reason is not just important to show why we should believe a particular theory; it also is a necessary part of the interpretation process. Even when people agree that Scripture is God's Word and contains ethical commands to which all are obligated, we still have to interpret these commands. This is, at least in part, a rational process. For example, a biblical injunction like "Thou shalt not kill" seems simple enough at first, but its meaning needs to be unpacked. Does the prohibition against killing refer to all living things, to animals or to humans only? If we decide that it is limited to human life only, is "Thou shalt not kill" a ban against self-defense or going to war? Does it eliminate capital punishment? Is abortion included? What about allowing someone to die by unplugging a respirator?

Let's take just one of these issues as a test. Christians believe that "Thou shalt not kill" should guide their actions, but how does it guide action, for example, on the question of warfare? Since there are no commands in Scripture to "be a pacifist," and since Scripture has no section listing the criteria for just war, faith alone does not seem to be enough. We must still use reason to know how and whether "Thou shalt not kill" applies to an opposing army. Even if we base our interpretation on other biblical commands, we must still depend on our logical capacities to determine which commands are relevant to the subject. Actually, the preceding paragraph simplifies the problem of interpretation because it deals only with commands. However, the vast majority of the material in Scripture does not come to us in the form of commands. Surely the noncommand parts of the Bible have some ethical significance. Mouw recognizes this situation:

> The Bible is much more than a compendium of imperatives; the sacred writings contain historical narratives, prayers, sagas, songs, parables, letters, complaints, pleadings, visions, and so on. The moral relevance of the divine commandments found in the Scriptures can only be understood by viewing them in their interrelatedness with these other types of writings. Divine commands must be evaluated and interpreted in this larger context.[11]

What is implied in the evaluation and interpretation of divine mandates "in this larger context" that Mouw refers to? At a minimum, it requires the use of reason. However, by eliminating any role for reason in the ethical process, divine command ethics undercuts the possibility of evaluating and interpreting the very commands on which right and wrong is constructed.

5. Why do non-Christians come up with the same laws? One of the most basic problems for divine command theory is the remarkable similarity in what most people believe to be morally obligatory. Both religious and nonreligious folks around the world agree on the value of human life, honoring commitments, loyalty toward friends and a whole host of other moral principles. It is also true that most people arrive at these principles without any help from Scripture. How does this happen if, as divine command ethics argues, the only means of knowing God's ethical obligations for humanity is to get God's Word through Scripture? Why does God command things in Scripture that just about everyone already knows independently of Scripture?

The universality of ethical virtues seems to indicate that human ethical ideals do not derive exclusively from commands found in the Bible. This, of course, does not mean that ethics can be separated from God. It could be that moral law is planted by God in our intuitions (virtue theory) or in nature (natural law). God may have created the world so that right and wrong is fused to the structure of reason (Kant), to our desire for happiness (utilitarianism) or to some other aspect of our experience. The point is that it is hard to avoid the observation that fundamental moral ideals are universal. An ethical system should explain why this is so, and voluntarism does not seem to be able to do this.

6. Do divine commands tell us enough? Imagine the following scenario. You and your spouse have always wanted children. More specifically, you want a boy and a girl. That's it. You now have a boy, so is it all right to use certain medical methods to improve your chances of conceiving a girl? Does the Bible have anything to say about gender selection of offspring?

The answer to the last question is no. Scripture does not envision using scientific means to increase the probability of having a child of a certain gender. So what does a follower of divine command theory do when there is no direct law? Other ethical theories used by Christians have other paths available when confronted with situations that have no directly corresponding biblical law. But the Bible's lack of specificity on issues like gender selection (or the propriety of first-strike nuclear capability, eavesdropping on the satellite communications of a hostile nation, etc.) is a problem for divine command ethics. It would seem invalid for the voluntarist to trust reason, intuition, happiness or any other standard to guide us through these issues, since morality is to be founded only on the divine commands.

Voluntarism considers ethical matters settled when God commands. However, when we cannot locate the "God said it" in relation to a whole list of moral questions we face, what are we to believe and do? Does this mean that advocates of divine command can speak only where Scripture speaks and must remain silent where Scripture is silent? The problem is that this conflicts with the belief that Scripture is relevant to all matters of morality.

Conclusion

Getting all of the pieces to fit is a difficult task. Divine command theory seems at first glance to put everything into a nice, neat package. It makes sense of a number of the big questions of life, especially the nature of God and human sinfulness, and brings them right into the middle of the ethical discussion. It is also attractive because there are none of those messy uncertainties that come with adding human elements. Moral commands come straight from God. All we have to do is listen and obey. There is something reassuring about the "that settles it" of divine command ethics.

However, it is always possible to press a good point so hard that other valuable points are excluded. We do want to include biblical commands in the ethical process, but unless we supplement them with other sources, we end up without anything to say about some important issues. We do want to highlight the role of faith, but when reason gets squeezed out completely, we have no means of justifying and expressing our faith.

We might be able to modify divine command theory in a way that would put some of the missing pieces back in. Certainly there are voluntarists who do this. However, that tends to make the package a little less neat than the basic view I have outlined here. A little "unsettledness" might not be all bad, though. In fact, the ambiguity that comes with human elements in the ethical process may be desirable. We will examine that possibility in the final chapter.

13

UNRAVELING THE OPTIONS

ONE OF MY FAVORITE READINGS is Plato's *Theaetetus*. On occasion I have assigned it to students, and I have to confess that they often do not like it as much as I do. The text is a dialogue between Socrates and Theaetetus, a young seeker of truth. Theaetetus wants to know whether anything is certain, and Socrates agrees to help him explore the options. The book ends without a positive conclusion. A number of possible answers are given and, one by one, discarded because of logical inconsistencies. The question of what can be known for certain is still open when the two men part ways. My students are often frustrated because after plowing through what is sometimes difficult reading in *Theaetetus*, they want answers, not just a new and more complex set of questions.

Why Does It Have to Be So Complicated?

That may be how you feel after going through this book. Matters have been left open-ended, and no system I have examined has been free of questions. With each ethical approach has come a series of potential problems. Instead of solving the moral dilemmas, looking at these potential problems only seems to make matters more complicated. When we read a book that ends without giving all the "right answers," it is not always clear what we are to make of it. It is not uncommon to feel frustrated or even a little angry. What is the point if we end up where we began?

Open-endedness can make us a little crazy because we crave certainty. Especially in the realm of ethics, where so much is on the line, we would like to find a theory beyond the reach of criticism. Moreover, when we begin by assuming the truth of Christianity as our basis, we might expect clear-cut answers on ethics. Since none of that was offered here, where do we go from here? Obviously, at least eleven different options are available, since there are people who support each one of the theories I have presented. However, when you notice that every system considered involves a set of difficult questions, you may give up on ever untangling the questions and finding answers. You may be tempted to go down one of two paths, both of which I find to be unhelpful.

First, some people will simply turn off all the questions, shut out any ideas that are unfamiliar and return to the comfortable bumper-sticker-sized slogans I introduced in the first chapter. This is understandable, because we have a natural aversion to clutter in our lives. We like our truths plain and simple, and going back to what is familiar and easy is the path of least resistance. Moreover, books like this seem to make simple matters much more complex than necessary. After all, have not people throughout history been capable of making ethical decisions without getting wrapped up in questions about behaviorism, narrative ethics, egoism or natural law? If people can get along without all this bother, why go through it? Why does it have to be so complicated?

Of course, it takes little thought to recognize that it is not the lack of reflection itself that allows some people to be morally successful. Some unreflective individuals live ethically disastrous lives. At the same time, it cannot be doubted that many people lead ethically sound lives without having thought much about ethics. When this works for particular people, it is usually because they are fortunate enough to have absorbed good ideas and habits. I know several such individuals, and you probably do too. However, even when a person exhibits moral integrity without having given much thought to the questions I have tried to address, it may be that something important is missing.

It is one thing to do what is good and right, but quite another to understand why what you are doing is good. And it seems worthwhile, when the opportunity is available, to think through carefully the most important things in our lives. We do this, or at least know we should, when it comes to career choices, major purchases, religious commitments, choosing our friends and similar matters. Since the way we are treated and how we treat others is one of those important aspects of life, it is a good idea to examine beliefs about ethics. In the end, we may not change what we do or believe, but we will then have personal owner-ship of it because we have considered the options. That is the aim of this book. Many things look good at first, and this is also true of the bumper sticker versions of ethical systems we have considered here. However, you may have discovered that the initial attractiveness of a particular ethical approach diminishes once you become acquainted with the implications of the system. It seems preferable, then, to choose a position after looking at what is available. Better to select a system after carefully considering the options, rather than to passively accept a system because you have absorbed its ideas unconsciously or because it sounds good or is the easiest way to go.

A second possible but unhelpful response to open-endedness is cyn-icism. Cynicism often appears to be a popular reaction to books that end without indicating a preference for one system over another. When people discover that no particular option will ever win everyone over, some are inclined to conclude that no claims to truth are valid. This attitude is attractive because it seems to put you safely beyond criticism. No one can dispute your views because you do not commit yourself to anything. Instead, you become the critic of anyone audacious enough to take a stand on ethical matters.

But this approach has its own problems. First, it can be a cheap posi-tion. To do nothing other than criticize the supposed faults in the belief systems of others gives a false sense of security. The possibility that others may be wrong never makes you right. And it is always much easier to locate the weaknesses of a belief system than to defend your own view, even if your view happens to be cynicism. Second, it is im-possible to drain ourselves of any convictions. People who only criticize other positions still assume a certain truth in their own criticisms. In reality, then, cynics do not play fair. They expect everyone else to de-fend their beliefs, but they keep their own out of sight.

The last point is important, because it brings us back to the question of truth. Even though I have not endorsed any specific position here, there are a number of indications that, rather than giving up the hope that some sort of ethical truth can be discovered, the entire process of inquiry assumes that truth is possible.

First, the very routine of critiquing various theories indicates that we have not rejected the notion of truth. In fact, criticism is actually a tribute to the idea of truth, because it is part of the search. Just as a construction worker will constantly measure and test a building in process to see whether things are "true," so we will want to keep measuring by means of questions to know whether the various elements fit properly.

Second, while locating a specific body of ideas that can be trusted is a difficult task, we can narrow our options, eliminating certain positions by looking for insurmountable problems. This is the purpose of critique. Knowing what is true begins with knowledge of what is not true. Moreover, while I examined the potential problems in each view, this was preceded by a statement about what a particular system has to offer in a positive sense. As I stated at the beginning of the book, though none of the systems may hang together as a whole, each one contains something worthwhile within it. When we isolate such positive points, we have located elements that may be integrated into our own view.

Finally, throughout this book I have assumed the validity of certain standards of truth: logical consistency, practical applicability and a few foundational doctrines of Christianity. These have been the North Star by which I have checked each approach. Thus, rather than critique being considered a denial of truth or an invitation to cynicism, questioning is part of the process of seeking truth.

One key to understanding the constructive purpose of this book is to recognize the nature of this book. This text is an introduction, and introductory texts involve certain necessary evils. The questioning process that is so much a part of this book is one of those necessary evils. Before we can know the answers, we have to ask the questions. However, inquiry can lead us into unfamiliar territory and require that we give up some of the comfort and control we once had. Some people like adventure and easily plunge into the uncertainty that comes with new possibilities. Others take the first road back to the familiar and vow never to leave again.

A second necessary evil in introductory texts is that authors do not have time to address a wide range of concerns. In this book I am able to give only very general descriptions of various ethical systems. Perhaps there are parts of an ethical theory not mentioned in this brief survey that would have made a particular system more credible. I also did not examine all of the possible variations of each system. This is one reason many scholars do not like to write introductory texts. They know that others will read it and say, "I'm a _____ [fill in the name of an ethical system], and that's not what I believe." And they will be right. I have given rather generalized pictures of various theories. However, for each theory, there are more nuanced versions that may sidestep or answer many of the complications discussed at the end of each chapter. Furthermore, it should be noted that the questions raised with regard to each system are only potential problems. The intent was to point out questions that are frequently raised in relation to a specific theory. However, raising a question is different from finding a fatal flaw in a position, and there are effective means of countering a great number of these objections.

Reaching a Conclusion

All this has been said to remind us that this text is not intended as the final word on ethical ideas but as a small step into the discipline. Actually, by examining ethical theories, we have moved into the middle of a larger process. Obviously, a book like this looks forward. Simply giving mental assent to a particular set of ethical ideas is not an end in itself. Once our theoretical bases are established, we still have to deal with the tricky matter of applying our ideas to actual circumstances. Good theories hold their value because they allow us to do things well. Any good theory will be a useful tool in the laboratory of life.

In addition, this book requires that we look again at beliefs that we already hold, and this may be the key to traversing the rather confusing maze of ideas I have considered. How you evaluate any given system will depend on a worldview you already believe. As you work through the diversity of thought, your own position will be informed by certain core beliefs that will guide you in reconstructing an ethical approach.

Let me illustrate how a person might work through these different theories. Imagine a hypothetical college student named Julie, who is searching for the best of all possible ethical systems. As she looks at the various options, her first inclination is to adopt a divine command position. This approach picks up two beliefs she thinks must be at the core of any moral system—that the moral nature of God has great importance for human morality, and that humans are morally and intellectually limited. However, one of Julie's friends disputes her choice by saying, "While parts of this system look good to me too, it gets us nowhere because not everyone believes in God." This bothers Julie briefly, but she decides her friend's objection is built on a mistake. Her friend is right about two things. First, not everyone is a theist. It is also true that without God, divine command theory falls apart. But this does not necessarily mean that divine command theory (or any other theistic ethics) is wrong. It only tells us that not everyone believes it.

From this process Julie begins to recognize something important: every system has foundational beliefs. God's existence is a foundational belief in several of the theories considered. Similarly, the tenet that the world is purely cause and effect is at the heart of behaviorism. The notion that evolutionary theory is sufficient to encompass even ethics is fundamental to evolutionary ethics. If we do not think that happiness is an indicator of moral rightness, we will not buy into utilitarianism. However, our lack of adherence to any of these foundational beliefs does not mean that these systems are not true. It just means that we do not believe they are true. In order to decide whether an ethical approach "gets us somewhere," we need to resolve the foundational questions. Julie is now clear about what she had known in only a vague way before. Her ethical conclusions will depend on answers to a number of other questions that are not primarily ethical questions. Does God exist? Is there any room for human choice? Is survival the fundamental moral value?

Julie now knows that many of her questions about ethical options have already been answered by what she has previously concluded about certain foundational questions. Given her foundational beliefs in a Christian worldview, which include a divine Creator who has a moral nature, Julie is unable to accept theories such as behaviorism, evolutionary ethics, ethical egoism or cultural relativism because they leave little room for such a Creator. However, she also notices that certain elements in these theories are consistent with her worldview, and she wants to incorporate these into the ethical system she finally adopts. For now, though, she decides to get back to the task of finding the best basic ethical theory.

As she turns her thoughts back to divine command theory, one problem keeps nagging at her. After all is said and done, just about all major belief structures end up with the same basic set of ethical principles. Divine command theory does not seem able to explain why lying, cheating and stealing are universally condemned, even by nontheistic belief systems. Moreover, she is becoming increasingly bothered that she cannot seem to get rid of human reason, as divine command theory requires. Perhaps reason and the universality of ethical norms fit together? Julie wonders whether it is reason that allows people the world around to come to these common moral norms.

One ethical system that allows Julie to connect a common knowledge of ethics and reason is Kant's. However, this theory has a significant fault, as measured by another one of Julie's foundational beliefs. Kant makes reason completely free of any higher authority and in this way overlooks human fallibility. Julie also is not able to accept the sharp divide Kant draws between duties and results. In her experience she recognizes that doing what is right generally leads to good results. Following moral rules brings about a longer and more satisfying life.

With this last point in mind, Julie wonders whether utilitarianism and situation ethics might be right on something. Perhaps rules are not absolute, but are simply good strategies. However, she backs away from this because both seem to pick one aspect of the good and collapse all the others into it. Virtue theory does a better job of recognizing the full spectrum of good, and Julie is especially attracted to the idea that goodness is not simply a matter of following rules. She knows too many legalists to put the entire weight of ethics on law alone. Motive and character seem to be important also to her understanding of Christianity.

The big negative in virtue ethics is that in its classical form it assumes that people can develop these virtues on their own. Hauerwas's version of narrative ethics gets around this problem, but to Julie's dismay, it also seems to eliminate any common ground for ethical discussions with those who do not buy into the Christian tradition.

In the end, everything points toward natural law for Julie. That approach includes a number of the things she finds attractive in other theories. Natural law answers the question of why everyone seems to have a fundamental agreement on moral principles without absolutizing reason. It adopts from utilitarianism or situationism the idea that good actions will have good results, and it seems quite easily blended with a virtue ethics approach, which focuses on a person's moral character. While placing a strong emphasis on human reason, it also pays attention to human fallenness and brings in divine law to answer the question of salvation. While Julie does not care for the egocentric approach in Rand's ethical egoism, natural law does allow a means of fulfilling our needs while caring for others as well. This perspective, with a bit of help from narrative ethics, also allows Julie to make sense of cultural diversity without completely relativizing all moral practices, as cultural relativism does. Thus, Julie's conclusion is that the best approach is a natural law theory with liberal doses of virtue and narrative ethics thrown in.

The story of Julie, as stated here, is not intended to provide what I believe is the best answer to ethics. We should also not assume that Julie was infallible in her process of sorting through the different ethical approaches. She may have missed some possible solutions to her objections to some views, and she could have overlooked some big problems that attend the conclusion she did adopt. And Julie will be the first to tell you that she still has some unanswered questions and that she has perhaps not yet asked certain questions she should have asked.

We should also note that Julie has done several things correctly. First, she did not give up on the process but kept sorting through different possibilities. Second, she began with her most basic beliefs in order to locate the best potential for a beginning point. Third, she has kept an open mind toward the positive points from other ethical approaches, even those she would have rather not liked at all, and has integrated them when possible. She was careful to make certain that the various elements would hang together and be consistent with other parts of her worldview. Finally, Julie did not feel that she had to have all the answers before committing herself to a position. Ideally, she will continue to refine her views and tie up the loose ends.

Even if you go through the same kind of process Julie went through, you still may not be clear where you come out on all the specifics. The best some people can do for now is to commit themselves to a broad outline of basic beliefs, with perhaps more questions than answers. This position leaves many Christians with an uncomfortable feeling. After all, aren't we after answers? At this point it may be helpful to recognize that your inability to come to specific conclusions may indicate that you have grasped another aspect of truth. Truth is not just a description of a certain body of facts that correspond to reality (although this should not be ignored), but it also describes the process we use to get there.

This brings us back to *Theaetetus*. The lack of conclusive answers at the end of *Theaetetus* has caused some to assume that Socrates finds little use for the concept of truth, but the reality is just the opposite. In fact, Socrates' strongest criticism was reserved for a group called the Sophists, who were cynical about the possibility of discovering what was good or right. Many of the Sophists gave up the search and reduced ethics to the realm of subjective opinion (a tendency that is very strong today as well). In contrast, Socrates says ethical rightness is objective and capable of discovery if we search faithfully enough and use the proper methods.

While Socrates was convinced that truth is available, he was also concerned about another aspect of truth: truthfulness in method. I am sure that there were times when he would have liked to take the easy route and accept answers that had initial plausibility. However, it was precisely because of his respect for truth that he rejected the bumper stickers of his age when they did not hold up to scrutiny.

Socrates can remind Christians of something valuable here. Many of us feel pressured to come up with the right answer right away. However, this can lead us to be dishonest in the process. Truthfulness, goodness and rightness need to characterize not only our conclusions but also the means by which we get to our conclusions. And if there is anyplace where Christians should be honest, it is the ethical process.

NOTES

Chapter 1: Bumper Stickers and Ethical Systems

[1]Philip E. Devine, *Relativism, Nihilism and God* (Notre Dame, Ind.: University of Notre Dame Press, 1989), p. 47.

Chapter 2: When in Rome, Do as the Romans Do

[1]*Relativism* and *skepticism* are often used interchangeably but should not be confused. Both deny absolute truth, but skepticism rejects the category of truth altogether, saying truth is either nonexistent or unknowable. Relativism says that we can speak of truth, but only truth that is relative to some nonabsolute standard.

[2]For a broader discussion of moral relativism, see chapter 5 in Steve Wilkens and Mark L. Sanford, *Hidden Worldviews: Eight Cultural Stories That Shape Our Lives* (Downers Grove, Ill.: InterVarsity Press, 2009).

[3]Not all cultural relativists are cognitive or conceptual relativists as well. However, because of the logical gap (see one paragraph earlier) that exists without the assumption of cognitive relativism, cultural relativism must either assume cognitive relativism or be willing to admit that the conclusion does not follow from the stated data. Furthermore, Roger Trigg makes a convincing argument that "conceptual relativism is not just one form of relativism, but is itself the logical outcome of any form of it." See Roger Trigg, *Reason and Commitment* (London: Cambridge University Press, 1973), p. 25.

[4]There is disagreement among cognitive relativists concerning whether objective reality exists. For our purposes, the result is the same—we have no absolute basis for judgments.

[5]Ruth Benedict, *Patterns of Culture*, 2nd ed. (Boston: Houghton Mifflin, 1934), p. 2.

[6]Phillipa Foot, "Moral Relativism," in *Relativism: Cognitive and Moral*, ed. Jack W. Meiland and Michael Krausz (Notre Dame, Ind.: University of Notre Dame Press, 1982), p. 155.

[7]Melville J. Herskovits, *Cultural Relativism: Perspectives in Cultural Pluralism*, ed. Frances Herskovits (New York: Random House, 1972), p. 33.

[8]D. Z. Phillips, *Faith and Philosophical Enquiry* (London: Routledge & Kegan Paul, 1970), p. 237, quoted in Trigg, *Reason and Commitment*, p. 22.

[9]Herskovits, *Cultural Relativism*, p. 22.

[10]Ibid., p. 33.

[11]It is important to notice also that the social and religious practices in both Judah and Israel are also subject to God's judgment (Amos 2:4-16).

[12]James Rachels, *The Elements of Moral Philosophy*, 2nd ed. (New York: McGraw-Hill, 1993), p. 25.

[13]Herskovits, *Cultural Relativism*, p. 59.

[14]John W. Cooper, "Reformed Apologetics and the Challenge of Post-modern Relativism," *Calvin Theological Journal* 28 (1993): 110.

Chapter 3: Look Out for Number One

[1]The negative connotations attached to the term *selfishness*, as well as the possibility of confusing the egoistic definition with other unintended meanings, lead some ethical egoists to avoid using this term altogether. See John Hospers, *An Introduction to Philosophical Analysis*, 3rd ed. (Englewood Cliffs, N.J.: Prentice-Hall, 1988), p. 351.

[2]Ayn Rand, *The Virtue of Selfishness* (New York: Signet, 1964), p. vii.

[3]Ibid., p. 14.

[4]Ayn Rand, *The Voice of Reason: Essays in Objectivist Thought*, ed. Leonard Peikoff (New York: New American Library, 1988), p. 18.

[5]It is for this reason that Rand prefers to call her philosophy "objectivism." This distinguishes it from other ethical approaches, which she considers subjectivistic.

[6]Rand, *Virtue of Selfishness*, p. 17.

[7]Ibid., p. 21. Here Rand distinguishes her view from Nietzschean egoism, which views life as fundamentally irrational. Rand's position is that egoism is not good simply because it is selfish. It becomes good when it is rational selfishness. See ibid., p. ix.

[8]Ibid., p. 22.

[9]Ibid., p. 17.

[10]Ayn Rand, *Philosophy: Who Needs It?* (Indianapolis: Bobbs-Merrill, 1982), p. 74.

[11]Hospers, *Introduction to Philosophical Analysis*, pp. 352-53.

[12]Rand says that while hedonism is correct in making happiness the goal, happiness cannot also be the standard of ethics. It is when we allow desire to set the standard that we must fear each other. See Rand, *Virtue of Selfishness*, pp. 29-30.

[13]Ibid., p. 31.

[14]Nathaniel Branden, *Honoring the Self* (Boston: Houghton Mifflin, 1983), pp. 220-21, quoted in Hospers, *Introduction to Philosophical Analysis*, p. 352.

[15]Rand, *Virtue of Selfishness*, pp. 44-45.

[16]Branden, *Honoring the Self*, pp. 220-21, quoted in Hospers, *Introduction to Philosophical Analysis*, p. 352.

[17]A good summary of Epicurean ethics can be found in his *Menoeceus*.

[18]It should be noticed that this scenario also illustrates how, rather than encouraging freedom, egoism undercuts it. Your coworker did not have the opportunity to engage in a "trading" situation, because your actions limited her options. In a sense her decisions are coerced, because she is led to believe circumstances are different from what they actually are.

[19]This criticism is found in somewhat different form in Richard B. Brandt, *Ethical Theory* (Englewood Cliffs, N.J.: Prentice-Hall, 1959), p. 374; and Brian Medlin, "Ultimate Principles and Ethical Egoism," in *Morality and Rational Self-Interest*, ed. David P. Gauthier (Englewood Cliffs, N.J.: Prentice-Hall, 1970), pp. 60-63.

[20]Rand, *Virtue of Selfishness*, p. viii.

[21]James Rachels, *The Elements of Moral Philosophy*, 2nd ed. (New York: McGraw-Hill, 1993), p. 88.

[22]Ibid., p. 89.

Chapter 4: I Couldn't Help Myself

[1]B. F. Skinner, *Science and Human Behavior* (New York: Free Press, 1965), p. 6.

[2]B. F. Skinner, *Beyond Freedom and Dignity* (New York: Bantam, 1971), p. 39.

[3]Skinner, *Science and Human Behavior*, p. 5.

[4]Skinner, *Beyond Freedom and Dignity*, p. 107.

[5]Ibid., p. 109.

[6]Ibid., p. 202.

[7]Ibid., p. 205.

[8]Ibid., p. 193.

[9]Ibid., p. 192.

[10]Skinner himself provides a catalog of such terms to note the prevalence of our illusion of freedom. Freedom is presupposed in terms such as *attitudes, pride, sense of responsibility, concern, will to power, paranoid delusion, mind, death instinct, nature, self-respect, initiative, frustration, sense of purpose, alienation, hopelessness, crisis of belief, loss of confidence* and *faith in man's inner capacities*. See *Beyond Freedom and Dignity*, pp. 7-8.

[11]Skinner, *Science and Human Behavior*, p. 446.

Chapter 5: Survival of the (Ethical) Fittest

[1]Charles Darwin, *The Descent of Man, and Selection in Relation to Sex*, 2nd ed. (New York: Burt, 1874), p. 143.

[2]Ibid., p. 80.

[3]Ibid., p. 142.

[4]Herbert Spencer, *First Principles* (New York: DeWitt Revolving Fund, 1958), p. 124.

[5]Herbert Spencer, *The Principles of Sociology* (New York: Appleton, 1898), 2:664.

[6]Edward O. Wilson, *Consilience: The Unity of Knowledge* (New York: Vintage, 1998), p. 262.

[7]Richard Dawkins, *The Selfish Gene* (New York: Oxford University Press, 1989), p. 1.

[8]Ibid., p. 19.

[9]Ibid., p. 20. See also E. O. Wilson, *Sociobiology: The New Synthesis* (New York: Belknap Press, 2000), p. 3.

[10]Dawkins, *Selfish Gene*, p. 2.

[11]Wilson, *Consilience,* p. 179.

[12]Ibid., p. 282.

[13]Ibid., p. 179.

[14]Ibid., pp. 141-42.

[15]Ibid., p. 273.

[16]Ibid., p. 288.

[17]Ibid., pp. 289-90.

[18]Ibid.

[19]Dawkins, *Selfish Gene,* p. 266.

[20]Stephen Jay Gould, *Rock of Ages* (New York: Ballantine Books, 2002), pp. 9-10.

[21]Wilson, *Consilience,* p. 136.

Chapter 6: The Greatest Happiness

[1]Aristotle, *Nicomachean Ethics* 1176b, in *The Basic Works of Aristotle,* ed. Richard McKeon (New York: Random House, 1941).

[2]Jeremy Bentham, *An Introduction to the Principles of Morals and Legislation* (New York: Hafner, 1948), chap. 1, par. 2. John Stuart Mill's formulation of this is similar. "Utility, or the 'greatest happiness principle' holds that actions are right in proportion as they tend to promote happiness; wrong as they tend to produce the reverse of happiness. By happiness is intended pleasure, and the absence of pain; by unhappiness, pain, and the privation of pleasure." John Stuart Mill, *Utilitarianism,* ed. George Sher (Indianapolis: Hackett, 1979), p. 7.

[3]Mill, *Utilitarianism,* p. 16.

[4]Ibid., p. 21. For an exposition of scholars who advocated early forms of theological utilitarianism, see chapter 1, section 4, in Anthony Quinton, *Utilitarian Ethics* (La-Salle, Ill.: Open Court, 1988).

[5]Bentham, *Introduction to the Principles,* chap. 4, pars. 1-5.

[6]Mill, *Utilitarianism,* p. 10.

Chapter 7: It's Your Duty

[1]Immanuel Kant, *Groundwork of the Metaphysics of Morals,* trans. H. J. Paton (New York: Harper & Row, 1964), p. 61.

[2]Immanuel Kant, "On the Supposed Right to Tell Lies from Benevolent Motives," in *Kant's Critique of Practical Reason and Other Works on the Theory of Ethics,* trans. Thomas Kingsmill Abbot (London: Longman, Green, 1927), p. 361.

[3]Kant, *Groundwork,* p. 82.

[4]Ibid.

[5]Ibid., p. 88.

[6]Kant defines a *maxim* as a "subjective principle of action." It is a rule by which we act, as opposed to a law, which is a rule by which we *should* act. See ibid., p. 88, n. 1.

[7]Ibid., p. 90.

[8]Ibid., p. 96.

[9]Kant also says suicide violates the first formulation of the Categorical Imperative.

The motive behind suicide is self-love. However, Kant says this is self-contradictory because the purpose of self-love is preservation of life. That which is intended to protect our life can never be validly used as a motive to end it. See ibid., p. 89.

[10]Ibid., p. 105.

[11]See Kant, "On the Supposed Right." He also uses this to demonstrate the problem of consequentialism. If you lied to the murderer and told him that his victim was in another location, unaware that the intended victim had slipped out and gone to precisely the place you had directed the murderer to, you might unintentionally facilitate a murder. The point is that we cannot be certain of results.

[12]Ibid., p. 363.

[13]Jacques Maritain, *Moral Philosophy: An Historical and Critical Survey of the Great Systems* (New York: Charles Scribner's, 1964), p. 106.

Chapter 8: Be Good

[1]For the three functions of the soul, see Plato, *Republic* 438-43.

[2]Plato speaks of the struggle of maintaining this balance in his analogy of the charioteer in *Phaedrus* 253c-54e.

[3]Aristotle, *Nicomachean Ethics* 1107a, in *The Basic Works of Aristotle*, ed. Richard McKeon (New York: Random House, 1941).

[4]Bernard Mayo, *Ethics and the Moral Life* (London: Macmillan, 1958), p. 215.

[5]Ibid.

[6]Aristotle, *Nicomachean Ethics* 1105a.

[7]Ibid., 1104b.

[8]Ibid., 1103a.

[9]Mayo, *Ethics and the Moral Life*, p. 214.

[10]Aristotle, *Nicomachean Ethics* 1098a.

[11]For a helpful comparison and discussion of differences in lists of virtues, see chapter 14 in Alasdair MacIntyre, *After Virtue: A Study in Moral Theory* (Notre Dame, Ind.: University of Notre Dame Press, 1980).

[12]Richard Taylor, "Ancient Wisdom and Modern Folly," *Midwest Studies in Philosophy* 13 (1988): 56.

[13]For example, see William Frankena, *Ethics*, 2nd ed. (Englewood Cliffs, N.J.: Prentice-Hall, 1973), pp. 65-67; and James Rachels, *The Elements of Moral Philosophy*, 2nd ed. (New York: McGraw-Hill, 1993), pp. 177-79.

Chapter 9: The Moral of the Story Is . . .

[1]Robert C. Roberts, "Narrative Ethics," in *Companion to Philosophy of Religion,* by Philip L. Quinn and Charles Taliaferro (New York: Wiley-Blackwell, 1999), p. 474.

[2]Martha C. Nussbaum, *Love's Language: Essays on Philosophy and Literature* (New York: Oxford University Press, 1990), p. 7.

[3]Stanley Hauerwas, *The Peaceable Kingdom: A Primer in Christian Ethics* (Notre Dame, Ind.: University of Notre Dame Press), p. 26.

[4]Ibid., p. 23.

[5]Stanley Hauerwas, *A Community of Character: Toward a Constructive Christian Social Ethic* (South Bend, Ind.: University of Notre Dame Press, 1981), p. 59.

[6]Stanley Hauerwas and William H. Willimon, *Resident Aliens: A Provocative Christian Assessment of Culture and Ministry for People Who Know That Something Is Wrong* (Nashville: Abingdon Press, 1989), p. 95.

[7]Hauerwas, *Peaceable Kingdom*, p. 27.

[8]Ibid., p. 31.

[9]Hauerwas, *Community of Character*, p. 56.

[10]Hauerwas lists and rejects several commonly used external tests for grounding Scripture's authority. "Therefore when Christians claim Scripture as authority for their community they are not claiming that the Bible is without error; or that the genres of the Bible are unique; or that the Bible contains a unique understanding of man, history, or even God as opposed to Greek or some other culture; or that the Bible manifests a unique *Weltanschauung* or contains an implicit metaphysics that still remains largely misunderstood; or that the Bible contains images without which we cannot achieve an adequate self understanding; and so on." Ibid., p. 63.

[11]Ibid.

[12]Stanley Hauerwas, *With the Grain of the Universe: The Church's Witness and Natural Theology* (Grand Rapids: Brazos, 2001), p. 214.

[13]Hauerwas, *Community of Character*, p. 50.

[14]Hauerwas, *With the Grain of the Universe*, p. 211.

[15]Stanley Hauerwas, "Abortion Theologically Understood," in *Virtues and Practices in the Christian Tradition*, ed. Nancey Murphy, Brad J. Kallenberg and Mark Thiessen Nation (Harrisburg, Penn.: Trinity Press International, 1997), pp. 231-32.

[16]Hauerwas, *Peaceable Kingdom*, p. 24.

[17]Ibid., p. xvii.

[18]Craig Boyd argues, and I think correctly, that while Hauerwas's criticisms toward post-Enlightenment versions of natural law hit the mark, they are less successful as a critique of Aquinas's version of natural law. Unlike more secularized versions, Aquinas's exposition of natural law sets ethics within a broader theological context and links it to the development of virtue. See Craig Boyd, *A Shared Morality: A Narrative Defense of Natural Law Ethics* (Grand Rapids: Brazos, 2007), pp. 234-47.

Chapter 10: All You Need Is Love

[1]For a brief summary and explanation of these six propositions, see Joseph Fletcher, *Moral Responsibility: Situation Ethics at Work* (Philadelphia: Westminster Press, 1967), pp. 14-27. A more extensive treatment is given in chapters 3-8 of Fletcher's *Situation Ethics: The New Morality* (Philadelphia: Westminster Press, 1966).

[2]Fletcher, *Situation Ethics*, p. 30.

[3]Ibid., p. 79.

[4]Ibid., p. 74.

[5]Ibid., p. 28.

[6]Ibid., p. 95.

[7]Ibid., p. 120. In addition to consequentialism, situationism has several points in common with utilitarian ethics. Like utilitarians, Fletcher argues that first principles are not subject to proof. Norms can be deduced only from higher norms; thus supreme norms cannot be proved (see *Situation Ethics*, p. 49). While utilitarianism puts forward happiness as its intrinsic good, Fletcher does not see this as a serious conflict with his ethics of love. "We need not try to assert some supposed mutual exclusions as between *agapē* and the 'happiness' that utilitarians want. All depends upon what we find our happiness in: all ethics are happiness ethics. . . . The Christian situationist's happiness is in doing God's will as it is expressed in Jesus' Summary" (see *Situation Ethics*, p. 96). Fletcher states that in social policy, situationism uses the same strategic principle as utilitarianism: "the greatest good of the greatest number."

[8]Fletcher sees this as one of the problems of antinomianism. Since the latter has no norms, there is complete relativity. However, it is questionable whether total relativity is logically coherent. For something to be relative, it must be relative to something. Fletcher says that this "something" is love.

[9]Fletcher, *Situation Ethics*, p. 104.

[10]James M. Gustafson, "How Does Love Reign?" in *The Situation Ethics Debate*, ed. Harvey Cox (Philadelphia: Westminster Press, 1968), p. 81.

[11]Fletcher, *Situation Ethics*, p. 69.

[12]Ibid., p. 156.

Chapter 11: Doing What Comes Naturally

[1]Thomas Aquinas, *Summa Theologica* 1-2.94.2c, trans. Fathers of the English Dominican Province (New York: Benziger Brothers, 1947-1948).

[2]This may sound like utilitarianism, but there is a significant difference. As Langan puts it, "For a utilitarian, if an action is conducive to the general happiness, then it is morally right; for Thomas, if an action is morally right, then it is conducive to happiness." John Langan, "Beatitude and Moral Law in St. Thomas," *Journal of Religious Ethics* 5 (1977): 186.

[3]Aquinas, *Summa Theologica* 1-2.94.2.

[4]Ibid., 1-2.94.3c.

[5]Ibid., 1-2.94.2c.

[6]Ibid., 1-2.94.4c.

[7]Ibid., 1-2.94.2.

[8]Ibid., 1-2.95.1.

[9]Ibid., 1-2.2.8c; 1-2.3.8c.

[10]Ibid., 1-2.91.4c.

[11]David Hume, *A Treatise of Human Nature* (London: Everyman's Library, 1961), 3.1.1.

[12]David Little, "Calvin and the Prospects for a Christian Theory of Natural Law," in *Norm and Context in Christian Ethics*, ed. Gene Outka and Paul Ramsey (New York:

Charles Scribner's, 1968), p. 176.

[13]Karl Barth, *Church Dogmatics* 2/1, ed. Geoffrey W. Bromiley and Thomas F. Torrance (Edinburgh: T & T Clark, 1957), p. 86.

[14]L. Thiry, "The Ethical Theory of Saint Thomas Aquinas: Interpretations and Misinterpretations," *Journal of Religion* 50 (1970): 180.

[15]John Paul II, *Veritatis Splendor*, p. 80. The complete text of this encyclical can be found in English translation in *Origins* 23 (1993).

[16]John Jefferson Davis, *Evangelical Ethics: Issues Facing the Church Today*, 2nd ed. (Phillipsburg, N.J.: Presbyterian & Reformed, 1993), p. 41.

Chapter 12: God Said It, I Believe It, That Settles It

[1]The term *voluntarism* comes from the Latin *voluntas*, which means "will." Thus "theological voluntarism" refers to the belief that what is good or evil is determined by God's expressed will on the matter.

[2]John Duns Scotus, *Commentary on the Sentences* 4.46.8, in *Divine Command Morality: Historical and Contemporary Readings*, ed. Janine Marie Idziak (New York: Mellen, 1979), p. 54.

[3]Richard J. Mouw, *The God Who Commands: A Study in Divine Command Ethics* (Notre Dame, Ind.: Notre Dame Press, 1990), pp. 41-42.

[4]John H. Sammis, "Trust and Obey" (1887).

[5]P. H. Nowell-Smith, "Morality: Religious and Secular," in *Divine Command Morality: Historical and Contemporary Readings*, ed. Janine Marie Idziak (New York: Mellen, 1979), pp. 272-79.

[6]Mouw, *God Who Commands*, p. 13.

[7]Ibid., p. 19.

[8]C. S. Lewis, *The Lion, the Witch and the Wardrobe* (New York: Collier, 1970), pp. 75-76.

[9]Plato, *Euthyphro* 10, in *The Collected Dialogues*, ed. Edith Hamilton and Huntington Cairns (Princeton, N.J.: Princeton University Press, 1961).

[10]Mouw, *God Who Commands*, p. 28.

[11]Ibid., p. 10.

Finding the Texbook You Need

The IVP Academic Textbook Selector
is an online tool for instantly finding the IVP books
suitable for over 250 courses across 24 disciplines.

www.ivpress.com/academic/textbookselector